The Discovery of Grounded Theory

OBSERVATIONS

A series edited by Howard S. Becker
Northwestern University

The Discovery of Grounded Theory
Strategies for Qualitative Research

BARNEY G. GLASER
AND
ANSELM L. STRAUSS
University of California
San Francisco Medical Center

ALDINE PUBLISHING COMPANY / *Chicago*

First published 1967 by
Aldine Publishing Company
320 West Adams Street
Chicago, Illinois 60606

Library of Congress Catalog Card Number 66–28314
Designed by Bernard Schliefer
Printed in the United States of America

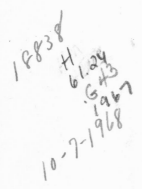

Preface

Mentioning the Department of Sociology at Columbia University brings to mind Merton's middle-range theory and Lazarsfeld's quantitative methodology. On the other hand, the "Chicago tradition" (from the 1920's to the 1950's) is associated with down-to-earth qualitative research, a less than rigorous methodology, and an unintegrated presentation of theory. By an ironic conjunction of careers, the authors of this book were trained, respectively, at Columbia and Chicago. The point is noted only to emphasize our conviction that neither of these traditions— nor any other in postwar sociology—has been successful at closing the embarrassing gap between theory and empirical research. The gap is as wide today as it was in 1941, when Blumer commented on it, and in 1949, when Merton optimistically suggested a solution.

Attempts to close the gap between theory and research have concentrated principally on the improvement of methods for testing theory, and sociologists, as well as other social and behavioral scientists, have been quite successful in that endeavor. Attempts to close the gap from the "theory side" have not been nearly so successful. In fact, "grand theory" is still so influential and prevalent that for many researchers it is synonymous with "theory"—and so they think of "theory" as having little relevance to their research. They have resolutely continued to focus on their empirical studies and on their efforts to improve the methodology of verification.

Our book is directed toward improving social scientists' capacities for generating theory that *will* be relevant to their research. Not everyone can be equally skilled at discovering theory, but neither do they need to be a genius to generate useful theory. What is required, we believe, is a different perspective on the canons derived from vigorous quantitative verification on such issues as sampling, coding, reliability, validity, indicators, frequency distributions, conceptual formulation, construction of hypotheses, and presentation of evidence. We need to develop canons more suited to the discovery of theory. These guides, along with associated rules of procedure, can help release energies for theorizing that are now frozen by the undue emphasis on verification.

We argue in our book for grounding theory in social research itself—for generating it from the data. We have linked this position with a general method of comparative analysis—different from the more specific comparative methods now current —and with various procedures designed to generate grounded theory. Although our emphasis is on generating theory rather than verifying it, we take special pains not to divorce those two activities, both necessary to the scientific enterprise. Although our book is directed primarily at sociologists, we believe it can be useful to anyone who is interested in studying social phenomena—political, educational, economic, industrial, or whatever—especially if their studies are based on qualitative data.

BARNEY G. GLASER
ANSELM L. STRAUSS

Acknowledgments

The Discovery of Grounded Theory was made possible by Public Health Service Research Grant NU-00047 from the Division of Nursing, Bureau of State Services–Community Health. Other books written under this grant and using the methods and position of this book are *Awareness of Dying* by Barney G. Glaser and Anselm L. Strauss (Aldine Publishing Company, 1965) and *The Nurse and the Dying Patient* by Jeanne C. Quint (Macmillan, 1967). A fourth book, *Time for Dying* (Aldine Publishing Company, forthcoming), deals with the course, or trajectory, of dying.

We wish to express our indebtedness to many colleagues for their general support of our total enterprise, their encouragement for its publication, and their specific commentaries and critiques, which we found invaluable for final revisions of the manuscript. Their comments indicated clearly that, while in general agreement, these colleagues felt in some controversy with us on several specific issues—issues that will doubtless be controversial in sociology for years to come. In short, we have taken their advice and support, but at the same time are fully responsible for our own position.

We wish to thank Howard S. Becker of Northwestern University, editor of the "Observations" series; Fred Davis and Leonard Schatzman of the University of California at San Francisco; Julius Roth of the University of California at Davis; Amitai Etzioni and Walter Klink of Columbia University; Herbert Blumer, Neil J. Smelser, Sheldon Messinger, and Aaron Cicourel of the University of California at Berkeley; George C.

Homans of Harvard University; Charles Fisher of Princeton University; and David Schneider of the University of Chicago. These colleagues put in several laborious hours of study on the manuscript in order to prepare their detailed comments. Other colleagues who have given general support to our venture are Kai Erikson, Rue Bucher, Berenice Fisher, Louis Schaw, Jeanne C. Quint, Virginia Olesen, and Egon Bittner.

We wish to express our gratitude to Bess Sonoda (now Mrs. H. Chang), Mrs. Kathleen Williams, and Elaine McLarin, the heroines who made possible two "rush jobs" of typing the manuscript.

B. G. G. and A. L. S.

Contents

The Discovery of
Grounded Theory

I

The Discovery of Grounded Theory

Most writing on sociological method has been concerned with how accurate facts can be obtained and how theory can thereby be more rigorously tested. In this book we address ourselves to the equally important enterprise of *how the discovery of theory from data—systematically obtained and analyzed in social research—can be furthered.* We believe that the discovery of theory from data—which we call *grounded theory*—is a major task confronting sociology today, for, as we shall try to show,' such a theory fits empirical situations, and is understandable to sociologists and layman alike. Most important, it works—provides us with relevant predictions, explanations, interpretations and applications.

As sociologists engaged in research soon discover, there are as yet few theories of this nature. And so we offer this book, which we conceive as a beginning venture in the development of improved methods for discovering grounded theory. Because this is only a beginning, we shall often state positions, counterpositions and examples, rather than offering clear-cut procedures and definitions, because at many points we believe our slight knowledge makes any formulation premature. A major strategy that we shall emphasize for furthering the discovery of grounded theory is a *general method of comparative analysis.*

Previous books on methods of social research have focused mainly on how to verify theories. This suggests an overemphasis in current sociology on the verification of theory, and a resultant de-emphasis on the prior step of discovering what concepts and hypotheses are relevant for the area that one wishes to research. Testing theory is, of course, also a basic task confronting sociology. We would all agree that in social research generating theory goes hand in hand with verifying it; but many sociologists have been diverted from this truism in their zeal to test either existing theories or a theory that they have barely started to generate.

Surely no conflict between verifying and generating theory is logically necessary during the course of any given research. For many sociologists, however, undoubtedly there exists a conflict concerning primacy of purpose, reflecting the opposition between a desire to generate theory and a trained need to verify it. Since verification has primacy on the current sociological scene, the desire to generate theory often becomes secondary, if not totally lost, in specific researches.

Our book—especially when we discuss the current emphasis on verification—will indicate many facets and forms that the resolution of this conflict takes among sociologists, but this discussion should not be taken as indicating that we endorse the existence of such a conflict. Rather, our position is that a conflict is created when sociologists do not clearly and consciously choose which will receive relative emphasis in given researches because of too great an adherence to verification as the chief mandate for excellent research.

Grounded Theory

The basic theme in our book is the discovery of theory from data systematically obtained from social research.[1] Every chapter deals with our beginning formulation of some of the processes

1. Merton never reached the notion of the discovery of grounded theory in discussing the "theoretic functions of research." The closest he came was with "serendipity"; that is, an unanticipated, anomalous, and strategic finding gives rise to a new hypothesis. This concept does not catch the idea of purposefully discovering theory through social research. It puts the discovery of a single hypothesis on a surprise basis. Merton was preoccupied with how verifications through research feed back into and modify theory. Thus, he was concerned with grounded modifying of theory, not grounded generating of theory. *Social Theory and Social Structure* (Glencoe, Ill.: Free Press, 1949), Chapter III.

of research for generating theory. Our basic position is that generating grounded theory is a way of arriving at theory suited to its supposed uses. We shall contrast this position with theory generated by logical deduction from *a priori* assumptions. In Chapter II we shall discuss what we mean by theory and compare it with other conceptions of theory.

The interrelated jobs of theory in sociology are: (1) to enable prediction and explanation of behavior; (2) to be useful in theoretical advance in sociology; (3) to be usable in practical applications—prediction and explanation should be able to give the practitioner understanding and some control of situations; (4) to provide a perspective on behavior—a stance to be taken toward data; and (5) to guide and provide a style for research on particular areas of behavior. Thus theory in sociology is a strategy for handling data in research, providing modes of conceptualization for describing and explaining. The theory should provide clear enough categories and hypotheses so that crucial ones can be verified in present and future research; they must be clear enough to be readily operationalized in quantitative studies when these are appropriate.[2] The theory must also be readily understandable to sociologists of any viewpoint, to students and to significant laymen. Theory that can meet these requirements must fit the situation being researched, and work when put into use. By "fit" we mean that the categories must be readily (not forcibly) applicable to and indicated by the data under study; by "work" we mean that they must be meaningfully relevant to and be able to explain the behavior under study.

To generate theory that fills this large order, we suggest as the best approach an initial, systematic discovery of the theory from the data of social research. Then one can be relatively sure that the theory will fit and work.[3] And since the categories are discovered by examination of the data, laymen involved in the area to which the theory applies will usually be able to under-

2. In principle any concept can be operationalized in quantitative ways, but the sociologist should develop his concepts to facilitate this operationalization.

3. Of course, the researcher does not approach reality as a *tabula rasa*. He must have a perspective that will help him see relevant data and abstract significant categories from his scrutiny of the data. We shall discuss this issue more fully in Chapters II and XI.

stand it, while sociologists who work in other areas will recognize an understandable theory linked with the data of a given area.

Theory based on data can usually not be completely refuted by more data or replaced by another theory. Since it is too intimately linked to data, it is destined to last despite its inevitable modification and reformulation. The most striking examples are Weber's theory of bureaucracy and Durkheim's theory of suicide. These theories have endured for decades, stimulating a variety of research and study, constantly exciting students and professors alike to try to modify them by clever ways of testing and reformulation. In contrast, logically deduced theories based on ungrounded assumptions, such as some well-known ones on the "social system" and on "social action" can lead their followers far astray in trying to advance sociology.[4] However, grounded theories—which take hard study of much data—are worth the precious time and focus of all of us in our research, study and teaching.

Grounded theory can help to forestall the opportunistic use of theories that have dubious fit and working capacity. So often in journals we read a highly empirical study which at its conclusion has a tacked-on explanation taken from a logically deduced theory. The author tries to give his data a more general sociological meaning, as well as to account for or interpret what he found. He uses this strategy because he has not been trained to generate a theory from the data he is reporting so that it will help interpret or explain the data in a general manner. He does this also because he has been trained only to research and verify his facts, not also to research and generate his explanation of them. The explanation is added afterward. For instance, many papers dealing with deviance conclude with an interpretation based on Merton's anomie theory, a classic example of this use of logically deduced theory. An author could, of course, borrow the grounded theory of another sociologist for its general relevance, but—since this kind of theory fits and works—it would readily be seen whether it is clearly applicable and relevant in this new situation. It cannot be tenu-

---

4. And also in trying to advance their personal careers, for one cannot empirically dissociate the need to generate theory from the need to advance careers in sociology.

ously connected, omitting of many other possible explanations, as a tacked-on explanation so often is.

Another opportunistic use of theory that cannot occur with grounded theory is what may be termed "exampling." A researcher can easily find examples for dreamed-up, speculative, or logically deduced theory after the idea has occurred. But since the idea has not been derived from the example, seldom can the example correct or change it (even if the author is willing), since the example was selectively chosen for its confirming power. Therefore, one receives the image of a proof when there is none, and the theory obtains a richness of detail that it did not earn.

There is also a middle zone between grounded and logico-deductive theorizing, in which the sociologist chooses examples systematically and then allows them to feed back to give theoretical control over his formulations; but often it is hard to figure out when this is happening, even when we are clearly told. Much of C. Wright Mills' work, we believe, is exampled with only little theoretical control, though he claimed that data disciplined his theory. In contrast, grounded theory is derived from data and then illustrated by characteristic examples of data.[5]

In contrasting grounded theory with logico-deductive theory and discussing and assessing their relative merits in ability to fit and work (predict, explain, and be relevant), we have taken the position that the adequacy of a theory for sociology today cannot be divorced from the process by which it is generated. Thus one canon for judging the usefulness of a theory is how it was generated—and we suggest that it is likely to be a better theory to the degree that it has been inductively developed from social research. We also believe that other canons for assessing a theory, such as logical consistency, clarity, parsimony, density, scope, integration, as well as its fit and its ability to work, are also significantly dependent on how the theory was generated. They are not, as some theorists of a logico-deductive persuasion would claim, completely independent of the processes of generation. This notion of independence too often ends up being taken as a license to generate theory from any source—

5. See, for example, Howard S. Becker *et al., Boys in White* (Chicago: University of Chicago Press, 1961).

happenstance, fantasy, dream life, common sense, or conjecture
—and then dress it up as a bit of logical deduction.

Probably we need to emphasize here what we shall discuss
later more explicitly. Generating a theory from data means that
most hypotheses and concepts not only come from the data, but
are systematically worked out in relation to the data during
the course of the research. *Generating a theory involves a
process of research.* By contrast, the *source* of certain ideas, or
even "models," can come from sources other than the data. The
biographies of scientists are replete with stories of occasional
flashes of insight, of seminal ideas, garnered from sources outside the data. But the generation of theory from such insights
must then be brought into relation to the data, or there is great
danger that theory and empirical world will mismatch. We shall
discuss this issue again more fully, particularly in Chapter XI
on "Insight, Theory Development, and Reality."

For many colleagues, our position will be at best a hypothesis, to be tested in the years to come; while for many others it
is proven fact, and for still others an article of faith. However
colleagues may respond, our position is not logical; it is phe-
nomenological. We could not suggest a process of generating
theory if we did not believe that people who might use it
would arrive at results that potentially may be judged as successful. Furthermore, we believe that grounded theory will be
more successful than theories logically deduced from *a priori*
assumptions. Our position, we hasten to add, does not at all
imply that the generation of new theory should proceed in
isolation from existing grounded theory. (We shall discuss this
in Chapter II.)

Purposes of This Book

This book is intended to underscore the basic sociological
activity that *only* sociologists can do: generating sociological
theory. Description, ethnography, fact-finding, verification (call
them what you will) are all done well by professionals in other
fields and by layman in various investigatory agencies. But
these people cannot generate sociological theory from their

work. Only sociologists are trained to want it, to look for it, and to generate it.

Besides reminding colleagues of a somewhat slighted task, we also are trying, through this book, to strengthen the mandate for generating theory, to help provide a defense against doctrinaire approaches to verification, and to reawaken and broaden the picture of what sociologists can do with their time and efforts. It should also help students to defend themselves against verifiers who would teach them to deny the validity of their own scientific intelligence. By making generation a legitimate enterprise, and suggesting methods for it, we hope to provide the ingredients of a defense against internalized professional mandates dictating that sociologists research and write in the verification rhetoric, and against the protests of colleagues who object to their freedom in research from the rigorous rules of verification (so stifling to the creative energies required for discovering theory).

In trying to stimulate all sociologists to discover grounded theory—from those who are only at the dissertation stage of their careers to those who are already "retired" professors—we hope to contribute toward the equalizing of efforts in generating theory, which are now often limited to the earlier stages of a sociological career. For example, Hammon, in presenting us with chronicles of some of the best sociological research (those with the highest theoretical yield), has chosen mainly chronicles of dissertations or studies done as soon as the dissertation was finished.[6] Similar studies could be done by mature sociologists, and with more speed (less fumbling, clearer purpose) and more sophisticated theoretical yields. Indeed, that the growth of a theorist is linked to the increasing sophistication of his output is clearly seen in the work of men like Goffman, Lipset and Wilbert Moore. Yet many sociologists as they mature disregard whatever fledgling potential for generating theory they showed in their dissertations and early monographs. They cease or slow up their research and writing of monographs and turn to scholarship and the mastery of others' works, particularly earlier "great man" theories. One respected scholar, by

6. Philip E. Hammond (Ed.), *Sociologists at Work* (New York: Basic Books, 1964).

virtue of his position and prominence, has encouraged this trend, by saying, in effect, at a recent sociological meeting, that he would like to see older sociologists cease writing their monographs and start worrying about teaching the next generation of students. We urge them to continue writing monographs and to try to generate theory!

Throughout this book we call for more theory, but not just any theory. The general comparative method for generating grounded theory that will be discussed in Part I provides criteria for judging the worth of all theory, as well as grounded theory. This theme pervades the whole book. It is our intent to give colleagues an effective means for evaluating the worth of any theory that they will teach, apply or use in research, for describing, explaining, predicting, interpreting and testing.

What about this book's usefulness for those sociologists who already are deeply involved in generating theory? Many may be able to use it effectively to help systematize their theorizing; for until they proceed with a bit more method their theories will tend to end up thin, unclear in purpose, and not well integrated (see Chapter VI). Our suggestions for systematizing should not curb anyone's creativity for generating theory; in contrast to the ways of verification, they should encourage it. Our strategies do not insist that the analyst engage in a degree of explicitness and overdrawn explanation in an effort to coerce the theory's acceptance by "drugging the reader's imagination and beating him into intellectual submission." [7] Our suggestions for systematizing the rendition of theory allow, even demand, room for including both propositions and the richness of information leading to them.[8]

Our principal aim is to stimulate other theorists to codify and publish their *own* methods for generating theory. We trust that they will join us in telling those who have not yet attempted to generate theory that it is not a residual chore in this age of verification. Though difficult, it is an exciting adventure.

In our own attempt to discuss methods and processes for discovering grounded theory, we shall, for the most part, keep

---

7. Melville Dalton, "Preconceptions in Methods in Men Who Manage," in Hammond, *op. cit.*, pp. 57-58.
8. Compare to Merton's strictures on codification of theory, which require leaving out the "irrelevant" richness of connotation! *Op. cit.*, p. 14.

the discussion open-minded, to stimulate rather than freeze thinking about the topic. Our suggestions are deliberately interspersed with occasional frank polemic—always, we hope, with purpose—though not at the expense of stopping the flow of suggested procedures or the logic lying behind them. In using examples from research, we have drawn heavily upon our own work—and for a very good reason. We know others' work as published product; we know our own better as work-in-process —and discovering *theory as a process* is, of course, the central theme of this book.

In the first section—*Comparative Analysis*—we shall present a strategy whereby sociologists can facilitate the discovery of grounded theory, both substantive and formal. This strategy involves the systematic choice and study of several comparison groups. In Chapter II we discuss the purpose of our use of comparative analysis. In Chapter III we discuss theoretical sampling—the process of collecting data for comparative analysis designed to generate substantive and formal theory. In Chapter IV we take up the transition from substantive to formal theory. And in Chapter V we offer our method for the comparative analysis of qualitative data. In Chapter VI we clarify and assess a number of previous comparative studies in terms of several important questions.

In the second part of the book—*The Flexible Use of Data*— we consider in detail the generation of theory from qualitative (especially documentary) and quantitative data (in Chapters VII and VII, respectively).

In the third part of the book—*Implications of Grounded Theory*—we consider the credibility of grounded theory (Chapter IX) and its practical implications (Chapter X). Lastly, in Chapter XI we discuss insight, theory development and reality. We close with an epilogue summarizing our position on the relations of theory to research.

Before moving on to these chapters, we shall discuss the contemporary emphasis on verification, the influential style of logico-deductive theorizing, which encourages the drive toward verification, and the distinction usually drawn between qualitative and quantitative data—a distinction useless for the generation of theory.

Verification and "Grand" Theory

Verification of theory is the keynote of current sociology. Some three decades ago, it was felt that we had plenty of theories but few confirmations of them—a position made very feasible by the greatly increased sophistication of quantitative methods.[9] As this shift in emphasis took hold, the discovery of new theories became slighted and, at some universities, virtually neglected. Those who still wished to generate theory had to brook the negative, sometimes punitive, attitudes of their colleagues or professors.

Part of the trend toward emphasizing verification was the assumption by many sociologists that our "great men" forefathers (Weber, Durkheim, Simmel, Marx, Veblen, Cooley, Mead, Park, etc.) had generated a sufficient number of outstanding theories on enough areas of social life to last for a long while. Although we, their sociological offspring, could never equal their genius, we did know how to modify and reformulate their theories with our new-found abilities in verification—and so that was the next job of sociology. As a result, many of our teachers converted departments of sociology into mere repositories of "great-man" theories and taught these theories with a charismatic finality that students could seldom resist. Currently, students are trained to master great-man theories and to test them in small ways, but hardly to question the theory as a whole in terms of its position or manner of generation. As a result many potentially creative students have limited themselves to puzzling out small problems bequeathed to them in big theories. A few men (like Parsons and Merton) have seen through this charismatic view of the great men sufficiently to generate "grand" theories on their own. But even these few have lacked methods for generating theory from data, or at any rate have not written about their methods. They have played "theoretical capitalist" to the mass of "proletariat" testers,

---

9. See Hans L. Zetterberg, *On Theory and Verification in Sociology* (Totowa, N.J.: Bedminster Press, 1963).

by training young sociologists to test their teachers' work but *not* to imitate it.[10]

In the face of this prevalent attitude, we contend, however, that the masters have not provided enough theories to cover all the areas of social life that sociologists have only begun to explore. Further, some theories of our predecessors, because of their lack of grounding in data, do not fit, or do not work, or are not·sufficiently understandable to be used and are therefore useless in research, theoretical advance and practical application. On the other hand, the great theorists have indeed given us models and guidelines for generating theory, so that with recent advances in data collection, conceptual systematization and analytic procedures, many of us can follow in their paths: from social research we can generate theories for new areas, as well as better theories for areas where previous ones do not work.[11]

We contend also that it does not take a "genius" to generate a useful grounded theory. It does take some codification of the method of doing it, as well as recognition of its legitimacy for student training and academic careers. Our book provides some of both. It is well known that in science the highest rewards have always gone to those who generate an important new

10. The following are the words of a young theoretical capitalist modestly asking the proletariat testers to correct his conjectured theory: "Whereas empirical tests would undoubtedly prove a good proportion of the inferred predictions to be incorrect, these negative findings would provide a basis for refining the theory, whereas as no such refinements are possible if a theory fails to yield operational hypotheses that can be negated by empirical evidence." Thus to encourage the testers he carefully writes his theory so it can be readily operationalized and proven wrong in several ways—a temptation for those who like to prove the theorist wrong. These proletariat testers do not realize that allowing themselves to be tempted simply puts the refined theory and the theorist on firmer ground, while they are soon forgotten. See Peter Blau, *Exchange and Power in Social Life* (New York: John Wiley and Sons, 1964), p. 9. We can only say that it is our position that theorists be responsible for the grounding of their theories from the start.

For another attempt at theoretical capitalism and request for colleagues to test him out, see Thomas J. Scheff, *Being Mentally Ill* (Chicago: Aldine Publishing Co., 1966), especially p. 101.

11. For example, this is happening in the study of deviance. See Marshall B. Clinard (Ed.), *Anomie and Deviant Behavior* (New York: Free Press of Glencoe, 1964).

theory (sociology *is* like physics in this regard).[12] Historical reasons, then, account for the paradox that more sociologists do not try their hand at generating theory and publishing it, thus achieving high rewards. We wish to help alleviate this condition by encouraging able sociologists to generate more and better theory with the type of comparative method discussed in our book, and, in turn, to start developing methods of their own for all of us to use.

Verification or Generation?

The following account is an example of the kind of historical circumstance that put the generation of grounded theory into second place, and made verification the dominant orientation in virtually all sociological work:

During 1938 the Social Science Research Council struck upon the idea of subjecting to critical appraisal a series of significant contributions to social science. In sociology, Herbert Blumer was assigned the task of appraising Thomas and Znaniecki's great monograph, *The Polish Peasant in Poland and America*.[13] A year later Blumer's critique was published by the Council.[14] The volume included comments on Blumer's analysis by Thomas and by Znaniecki, as well as a reprinting of the proceedings of a conference that discussed the analysis (the conference included such participants as Murdock, Wirth, Bain, Wiley and Waller).

Blumer noted that Thomas and Znaniecki had been much concerned with methodological issues and had taken a stand against several types of knowledge then much advocated. These latter included "common sense generalization," "planless empiricism," "mere statements of uniformities of social behavior in response to social influences," "statements of causal influences which hold true 'on the average,' or 'in a majority of cases,'" and a type of misleading oversimplification in which "effort is made to resolve what must be taken as a primary relation into

12. For example, six of the eight MacIver Awards have gone to sociologists for generating grounded theory.
13. Thomas and F. Znaniecki (New York: Alfred A. Knopf, 1918).
14. Appraisal of Thomas and Znaniecki's *The Polish Peasant in Europe and America* (New York: Social Science Research Council, 1939).

simpler elements." In contrast, the monograph was directed at furthering general sociological theory and giving a very detailed interpretation of Polish peasant society in Europe and America.

Blumer's principal criticism of *The Polish Peasant* was directed at what he believed was an important methodological flaw in it—one that needed to be discussed as an issue basic to sociological research rather than as pertinent merely to this particular monograph. The authors claimed that their analyses rested largely on numerous "human documents": letters, agency records, life histories, court records. Blumer noted first that not all—perhaps not even the major—theoretical conceptions used by Thomas and Znaniecki were grounded on those documents. Indeed, "the major outlines are foreshadowed in the previous writings of Thomas," and even "their *particular* interpretations of Polish peasant life were not formed solely from the materials they present; we have to assume that the familiarity with Polish peasant life which enabled their interpretations was made in a wide variety of ways."

But this was only a minor criticism. Blumer's major concern was this: "the important question is whether the materials adequately test the generalizations (regardless of their source) which are being applied to the materials. . . ." But "the answer is very inconclusive." Some interpretations seemed to him to be borne out by the materials; some did not. Worse yet, usually one could not say that "the interpretation is either true or not, even though it is distinctly plausible," (pp. 74-75). Blumer agreed that these plausible interpretations made the materials more significant and made "theoretical interpretation more understandable." Yet the very puzzling issue of plausible interpretation versus genuine verification remained.

Therefore Blumer concluded, first, that the materials were not a decisive test of theoretical interpretations, although they did more than simply illustrate them; second, that a test of "theory would have to come in other ways, such as in its internal consistency, in the character of its assumptions, in its relation to other theories, in its consistency with what seems to be 'human,' or in other kinds of data than those provided by human documents"; and, third, that the authors' use of human documents would seemingly imply that their essential function "would be to . . . yield to a sensitive and inquiring mind

hunches, insights, questions suitable for reflection, new perspectives, and new understandings" (pp. 75-76). In short, the
data were useful for theorizing but not adequate for verification.

Blumer's critique was written during the period when
Stouffer, Chapin, Lazarsfeld, Guttman and other advocates of
better (quantitative) measures for checking theory began to
exert great influence in sociology. The emphasis in Blumer's
critique on verification, then, fit the mood of the day. Yet the
enormous influence of *The Polish Peasant* for two decades was
less the result of its demonstrable findings than of its stimulating
theory. With hindsight, we can wonder what might have happened if Blumer had focused less on the problem of verification
and more on generation. He did, of course, come close to
emphasizing the latter, since he raised the issue of how to
theorize from data rather than from the armchair. But, as we
see it, whatever his intent, Blumer threw the weight of his
analysis toward an examination of verification, rather than
toward the question of how to generate grounded theory. He
left that latter problem largely untouched, apparently assuming
that the most one could say was that good theory is produced
by a fortunate combination—an inquiring mind, rich experience,
and stimulating data.[15]

Znaniecki's rejoinder to Blumer's critique on the verification
issue is also instructive. He agreed that his monograph's materials did not always provide a good test of the theoretical formulations, but he attributed this to "the inadequacy of that general
conceptual framework with which we approached our data."

15. A year later, Blumer published an admirable article,· addressing
himself to the gap between ungrounded theories and the countless empirical studies unguided by any theories. Operationalism was then coming into
dominance, and he attacked it effectively as not offering a solution to closing the gap. Closing it, he believed, would depend on "developing a rich
and intimate familiarity with the kind of conduct being studied and in employing whatever relevant imagination observers may fortunately possess.
The improvement in judgment, in observation, and in concept will be in
the future, as . . . in the past, a slow maturing process." His emphases on
the meaning of the theory-data gap and on the requisite need for good
qualitative data, we agree with thoroughly. Blumer's solution to getting
better theory, and in close relation to data, was—again—blunted because
he was poised in too sharp a posture against verification (operationalism in
this instance), and too ready to give up on the problem of how to generate
better theory except by the general formula of sticking close to the data
being studied. See his "The Problem of the Concept in Social Psychology,"
American Journal of Sociology (1940), 707-19; the quotes are from pp.
718-19.

By "framework," Znaniecki referred to the "excessive simplicity of the 'attitude-value' conceptual combinations"—the principal theoretical conception that organized the monograph. Znaniecki would substitute a more sophisticated conception involving "system" and "pattern" (which he believed had been implicit anyhow in the monograph) which would have demanded fuller qualitative data of various kinds. He was still thinking of the generation of theory largely in terms of a pre-existent conceptualization; he was still not emphasizing methods for generating *grounded* theory.

Qualitative vs. Quantitative Data

Historically linked with the change in relative emphasis from generation to verification of theory was the clash between advocates of quantitative and qualitative data. The generators of theory in the late 1930's, by and large, had used qualitative data in a nonsystematic and nonrigorous way (when they used data at all), in conjunction with their own logic and common sense. In addition, monographs based on qualitative data consisted of lengthy, detailed descriptions which resulted in very small amounts of theory, if any.[16] The effort in these monographs was to "get the story straight." In short, the work based on qualitative data was either not theoretical enough or the theories were too "impressionistic."

Meanwhile, beginning in the late 1930's, and especially after World War II, quantitative researchers made great strides both in producing accurate evidence and in translating theoretical concepts into research operations. The result was an ability to begin the challenge of testing theory rigorously.

Thus, advances in quantitative methods initiated the zeal to test unconfirmed theories with the "facts." Qualitative research, because of its poor showing in producing the scientifically reproducible fact, and its sensitivity in picking up everyday facts about social structures and social systems, was relegated, by men like Stouffer and Lazarsfeld, to preliminary, exploratory, groundbreaking work for getting surveys started. Qualitative research was to provide quantitative research with a few sub-

16. For example, see the various studies of the Chicago school on the gang, the ghetto, the taxi-dance hall, the hoboes, etc.

stantive categories and hypotheses. Then, of course, quantitative research would take over, explore further, discover facts and test current theory.

The strength of this position, which soon swept over American sociology, was based on the emerging systematic canons and rules of evidence of quantitative analysis: on such issues as sampling, coding, reliability validity, indicators, frequency distributions, conceptual formulization, hypothesis construction, and parsimonious presentation of evidence. The methods of qualitative researchers on these issues had not been developed to the point where they offered any assurance of their ability to assemble accurate evidence and to test hypotheses. Indeed, in sociology the only qualitative methods receiving much development were for the quantification of qualitative data! The assumption behind, and because of, these developments was that sociology was embarked on a straight-line course of progress towards becoming a science, by virtue of quantitative verifications of hypotheses.

A smaller number of sociologists did take other positions, in their research and teaching, but they began—and still continue today—to use the verification rhetoric in talking of qualitative data (testing, proving, tentativeness, demonstrating, and so forth). One position was "since we are so accustomed to qualitative data, let's verify with such data, as they do with quantitative data." These advocates tried to systematize the ways they collected, assembled and presented qualitative materials. Sometimes they used quantifying techniques, but their systemization was far broader. Virtually every maneuver was accomplished according to precise patterns—for example, how interviews or observation were recorded, coding procedures accomplished, modeled analyses done, and concepts clarified. The path to systematization was guided (as this book has been) by the pressure that quantitative verifications had put on all sociologists to clarify and codify all research operations, no matter what the type of data or the content of the research report.[17]

17. For clarifications and codifications of qualitative methods see, for example, the articles in Richard N. Adams and Jack J. Preiss (Eds.), *Human Organization Research* (Homewood, Ill.: Dorsey Press, 1960). The call to codify and clarify all methods, including qualitative research was earlier given in 1949 by Robert K. Merton, *op. cit.*, p. 390.

Another position taken by advocates of qualitative data has been that these data were their media and therefore were still the best and richest for theorizing about social structures and social systems. Also, qualitative method still was the only way to obtain data on many areas of social life not amenable to the techniques for collecting quantitative data. The fascinating fact about people who have taken this stand is that they have continued to generate theories from qualitative data, realizing its importance, and yet they have not explicitly referred to their work as generating theory (or have not described how they generated theory or how it was relevant) because they have been too concerned with formulating their ideas within the rhetoric of verification! In reading their writings, one constantly finds that they make qualifications using the verification terminology, such as "the hypothesis is tentative," "we had only a few cases," "we need more denite proofs in future research," and "we checked this out many times." We cannot evaluate how well their theories were generated, because we are seldom told of what use the theories are in prediction, application and explanation, or what procedures led to suggested hypotheses.

The position of the logico-deductive theorists also became subordinated to the rhetoric of verification. Since they did not use data for generating theory anyway, they supported quantitative verifications as the best way to reformulate and modify their theories. This meant, of course, that they supported the trend in sociology that pointed toward the perfection of their own theories by other men. They could not lose. As we have remarked earlier, they never mentioned the lost emphasis on generating theory, since perhaps they wanted their work to be tested and only slightly modified rather than replaced.

Our position in this book is as follows: there is no fundamental clash between the purposes and capacities of qualitative and quantitative methods or data. What clash there is concerns the primacy of emphasis on verification or generation of theory— to which heated discussions on qualitative *versus* quantitative data have been linked historically.[18] We believe that *each form*

18. In the 1930's, men like E. W. Burgess attempted to mediate between the antagonists, using both types of data in their research. But inevitably they leaned toward the Stouffer-Lazarsfeld position that qualitative data was exploratory in function, thus neutralizing its generative possibilities.

of data is useful for both verification and generation of theory,
whatever the primacy of emphasis. Primacy depends only on
the circumstances of research, on the interests and training of
the researcher, and on the kinds of material he needs for his
theory.

In many instances, both forms of data are necessary—not
quantitative used to test qualitative, but both used as supple-
ments, as mutual verification and, most important for us, as
different forms of data on the same subject, which, when compared, will each generate theory (see Chapter III).

To further this view, we seek in this book to further the
systematization of the collection, coding and analysis of qualitative data for the generation of theory. We wish particularly
to get library and field research off the defensive in social
research, and thereby encourage it. Although the emphasis on
qualitative data is strong in our book, most chapters also can
be used by those who wish to generate theory with quantitative
data, since the process of generating theory is independent of
the kind of data used. (See particularly Chapters II and VIII,
on theoretical sampling and quantitative data.)

We focus on qualitative data for a number of other reasons:
because the crucial elements of sociological theory are often
found best with a qualitative method, that is, from data on
structural conditions, consequences, deviances, norms, processes,
patterns, and systems [19]; because qualitative research is, more
often than not, the end product of research within a substantive
area beyond which few research sociologists are motivated to
move; and because qualitative research is often the most "adequate" and "efficient" way to obtain the type of information required and to contend with the difficulties of an empirical situation. We wish also through this book to provide sociologists
with a set of categories for writing their theories within a
rhetoric of generation, to balance out that of verification.

19. See James Coleman's discussion of the relative merits of qualitative
and quantitative research in analyzing the "working parts of a system,"
"Research Chronicle: The Adolescent Society," in Philip E. Hammond, *op.
cit.*, pp. 190-193, 206. Coleman agrees with us, but he is not aware that
the benefits that he suggests for a "comparative quantitative analysis" can
also be obtained with a "comparative qualitative analysis," as we shall show
in this book.

PART I:

GENERATING THEORY BY COMPARATIVE ANALYSIS

II

Generating Theory

The term *comparative analysis*—often used in sociology and anthropology—has grown to encompass several different meanings and thereby to carry several different burdens. Many sociologists and anthropologists, recognizing the great power of comparative analysis, have employed it for achieving their various purposes. To avoid confusion, we must, therefore, be clear at the outset as to our own use for comparative analysis —the generation of theory. We shall first contrast our use of this method with certain other uses.[1] Then we shall define and describe what kind of theory can be generated through comparative analysis.

Comparative analysis is a general method, just as are the experimental and statistical methods. (All use the logic of comparison.) Furthermore, comparative analysis can, like those other methods, be used for social units of *any* size. Some sociologists and anthropologists customarily use the term comparative analysis to refer only to comparisons between large-scale social units, particularly organizations, nation, institutions, and large regions of the world. But such a reference restricts a general method to use with one specific class of social units to which it has frequently been applied. Our discussion of comparative analysis as a strategic method for *generating theory* assigns the method its fullest generality for use on social units of any size, large or small, ranging from men or their roles to

1. In Chapter VI, we discuss in detail a number of studies in which "comparative method" was used, examining them for their specific purposes and distinguishing them from our own suggested purpose.

nations or world regions. Our own recent experience has demonstrated the usefulness of this method for small organizational units, such as wards in hospitals or classes in a school.[2]

Before distinguishing our purpose in using comparative analysis from other purposes, we should mention one unfortunate use of comparisons: to debunk, disprove, or discount the work of colleagues. From his own readings, a sociologist can almost always find, if he wants to, some piece of data that disproves the fact on which his colleague has based a theoretical notion. Many sociologists do! If each debunker thought about the potential value of comparative analysis, instead of satisfying his urge to "put down" a colleague, he would realize that he has merely posed another comparative datum for generating another theoretical property or category. That is all he has done. Nothing is disproved or debunked, despite what those who are overly concerned with evidence constantly believe. Kinder colleagues, who present a sociologist with one or more negative case but are afraid of impairing his motivation, usually will suggest that some qualification in his theoretical assertion may be advisable. Their comparative analysis aids him in rounding out his own comparative analysis and further generating his theory.

We also intend to hold a dialogue with those who "put down" the comparative strategy as "not especially original." True, the general notion of comparative analysis was developed by our sociological forefathers—Weber, Durkheim, Mannheim— and by social anthropologists. We can only trust that our readers will absorb enough details of comparative analysis as rendered in this book to be able to spot the advances in the strategy that should make a world of difference in its use.

Purposes of Comparative Analyses

The distinction made earlier between relative emphasis on generating and verifying can be illuminated further by considering the typical uses of evidence obtained through comparative studies.

2. Barney G. Glaser and Anselm L. Strauss, *Awareness of Dying* (Chicago: Aldine Publishing Co., 1965).

Accurate Evidence

On the factual level, evidence collected from other comparative groups—whether nations, organizations, counties, or hospital wards—is used to check out whether the initial evidence was correct. Is the fact a fact? Thus, facts are replicated with comparative evidence, either internally (within a study), externally (outside a study), or both. Sociologists generally agree that replications are the best means for validating facts.

Although this use of comparative analysis is not, of itself, our goal, it is definitely subsumed under our goal. Naturally we wish to be as sure of our evidence as possible, and will therefore check on it as often as we can. However, even if some of our evidence is not entirely accurate this will not be too troublesome; for in generating theory it is not the fact upon which we stand, but the *conceptual category* (or a *conceptual property* of the category) that was generated from it. A concept may be generated from one fact, which then becomes merely one of a universe of many possible diverse indicators for, and data on, the concept.[3] These indicators are then sought for the comparative analysis. (See Chapters III and IV.)

In discovering theory, one generates conceptual categories or their properties from evidence; then the evidence from which the category emerged is used to illustrate the concept. The evidence may not necessarily be accurate beyond a doubt (nor is it even in studies concerned only with accuracy), but the concept is undoubtedly a relevant theoretical abstraction about what is going on in the area studied. Furthermore, the concept itself will not change, while even the most accurate facts change. Concepts only have their meanings respecified at times because other theoretical and research purposes have evolved.

For example, one theoretical category related to the care of dying patients is their social loss—loss to family and occupation.[4] This category clearly affects how nurses care for dying

3. We are applying here Lazarsfeld's rule of "interchangeability of indices" in a new connection. See Paul F. Lazarsfeld and Wagner Thielens, *The Academic Mind* (New York: Free Press of Glencoe, 1958), pp. 402-407.

4. For an explication and theoretical discussion of the category of social loss, see Barney G. Glaser and Anselm L. Strauss, "The Social Loss of Dying Patients," *American Journal of Nursing*, 64 (June 1964), pp. 119-22.

patients. The category of "social loss" can be generated from either the observation that VIP's receive special care on intensive care units or that lower-class Negroes often are neglected on city hospital emergency wards. Even if the evidence changes (or is different in other hospitals for various other reasons), we can be sure that social loss is a category related to nursing care, and we can make predictions on its basis. We can predict that patients who have high social loss will receive better care than those who have low social loss. If that prediction proves incorrect, then we are likely to find out next what structural conditions have tended to negate this relationship; for example, how the medical staff has overcome this socially induced tendency in one type of hospital. In short, the discovered theoretical category lives on until proven theoretically defunct for any class of data, while the life of the accurate evidence that indicated the category may be short.

Empirical Generalizations

Another standard use of comparative studies is to establish the generality of a fact. Does the incest taboo exist in all societies? Are almost all nurses women? Is basic research the most revered goal of scientists in all research organizations? Accuracy is not at stake so much as establishing the structural boundaries of a fact: where is the fact an accurate description? For some sociologists and anthropologists this purpose becomes a quest for "universals"—facts and their explanations by other facts— that apply to all men irrespective of their society or culture.

Our goal of generating theory also subsumes this establishing of empirical generalizations, for the generalizations not only help delimit a grounded theory's boundaries of applicability; more important, they help us broaden the theory so that it is more generally applicable and has greater explanatory and predictive power. By comparing where the facts are similar or different, we can generate properties of categories that increase the categories' generality and explanatory power.

For example, dying of cancer in America can be characterized as occurring in a "closed awareness context"—while the hospital staff does, the patient does not know he is dying. Most doctors do not tell their patients that their illness is terminal, and patients find that cues that might alert them that they are dying are vague and hard to read until the last stages of their dying.[5] In a Japanese hospital we once visited, cancer patients typically know they are dying (an "open awareness context"). Why? Because the hospital ward is openly labeled "Cancer." The patient entering the ward reads a clear cue that makes him aware that he is dying. While in America the cues tend to be vague and fleeting, we discovered through the Japanese example that they can be clear even at the beginning stage of a long term of dying. Until then, we had not realized that cues can vary in clarity at the beginning of such a disease as cancer. We had thought that clear cues emerged only during the final stages; for example, when the priest arrives, or the patient's pain is beyond endurance, or massive bodily degeneration occurs.

This comparative data from Japan stimulated us to find locations in America where clear cues are provided at the start of dying. We found that in a veterans' hospital and in a prison medical ward, patients from the outset were given clear cues that they had cancer. Thus we discovered that under the structural condition of being a captive patient in a government hospital, one tends to die in an open awareness context. But most patients in America do not die under such circumstances.

Specifying a Concept

Another (usually detailed and painstaking) use of comparative data is to specify a unit of analysis for a one-case study. This is done by specifying the dimensions of the concept designating the unit. To make certain the reader understands what a given monograph will be about, in comparison with seemingly similar units, the author compares his unit for analysis with these other units. His comparison brings out the distinctive elements or nature of the case he has studied. For instance, Cressey painstakingly compared taxi-dance halls with all other forms of dance halls before proceeding with his analysis.[6] Lipset,

---

5. Glaser and Strauss, *Awareness* . . . , *op. cit.*, Chapters 3 and 8.
6. Paul Cressey, *The Taxi-Dance Hall* (Chicago: University of Chicago Press, 1932).

Trow and Coleman compared the distinctive political nature of the ITU with the characteristic political structure of other unions to establish their "deviant" case study.[7] Wirth compared the Chicago ghetto with the European to establish distinctive changes in the new-world ghetto.[8] Coleman, with the aid of IBM equipment, carefully distinguished between types of high schools on three dimensions, themselves checked out empirically to assure us that they are different in more than script.[9]

This standard, required use of comparative analysis is accomplished early in the presentation of a study for the purpose of getting the ensuing story straight. This use is, of course, subsumed under the purpose of generating theory. However, when the analyst's purpose is only the specifying of a unit of analysis, he stifles his chances for generating to a greater degree than with any other use of comparative analysis. The distinctive empirical elements distinguishing the units of comparison are kept on the level of data, to insure clear understanding of differential definitions. As a consequence, the units' general properties in common, which might occur to the analyst as he compares, are carefully unattended. No ambiguity of similarity, such as a general underlying property pervading all of them, is allowed between the competing units. Comparative analysis, then, is carefully put out of the picture, never to "disrupt" the monologue again.

Verifying Theory

When the analyst turns to theoretical concerns, evidence is invariably used as a test of his hypotheses—and thereby of the relevance of his categories; comparative data give the best test. Both implicitly and explicitly, the analyst continually checks out his theory as the data pour in. Explicit verification beyond testing his hypotheses may lead to establishing major uniformi-

7. S. M. Lipset, Martin Trow and James S. Coleman, *Union Democracy* (New York: Free Press of Glencoe, 1956).

8. Louis Wirth, *The Ghetto* (new ed.) (Chicago: University of Chicago Press, 1962).

9. James Coleman, *The Adolescent Society* (New York: Free Press of Glencoe, 1961).

ties and universals, to strategic variations of theory under different conditions,[10] and to grounded modifications of theory.[11]
A touch of generation may be included, but the researcher's
focus is on verifying; he generates theory only in the service of
modifying his original theory as a result of the tests. And most
of this work is done with existing theories; for example, Blauner's
work with Marxian theory or Lipset's work with Michel's
theory.[12]

Some analysts focus on verifying the new theory that
emerges in their data.[13] Thus, in their work, theory is generated,
but its emergence is taken for granted; what is intentionally
worked for is the verification of this emergent theory. The analysts are preoccupied with "checking out" the "emergent set of
propositions." Their favorite technique is looking for negative
cases or setting out deliberately to accumulate positive ones to
gain further evidence for their hypotheses. And while, as in
Dalton's research, great trouble may be taken in actively seeking
comparative groups, other analysts may use comparative groups
incidentally or even implicitly.

These researchers in specific studies do not seem to have
focused directly on how their theory emerged; as a result, they
have not explored how they could have generated more of it
more systematically, and with more conceptual generality and
scope. A focus on testing can thus easily block the generation
of a more rounded and more dense theory (see Chapter VI).
Ordinarily, we are presented with well-tested theory fragments,
which can only partially account for what is happening in the
researched situation. Also, we are presented with plenty of
evidence, coupled with at least implicit assurances that there
were mountains more for verification—because evidence is still
most important to the analyst as the means for testing how he

10. For example, Robert Blauner, *Alienation and Freedom* (Chicago:
University of Chicago Press, 1964).

11. See Robert K. Merton, *Social Theory and Social Structure* (New
York: Free Press of Glencoe, 1957), Chapter III.

12. See Blauner, *op. cit.* and Lipset *et al., op. cit.*

13. See, for example, Melville Dalton, *Men Who Manage* (New York:
John Wiley and Sons, 1959); and Howard S. Becker, Blanche Geer, Everett
Hughes and Anselm L. Strauss, *Boys In White* (Chicago: University of
Chicago Press, 1961).

knew his theory was "right." [14] This focus on evidence para-
doxically allows cantankerous colleagues, with their own different comparative evidence or personal experience, to "pooh-
pooh" his theory, wholly or in part.

Generating Theory

While verifying is the researcher's principal and vital task
for existing theories, we suggest that his main goal in developing new theories is their purposeful systematic generation from
the data of social research. Of course, verifying as much as
possible with as accurate evidence as possible is requisite
while one discovers and generates his theory—but *not* to the
point where verification becomes so paramount as to curb generation. Thus, generation of theory through comparative analysis both subsumes and assumes verifications and accurate
descriptions, but *only* to the extent that the latter are in the
service of generation. Otherwise they are sure to stifle it. To be
sure, the urge to generate is normal; and sociologists, students
and professors alike, if they are not "hooked" on verifying, tend
to give themselves enthusiastically to generating. But when
generating is not clearly recognized as the main goal of a
given research, it can be quickly killed by the twin critiques of
accurate evidence and verified hypotheses. This happens especially when the critiques are made by an influential colleague
or professor. The analyst's confidence is destroyed because
everyone involved fails to realize that accurate description and
verification are not so crucial when one's purpose is to generate
theory. This is especially true because evidence and testing
never destroy a theory (of any generality), they only modify it.
A theory's only replacement is a better theory.[15]

When the vital job of testing a newly generated theory
begins, the evidence from which it was generated is quite likely

---

14. Becker *et al.* (*ibid.*) tells of "5000 single-spaced typed pages" of
field notes and interviews (p. 30); and Dalton (*ibid.*) tells of his research
"which continued over a decade." They imply that one cannot doubt notions
and findings based on such mountains of time and evidence.

15. This is a basic finding in Thomas S. Kuhn, *The Structure of Scientific Revolutions* (Chicago: University of Chicago Press, 1962). We believe
it applies more to a grounded theory than a logico-deductive one.

to be forgotten or ignored. Now, the focus is on the new evidence that will be used for verifying only a part of the theory. Furthermore, sociologists will find it worthwhile to risk a period in their careers in order to test grounded theories, since these theories are certain to be highly applicable to areas under study. This situation is in contrast to the risk of testing a logico-deductive theory, which is dubiously related to the area of behavior it purports to explain, since it was merely thought up on the basis of *a priori* assumption and a touch of common sense, peppered with a few old theoretical speculations made by the erudite.[16] The verifier may find that the speculative theory has nothing to do with his evidence, unless he *forces* a connection.[17]

Generating theory carries the same benefit as testing theory, plus an additional one. Verifying a logico-deductive theory generally leaves us with at best a reformulated hypothesis or two and an unconfirmed set of speculations; and, at worst, a theory that does not seem to fit or work (and perhaps the uncomfortable feeling that some "thinker" might have been playing with us). A grounded theory can be used as a fuller test of a logico-deductive theory pertaining to the same area by comparison of both theories than an accurate description used to verify a few propositions would provide. Whether or not there is a previous speculative theory, discovery gives us a theory

16. As one example, in his book of conjecture-based theory, Blau states: "The idea and analysis presented in this book have been strongly influenced by the works of other social scientists, and they often have their ultimate source in the insights into social life presented by social philosophers and thinkers of long ago." Peter Blau, *Exchange and Power in Social Life* (New York: John Wiley and Sons, 1964), p. vii.

17. The analyst may, indeed, force this connection because he was taught to think that science is applying an analytic framework to an area of study—not to force is to stray from science. "Unless the researcher is extremely cautious he is quite likely to find himself straying from his original working hypotheses, since he is obliged to move 'wherever the data take him,'" warns one researcher about declining to force in favor of fitting the hypotheses to data. See Stanley H. Udy, Jr., "Cross Cultural Analysis: A Case Study," in Philip Hammond (Ed.), *Sociologists at Work* (New York: Basic Books, 1964), pp. 174-75. Or he may force the connection to ensure his promotion in an organization staffed with colleagues who feel there ought to be such a relation, because a "great man" said one existed. Needless to say, we believe that forcing the connection between theory and data is completely opposed to our emphasis on a fit between them.

that "fits or works" in a substantive or formal area (though further testing, clarification, or reformulation is still necessary), since the theory has been derived from data, not deduced from logical assumptions.

Since accurate evidence is not so crucial for generating theory, the kind of evidence, as well as the number of cases, is also not so crucial. A single case can indicate a general conceptual category or property; a few more cases can confirm the indication. As we note in the next chapter on theoretical sampling, generation by comparative analysis requires a multitude of carefully selected cases, but the pressure is *not* on the sociologist to "know the whole field" or to have all the facts "from a careful random sample." His job is not to provide a perfect description of an area, but to develop a theory that accounts for much of the relevant behavior. The sociologist with theoretical generation as his major aim need not know the concrete situation better than the people involved in it (an impossible task anyway). His job and his training are to do what these laymen cannot do—generate general categories and their properties for general and specific situations and problems. These can provide theoretical guides to the layman's action (see Chapter X on practical applications). The sociologist thereby brings sociological theory, and so a different perspective, into the situation of the layman. This new perspective can be very helpful to the latter.

Sociologists who conceive of this task as their job are not plagued (as are those who attempt to report precise description) by thoughts such as "everybody knows it, why bother to write a book" [18]; or feelings that description is not enough: a good sociologist from Chicago must do more, but what?" [19] Sociologists who set themselves the task of generating theory from the data of social research have a job that can be done only by the sociologist, and that offers a significant product to laymen and colleagues alike. Research sociologists in their driving efforts to get the facts tend to forget that, besides methodology, the distinctive offering of sociology to our society is sociological

18. Blanche Geer, "First Days in the Field," in Hammond, *op. cit.*, p. 322.

19. David Reisman and Jeanne Watson, "The Sociability Project: A Chronicle of Frustration and Achievement," in Hammond, *op. cit.*, p. 292.

theory, not only researched description.[20] Indeed, the market, corporate, and government fact-finding agencies can easily outdo any sociologist in researched descriptions through sheer resources, if they care to. Where the sociologist can help these agencies is by providing them with theory that will make their research relevant. And, as a brief reading of typical fact-finding and market-research reports indicates, sociological relevance is sorely needed both for understanding the "dust heap" of data piled up by agencies and for correcting the conventional ideology that guides this piling up of data.[21]

What Theory Is Generated

This book is about the process of generating grounded theory, and so our polemic is with other processes of arriving at theory, particularly the logico-deductive. Grounded theory, it should be mentioned, may take different forms. And although we consider the *process* of generating theory as related to its subsequent use and effectiveness, the *form* in which the theory is presented can be independent of this process by which it was generated. Grounded theory can be presented either as a well-codified set of propositions or in a running theoretical discussion, using conceptual categories and their properties.[22]

20. We are in complete agreement with Zetterberg on this issue of whether sociology will advance more by concentrating on theory or on methodology. But we feel that a methodology of generating it is needed for theoretical advance. See Hans L. Zetterberg, *On Theory and Verification in Sociology* (Totowa, N.J.: Bedminster Press, 1963), Preface.

21. A good instance is the sociological relevance of vast amounts of governmental statistics on the differential medical care of socioeconomic strata in America. The common-sense meaning of these statistics is almost self evident, but deeper sociological significance neither guides these governmental surveys nor much affects agency policies. What sociologists know about socioeconomic life styles and about the organization of medical facilities can easily be brought to bear upon government data. See policy paper on medical care by Anselm Strauss, written for the Institute for Policy Studies (Washington, D.C., July, 1965).

22. This choice is not news, since most theory is written this way, whether grounded or logico-deductive. But we have noted this decision, on the request of several colleagues, to fend off the critique that the only true theory is the one written, by the numbers, as an integrated set of propositions. The form in which a theory is presented does not make it a theory; it is a theory because it explains or predicts something.

We have chosen the discussional form for several reasons. Our strategy of comparative analysis for generating theory puts a high emphasis on *theory as process;* that is, theory as an ever-developing entity, not as a perfected product. (The reader will see further what we mean in Chapters III and IV.) To be sure, theory as process can be presented in publications as a momentary product, but it is written with the assumption that it is still developing. Theory as process, we believe, renders quite well the reality of social interaction and its structural context.

The discussional form of formulating theory gives a feeling of "ever-developing" to the theory, allows it to become quite rich, complex, and dense, and makes its fit and relevance easy to comprehend. On the other hand, to state a theory in propositional form, except perhaps for a few scattered core propositions, would make it less complex, dense, and rich, and more laborious to read. It would also tend by implication to "freeze" the theory instead of giving the feeling of a need for continued development. If necessary for verificational studies, parts of the theoretical discussion can at any point be rephrased as a set of propositions. This rephrasing is simply a formal exercise, though, since the concepts are already related in the discussion. Also, with either a propositional or discussional grounded theory, the sociologist can then logically deduce further hypotheses. Indeed, deductions from grounded theory, as it develops, are the method by which the researcher directs his theoretical sampling (see Chapter III).

Substantive and Formal Theory

Comparative analysis can be used to generate two basic kinds of theory: substantive and formal. By substantive theory, we mean that developed for a substantive, or empirical, area of sociological inquiry, such as patient care, race relations, professional education, delinquency, or research organizations. By formal theory, we mean that developed for a formal, or conceptual, area of sociological inquiry, such as stigma, deviant behavior, formal organization, socialization, status congruency, authority and power, reward systems, or social mobility. Both types of theory may be considered as "middle-range." That is, they fall between the "minor working hypotheses" of everyday life and the "all-inclusive" grand theories.[23]

Substantive and formal theories exist on distinguishable levels of generality, which differ only in terms of degree. There- fore, in any one study, each type can shade at points into the other. The analyst, however, should focus clearly on one level or other, or on a specific combination, because the strategies vary for arriving at each one. For example, in our analysis of dying as a nonscheduled status passage, the focus was on the substantive area of dying, not on the formal area of status pas- sage.[24] With the focus on a substantive area such as this, the generation of theory can be achieved by a comparative analysis between or among groups within the same substantive area. In this instance, we compared hospital wards where patients characteristically died at different rates. The substantive theory also could be generated by comparing dying as a status passage with other substantive cases within the formal area of status passage with other substantive cases within the formal area of status passage, whether scheduled or not, such as studenthood or engagement for marriage. The comparison would illuminate the substantive theory about dying as a status passage.

However, if the focus were on formal theory, then the com- parative analysis would be made among different kinds of sub- stantive cases which fall within the formal area, without relating them to any one substantive area. The focus of comparisons is now on generating a theory of status passage, not on generating theory about a single substantive case of status passage.

Both substantive and formal theories must be grounded in data. Substantive theory faithful to the empirical situation can- not, we believe, be formulated merely by applying a few ideas from an established formal theory to the substantive area. To be sure one goes out and studies an area with a particular sociological perspective, and with a focus, a general question, or a problem in mind. But he can (and we believe should) also study an area without any preconceived theory that dictates, prior to the research, "relevancies" in concepts and hypotheses.

23. See Merton, *op. cit.*, pp. 5-10.
24. Barney G. Glaser and Anselm L. Strauss, "Temporal Aspects of Dying as a Non-Scheduled Status Passage," *American Journal of Sociology,* LXXI (July, 1965), pp. 48-59.

Indeed it is presumptuous to assume that one begins to know the relevant categories and hypotheses until the "first days in the field," at least, are over.[25] A substantive theory generated from the data must first be formulated, in order to see which of diverse formal theories are, perhaps, applicable for furthering additional substantive formulations.

Ignoring this first task—discovering substantive theory relevant to a given substantive area—is the result, in most instances, of believing that formal theories can be applied directly to a substantive area, and will supply most or all of the necessary concepts and hypotheses. The conseqence is often a forcing of data, as well as a neglect of relevant concepts and hypotheses that may emerge. Our approach, allowing substantive concepts and hypotheses to emerge first, on their own, enables the analyst to ascertain which, if any, existing formal theory may help him generate his substantive theories. He can then be more faithful to his data, rather than forcing it to fit a theory. He can be more objective and less theoretically biased. Of course, this also means that he cannot merely apply Parsonian or Mertonian categories at the start, but must wait to see whether they are linked to the emergent substantive theory concerning the issue in focus.

Substantive theory in turn helps to generate new grounded formal theories and to reformulate previously established ones. Thus it becomes a strategic link in the formulation and development of formal theory based on data. For example, in our theory bearing on "awareness contexts" relevant to dying, two important properties are *cues* leading to awareness and the personal *stakes* involved in the various parties' becoming aware. Currently, in generating a formal theory of awareness contexts, we are developing the generalities related to stakes and cues by studying such groups as spies and building subcontractors. A dying patient or a spy has a great stake in any type of awareness context, and a subcontractor has a quantifiable or monetary stake. In Chapter IV, we shall discuss more fully the generation of grounded formal theory. Suffice it to say that we use the word *grounded* here to underline the point that the formal theory we are talking about must be contrasted with "grand" theory

25. Geer, *op. cit.*

that is generated from logical assumptions and speculations about the "oughts" of social life.

Within these relations existing among social research, substantive theory and formal theory is a design for the cumulative nature of knowledge and theory. The design involves a progressive building up from facts, through substantive to grounded formal theory. To generate substantive theory, we need many facts for the necessary comparative analysis; ethnographic studies, as well as direct gathering of data, are immensely useful for this purpose. Ethnographic studies, substantive theories and direct data collection are all, in turn, necessary for building up by comparative analysis to formal theory. This design, then, locates the place of each level of work within the cumulation of knowledge and theory, and thereby suggests a division of labor in sociological work.

This design also suggests that many ethnographic studies and *multiple theories* are needed so that various substantive and formal areas of inquiry can continue to build up to more inclusive formal theories. Such a call for multiple theories is in contrast to the directly monopolistic implications of logico-deductive theories, whose formulators claim there is only one theory for an area, or perhaps even one sociological theory for all areas. The need for multiple theories on the substantive level may be obvious, but it is not so obvious on the formal level. Yet multiple formal theories are also necessary, since one theory never handles all relevancies, and because by comparing many theories we can begin to arrive at more inclusive, parsimonious levels. The logico-deductive theorist, proceeding under the license and mandate of analytic abstraction, engages in premature parsimony when arriving at his theory. (In Chapters III, IV and V we shall discuss in more detail the relations of research to the generation of substantive and formal theory.)

Elements of the Theory

As we shall discuss and use them, the elements of theory that are generated by comparative analysis are, first, conceptual categories and their conceptual properties; and second, hypotheses or generalized relations among the categories and their properties.

Categories and properties. Making a distinction between category and property indicates a systematic relationship between these two elements of theory. A category stands by itself as a conceptual element of the theory. A property, in turn, is a conceptual aspect or element of a category. We have, then, both categories and their properties. For example, two categories of nursing care are the nurses' "professional composure" and their "perceptions of social loss" of a dying patient that is, their view of what degree of loss his death will be to his family and occupation.[26] One property of the category of social loss is "loss rationales"—that is, the rationales nurses use to justify to themselves their perceptions of social loss. All three are interrelated: *loss rationales* arise among nurses to explain the death of a patient whom they see as a high *social loss,* and this relationship helps the nurses to maintain their *professional composure* when facing his death.

It must be kept in mind that *both* categories and properties are concepts indicated by the data (and not the data itself); also that both vary in degree of conceptual abstraction. Once a category or property is conceived, a change in the evidence that indicated it will not necessarily alter, clarify or destroy it. It takes much more evidence—usually from different substantive areas—as well as the creation of a better category to achieve such changes in the original category. In short, conceptual categories and properties have a life apart from the evidence that gave rise to them.

The constant comparing of many groups draws the sociologist's attention to their many similarities and differences. Considering these leads him to generate abstract categories and their properties, which, since they emerge from the data, will clearly be important to a theory explaining the kind of behavior under observation. Lower level categories emerge rather quickly during the early phases of data collection. Higher level, overriding and integrating, conceptualizations—and the properties that elaborate them—tend to come later during the joint collection, coding and analysis of the data.

Although categories can be borrowed from existing theory, provided that the data are continually studied to make certain

26. See Barney G. Glaser and Anselm L. Strauss, "The Social Loss of Dying Patients," *American Journal of Nursing,* 64 (June, 1964), pp. 119-22.

that the categories fit, generating theory does put a premium on emergent conceptualizations. There are a number of reasons for this. Merely selecting data for a category that has been established by another theory tends to hinder the generation of new categories, because the major effort is not generation, but data selection. Also, emergent categories usually prove to be the most relevant and the best fitted to the data. As they are emerging, their fullest possible generality and meaning are continually being developed and checked for relevance. Also the adequacy of indicators for emergent categories is seldom a problem.

By contrast, when we try to fit a category from another theory to the situation under study, we can have much trouble in finding indicators and in getting agreement among colleagues on them. The result is that our forcing of "round data" into "square categories" is buttressed by a long justificatory explanation for the tentative relationship between the two. Forcing data to apply to categories or properties is sure to arouse the disbelief of both colleagues and laymen from the start.[27] Working with borrowed categories is more difficult since they are harder to find, fewer in number, and not as rich; since in the long run they may not be relevant, and are not exactly designed for the purpose, they must be respecified. In short, our focus on the emergence of categories solves the problems of fit, relevance, forcing, and richness. An effective strategy is, at first, literally to ignore the literature of theory and fact on the area under study, in order to assure that the emergence of categories will not be contaminated by concepts more suited to different areas. Similarities and convergences with the literature can be established after the analytic core of categories has emerged.

While the verification of theory aims at establishing a relatively few major uniformities and variations on the same conceptual level, we believe that the generation of theory should aim at achieving much *diversity* in emergent categories, synthesized at as *many levels* of conceptual and hypothetical generalization as possible. The synthesis provides readily apparent connections between data and lower and higher level conceptual abstractions of categories and properties.

This position on the diversity of conceptual level has impor-

27. See the case history on this problem confronted by Reisman and Watson, *op. cit.*, pp. 305-09.

tant consequences both for the sociologist and for sociology. As the sociologist uses standard sociological concepts, he soon discovers that they usually become very differently defined, dimensioned, specified, or typed. Typical boundaries of the standard concept become broken. Furthermore, the boundaries of the established battery of sociological concepts are also broken. As he discovers new categories, the sociologist realizes how few kinds of behavior can be coped with by many of our concepts, and recognizes the need to develop more concepts by straying out of traditional research areas into the multitude of substantive unknowns of social life that never have been touched —to give only a few examples, building subcontracting, auctioneering, mortgaging, or the producing of plays by amateur theater groups.

As one thinks about the broad spectrum of social life, one realizes that sociologists (with the focused aid of foundations) have really worked in only a small corner of it when posing the larger questions of deviance, social problems, formal organizations, education, mental health, community government, underdeveloped countries, and so forth. One also realizes that a great many more formal theories of sociology have yet to be generated about such additional areas as loneliness, brutality, resistance, debating, bidding systems, transportation, mail-order distribution, corporate collusion, financial systems, diplomacy, and world interdependence through business systems. One strategy for bringing the generation of theory to greater importance is to work in non-traditional areas where there is little or no technical literature. Finding non-traditional areas is also a strategy for escaping the shackles of existing theory and contemporary emphasis. The sociologist who does so can easily find himself not merely generating a new theory but also opening a new area for sociological inquiry—virtually initiating a new portion of sociology. Whether he studies less or more traditional areas, however, the first requirement for breaking the bounds of established sociology is to generate theory from data.

The type of concept that should be generated has two, joint, essential features. First, the concepts should be *analytic*—sufficiently generalized to designate characteristics of concrete entities, not the entities themselves. They should also be *sensitizing* —yield a "meaningful" picture, abetted by apt illustrations that enable one to grasp the reference in terms of one's own experience.[28] To make concepts both analytic and sensitizing helps the reader to see and hear vividly the people in the area under study, especially if it is a substantive area. This perception, in turn, helps the reader to grasp the theory developed for the area. To formulate concepts of this nature, bringing together the best of two possible worlds, takes considerable study of one's data and requires considerable data collection of incidents bearing on a category. If, when a category is but scarcely established, the sociologist turns to collecting data for another potential category, slighting the newly established one, the latter is likely to lack development both in sensitizing and in some of its analytic aspects. A balance must be struck between the two lines of effort in accordance with the theoretical saturation of categories (a strategy we shall discuss in Chapter III).

Hypotheses. The comparison of differences and similarities among groups not only generates categories, but also rather speedily generates generalized relations among them. It must be emphasized that these hypotheses have at first the status of suggested, not tested, relations among categories and their properties, though they are verified as much as possible in the course of research.

Whether the sociologist, as he jointly collects and analyzes qualitative data, starts out in a confused state of noting almost everything he sees because it all seems significant, or whether he starts out with a more defined purpose, his work quickly leads to the generation of hypotheses. When he begins to hypothesize with the explicit purpose of generating theory, the researcher is no longer a passive receiver of impressions but is drawn naturally into actively generating and verifying his hypotheses through comparison of groups. Characteristically, in this kind of joint data collection and analysis, multiple hypotheses are pursued simultaneously. Some are pursued over long periods of time because their generation and verification are linked with developing social events. Meanwhile, new hypotheses are continually sought.

Generating hypotheses requires evidence enough only to

28. On sensitizing concepts see Herbert Blumer, "What is Wrong with Social Theory," *American Sociological Review,* 19 (February, 1964), pp. 3-10.

establish a suggestion—not an excessive piling up of evidence to establish a proof, and the consequent hindering of the generation of new hypotheses. In field work, however, general relations are often discovered in vivo; that is, the field worker literally sees them occur. This aspect of the "real life" character of field work deserves emphasis, for it is an important dividend in generating theory. (We shall say more about this point when discussing the credibility of analyses of qualitative field data in Chapter IX).

In the beginning, one's hypotheses may seem unrelated, but as categories and properties emerge, develop in abstraction, and become related, their accumulating interrelations form an integrated central theoretical framework—*the core of the emerging theory*. The core becomes a theoretical guide to the further collection and analysis of data. Field workers have remarked upon the rapid crystallization of that framework, as well as the rapid emergence of categories.[29] When the main emphasis is on verifying theory, there is no provision for discovering novelty, and potentially illuminating perspectives, that do emerge and might change the theory, actually are suppressed. In verification, one feels too quickly that he has the theory and now must "check it out." When generation of theory is the aim, however, one is constantly alert to emergent perspectives that will change and help develop his theory. These perspectives can easily occur even on the final day of study or when the manuscript is reviewed in page proof: so the published word is not the final one, but only a pause in the never-ending process of generating theory. When verification is the main aim, publication of the study tends to give readers the impression that this is the last word.

Integration. Integration of the theory—which takes place at the many levels of generality that emerge—does *not* necessitate a distinction between "working" (or "ordinary") and theoretical hypotheses.[30] Our emphasis on integration takes into considera-

---

29. Our colleague, Leonard Schatzman, has called this the "momentum effect." The emergence of categories and theoretical perspective gains such momentum that a researcher must usually retire from the field after the first few days to appraise the data and establish an order for what is happening. He stops being drowned by the flood of data and starts to plan his theoretical sampling.

30. Zetterberg, *op. cit.*, p. 21, and *passim*.

tion the fullest range of conceptual levels; anyone who uses the integrated theory can start at a more general level and, focusing upon a specific area within the theory, work down to data, still guided by hypotheses for limited, specific situations. For those who use the theory, these less information-packed hypotheses may be as important as the more general theoretical ones; for instance, a sociologist studying the awareness of dying patients on a surgical ward, or nurses trying to apply awareness theory to family relations as observed on an emergency ward (although not on all wards).

It must be emphasized that integration of the theory is best when it emerges, like the concepts. The theory should never just be put together, nor should a formal-theory model be applied to it until one is sure it will fit, and will not force the data. Possible use of a formal model of integration can be determined only after a substantive model has sufficiently emerged. The truly emergent integrating framework, which encompasses the fullest possible diversity of categories and properties, becomes an open-ended scheme, hardly subject to being redesigned. It is open-ended because, as new categories or properties are generated and related, there seems always to be a place for them in the scheme. For substantive theory, the analyst is very likely to discover an integrating scheme within his data, since the data and the interrelations of his theory lie so close together.[31]

However, the comparative analysis of diverse kinds of substantive groups, though aimed at generating "grounded" formal theory, can take the researcher far from from emergent substantive integrations. Then existing formal models of process and structure and analysis become useful guides to integrating the categories of a formal theory—provided that integration is not forced on the theory. Models of integration for substantive theory that are derived from the data are not necessarily applicable to other substantive areas. Their transfer should be attempted with great caution, and only after trying to discover an emergent integration first.

For example, our integration of substantive theory on the

31. For example consider the integration scheme of "Awareness and the Nurse's Composure," Chapter 13 in Glaser and Strauss, *Awareness of Dying*.

social loss of dying patients—under the major categories of calculating social loss, social loss stories and the impact of social loss—includes the effect of the social loss of dying patients on nurses' attitudes and behavior.[32] We cannot say whether or not this same scheme of interrelations would apply to other substantive theories that deal with the social value of people served by experts. Our substantive integration, however, would provide a useful beginning for integrating a formal theory about the distribution of services as affected by the social value of the people.[33] The move from substantive to formal levels of theorizing is referred to in Chapter III and will be explicitly discussed in Chapter IV.

Paying heed to these strictures on emergence and the application of integrative schemes, as well as to strictures on the emergence of concepts can insure that substantive and formal theories will correspond closely to the "real" world. These rules are beginning descriptions of a process—which we cannot emphasize too strongly—whereby substantive and formal theories that "work" (predict and explain—and do not sound "windy") are generated from data.

The following chart provides examples of elements of the two kinds of theory that we have discussed:

Elements of Theory	*Type of Theory*	
	Substantive	*Formal*
Category	Social loss of dying patients	Social value of people
Properties of Category	*Calculating* social loss on basis of *learned* and *apparent* characteristics of patient	Calculating social value of person on basis of *learned* and *apparent* characteristics
Hypotheses	The higher the social loss of a dying patient, (1) The better his care, (2) The more nurses develop loss rationales to explain away his death	The higher the social value of a person the less delay he experiences in receiving services from experts

32. Glaser and Strauss, "The Social Loss of Dying Patients," *op. cit.*
33. The way we have integrated a theory of dying as a non-scheduled status passage—legitimating, announcing and coordinating the passage—would provide a useful beginning to the study of status passage in general, "Temporal Aspects of Dying as a Non-Scheduled Status Passage," *op. cit.*

In concluding this chapter, we wish to emphasize one highly important aspect of generating theory that pervades this and other chapters of our book. Joint collection, coding, and analysis of data is the underlying operation. The generation of theory, coupled with the notion of theory as process, requires that all three operations be done together as much as possible. They should blur and intertwine continually, from the beginning of an investigation to its end. To be sure, in any investigation the tendency is to do all three simultaneously; but in many (if not most) studies of description and verification, there is typically such a definite focus on one operation at a time that the others are slighted or ignored. This definite separation of each operation hinders generation of theory. For example, if data are being coded and a fresh analytic idea emerges that jolts the operation, the idea may be disregarded because of pre-established rules or plain routine—thus stifling at that moment the generation of theory. To pursue this vital tactic further, in Chapter III we discuss the relations between data collection and analysis, which imply considerable coding; in Chapter V, the discussion will focus on the relations between joint coding and analysis, as data are collected.

III

Theoretical Sampling

Theoretical sampling is the process of data collection for generating theory whereby the analyst jointly collects, codes, and analyzes his data and decides what data to collect next and where to find them, in order to develop his theory as it emerges. This process of data collection is *controlled* by the emerging theory, whether substantive or formal. The initial decisions for theoretical collection of data are based only on a general sociological perspective and on a general subject or problem area (such as how confidence men handle prospective marks or how policemen act toward Negroes or what happens to students in medical school that turns them into doctors). The initial decisions are not based on a preconceived theoretical framework.

The sociologist may begin the research with a partial framework of "local" concepts, designating a few principal or gross features of the structure and processes in the situations that he will study. For example, he knows before studying a hospital that there will be doctors, nurses, and aides, and wards and admission procedures. These concepts give him a beginning foothold on his research. Of course, he does not know the relevancy of these concepts to his problem—this problem must emerge—nor are they likely to become part of the core explanatory categories of his theory. His categories are more likely to be concepts about the problem itself, not its situation. Also, he discovers that some anticipated "local" concepts may remain unused in the situations relevant to his problem—doctors may, for the problem, be called therapists—and he discovers many more structural and processional "local" concepts than he could have anticipated before his research.

The sociologist should also be sufficiently *theoretically sensitive* so that he can conceptualize and formulate a theory as it emerges from the data. Once started, theoretical sensitivity is forever in continual development. It is developed as over many years the sociologist thinks in theoretical terms about what he knows, and as he queries many different theories on such questions as "'What does the theory do? How is it conceived? What is its general position? What kinds of models does it use?" Theoretical sensitivity of a sociologist has two other characteristics. First, it involves his personal and temperamental bent. Second, it involves the sociologist's ability to have theoretical insight into his area of research, combined with an ability to make something of his insights (see Chapter XI).

These sources of developing theoretical sensitivity continually build up in the sociologist an armamentarium of categories and hypotheses on substantive and formal levels. This theory that exists within a sociologist can be used in generating his specific theory if, after study of the data, the fit and relevance to the data are emergent. A discovered, grounded theory, then, will tend to combine mostly concepts and hypotheses that have emerged from the data with some existing ones that are clearly useful. We have put most emphasis on the emergent concepts—those coming from the data. Still, whether the theoretical elements are emergent or already exist with fit and relevance that emerges, the strategies of comparative analysis presented in this and the next two chapters apply.

Potential theoretical sensitivity is lost when the sociologist commits himself exclusively to one specific preconceived theory (*e.g.*, formal organization) for then he becomes doctrinaire and can no longer "see around" either his pet theory or any other. He becomes insensitive, or even defensive, toward the kinds of questions that cast doubt on his theory; he is preoccupied with testing, modifying and seeing everything from this one angle. For this person, theory will seldom truly emerge from data. In the few instances where theory does emerge, the preconceived theory is likely to be readily dropped or forgotten because it now seems irrelevant to the data.[1]

Beyond the decisions concerning initial collection of data, further collection cannot be planned in advance of the emerging theory (as is done so carefully in research designed for verification and description). The emerging theory points to the next steps—the sociologist does not know them until he is guided by emerging gaps in his theory and by research questions suggeted by previous answers.[2]

The basic question in theoretical sampling (in either substantive or formal theory) is: *what* groups or subgroups does one turn to *next* in data collection? And for *what* theoretical purpose? In short, how does the sociologist select multiple comparison groups?[3] The possibilities of multiple comparisons are infinite, and so groups must be chosen according to theoretical criteria.

In actuality, many sociologists escape this problem of selecting groups by studying only one group during a given research, with some slight effort at delineating subgroups, and with occasional references (usually in footnotes) to comparative findings on another group, typically followed by a brief description of differences, but not by a theoretical analysis. In other studies, particularly survey research, comparisons are usually, and quite arbitrarily, based on only one different substantive group (such as natural scientists compared with social scientists, or scientists with engineers); or the comparisons are based on several subgroups within the substantive group. And in "comparative studies" of more than two groups, the sociologist usually tries to compare as many as he can of the groups for which he can

1. For an excellent discussion of this phenomenon see James Coleman, "Research Chronicle: The Adolescent Society," in Philip Hammond (Ed.), *Sociologists at Work* (New York: Basic Books, 1964), pp. 198-204.

2. For example, in our study of the patient's awareness of dying related to medical staff-patient interaction, after we had saturated the various contexts in which this occurred, we realized that we should collect data on additional situations where patient awareness is discounted. So we looked closely for this at staff-patient interaction on an emergency ward. See Barney G. Glaser and Anselm L. Strauss, *Awareness of Dying* (Chicago: Aldine Publishing Co., 1965), Chapter 7.

3. The reader may consider aggregates or single people as the equivalents of groups, with respect to the strategies of comparative analysis.

obtain data within the limits of his own time and money and his degree of access to those groups.[4] The resulting set of groups is then justified by citing common factors and relevant differences, stating that this constitutes all the available data anyhow. Further comparisons are left to future researchers.

Although these methods of choosing groups yield worthwhile research, they do not employ the criteria for theoretical sampling that we shall discuss in this chapter. Our criteria are those of *theoretical purpose and relevance*—not of structural circumstance. Though constrained by the same structural circumstances of research, we do not base research on them. The criteria may appear flexible (too much so for validity, one critic has said), but the reader must remember that our main purpose is to generate theory, not to establish verifications with the "facts." We trust that these criteria will also appear to create a more systematic, relevant, impersonal control over data collection than do the preplanned, routinized, arbitrary criteria based on the existing structural limits of everyday group boundaries. The latter criteria are used in studies designed to get the facts and test hypotheses. One reason for emphasizing this difference in control is immediately apparent. The criteria of theoretical sampling are designed to be applied in the ongoing joint collection and analysis of data associated with the generation of theory. Therefore, they are continually tailored to fit the data and are applied judiciously at the right point and moment in the analysis. The analyst can continually adjust his control of data collection to ensure the data's relevance to the impersonal criteria of his emerging theory.   ·

By contrast, data collected according to a preplanned routine are more likely to force the analyst into irrelevant directions and harmful pitfalls. He may discover unanticipated contingencies in his respondents, in the library and in the field, but is unable to adjust his collection procedures or even redesign his whole project. In accordance with conventional practice, the researcher is admonished to stick to his prescribed research

4. For examples see: Coleman, *op. cit.*, and *The Adolescent Society* (New York: Free Press of Glencoe, 1961); Morris Janowitz, *The Military in the Political Development of New Nations* (Chicago: University of Chicago Press, 1964), or Seymour Martin Lipset and Reinhard Bendix, *Social Mobility in Industrial Society* (Berkeley: University of California Press, 1959).

design, no matter how poor the data. If he varies his task to meet these unanticipated contingencies, readers may judge that his facts have been contaminated by his personal violation of the preconceived impersonal rules. Thus he is controlled by his impersonal rules and has no control over the relevancy of his data, even as he sees it go astray.[5]

Selecting Comparison Groups

In this section we focus on two questions: which groups are selected, why and how?

Which Groups?

The basic criterion governing the selection of comparison groups for discovering theory is their *theoretical relevance* for furthering the development of emerging categories. The researcher chooses any groups that will help generate, to the fullest extent, as many properties of the categories as possible, and that will help relate categories to each other and to their properties. Thus, as we said in Chapter II, group comparisons are conceptual; they are made by comparing diverse or similar evidence indicating the same conceptual categories and properties, *not* by comparing the evidence for its own sake. Comparative analysis takes full advantage of the "interchangeability" of indicators, and develops, as it proceeds, a broad range of acceptable indicators for categories and properties.[6]

Since groups may be chosen for a single comparison only, there can be no definite, prescribed, preplanned set of groups that are compared for all or even most categories (as there are

5. For example, "The entire design of the study did not permit me to propose hypotheses . . . it simply permitted me to describe what I found," Stanley H. Udy, Jr., "Cross Cultural Analysis: A Case Study," Hammond, *op. cit.*, p. 173, and *passim* for more examples. Merton has developed a research design for interweaving the standard procedures of preplanned data collection and data analysis in order to keep adjusting to discovered relevances. For a synopsis see Hanan C. Selvin, "The Interplay of Social Research and Social Policy in Housing," *Journal of Social Issues,* Vol. VII, (1951), pp. 180-81.

6. Paul F. Lazarsfeld and Wagner Theileus, Jr., *Academic Mind* (New York: Free Press of Glencoe, 1958), pp. 402-08.

in comparative studies made for accurate descriptions and verification). In research carried out for discovering theory, the
sociologist cannot cite the number and types of groups from
which he collected data *until* the research is completed. In an
extreme case, he may then find that the development of each
major category may have been based on comparisons of different sets of groups. For example, one could write a substantive
theory about scientists' authority in organizations, and compare
very different kinds of organizations to develop properties associated with the diverse categories that might emerge: authority
over clients, administration, research facilities, or relations with
outside organizations and communities; the degree or type of
affiliation in the organization; and so forth. Or the sociologist
may wish to write a formal theory about professional authority
in organizations; then the sets of comparison groups for each
category are likely to be much more diverse than those used
in developing a substantive theory about scientists, since now
the field of possible comparison is far greater.

Our logic of *ongoing inclusion* of groups must be differentiated from the logic used in comparative analyses that are
focused mainly on accurate evidence for description and verification. That logic, one of preplanned inclusion and exclusion,
warns the analyst away from comparing "non-comparable"
groups. To be included in the planned set, a group must have
"enough features in common" with the other groups. To be
excluded, it must show a "fundamental difference" from the
others.[7] These two rules represent an attempt to "hold constant"
strategic facts, or to disqualify groups where the facts either
cannot actually be held constant or would introduce more un-
wanted differences. Thus in comparing variables (conceptual
and factual), one hopes that, because of this set of "purified
groups," spurious factors now will not influence the findings
and relationships and render them inaccurate. This effort of purification is made for a result impossible to achieve, since one
never really knows what has and has not been held constant.

7. For example see Janowitz, *op. cit.*, Preface and Chapter 1; and Ed-
ward A. Shils, "On the Comparative Study of New States" in Clifford
Geertz (Ed.), *Old Societies and New States* (New York: Free Press of
Glencoe, 1963), pp. 5, 9.

To be sure, these rules of comparability are important when accurate evidence is the goal, but they hinder the generation of theory, in which "non-comparability" of groups is irrelevant. They prevent the use of a much wider range of groups for developing properties of categories. Such a range, necessary for the categories' fullest possible development, is achieved by comparing *any* groups, irrespective of differences or similarities, as long as the data apply to a similar category or property. Furthermore, these two rules divert the analyst's attention away from the important sets of fundamental differences and similarities, which, upon analysis, become important qualifying conditions under which categories and properties vary. These differences should be made a vital part of the analysis, but rules of comparability tend to make the analyst inattentive to conditions that vary findings by allowing him to assume constants and to disqualify basic differences, thus nullifying their effort before the analysis.

It is theoretically important to note to what degree the properties of categories are varied by diverse conditions. For example, properties of the effect of awareness contexts on the interaction between the nurse and the dying patient within a hospital can usefully be developed by making comparisons with the same situation in the home, in nursing homes, in ambulances, and on the street after accidents. The similarities and differences in these conditions can be used to explain the similar and diverse properties of interaction between nurse and patient.

The principal point to keep clear is the purpose of the research, so that rules of evidence will not hinder discovery of theory. However, these goals are usually not kept clear (a condition we are trying to correct) and so typically a sociologist starts by applying these rules for selecting a purified set of groups to achieve accurate evidence. He then becomes caught up in the delights of generating theory, and so compares everything comparable; but next he finds his theory development severely limited by lack of enough theoretically relevant data, because he has used a preplanned set of groups for collecting his information (see Chapter VI). In allowing freedom for comparing any groups, the criterion of theoretical relevance used for each comparison in systematically generating theory controls data collection without hindering it. Control by this criterion assures that ample data will be collected and that the data collection makes sense (otherwise collection is a waste of time). However, applying theoretical control over choice of comparison groups is more difficult than simply collecting data from a preplanned set of groups, since choice requires continuous thought, analysis and search.

The sociologist must also be clear on the basic *types* of groups he wishes to compare in order to control their effect on generality of both *scope* of population and *concepiual level* of his theory. The simplest comparisons are, of course, made among different groups of exactly the same substantive type; for instance, federal bookkeeping departments. These comparisons lead to a substantive theory that is applicable to this one type of group. Somewhat more general substantive theory is achieved by comparing different types of groups; for example, different kinds of federal departments in one federal agency. The scope of the theory is further increased by comparing different types of groups within different larger groups (different departments in different agencies). Generality is further increased by making these latter comparisons for different regions of a nation or, to go further, different nations. *The scope of a substantive theory can be carefully increased and controlled by such conscious choices of groups.* The sociologist may also find it convenient to think of subgroups within larger groups, and of internal and external groups, as he broadens his range of comparisons and attempts to keep tractable his substantive theory's various levels of generality of scope.

The sociologist developing substantive or formal theory can also usefully *create* groups, provided he keeps in mind that they are an artifact of his research design, and so does not start assuming in his analysis that they have properties possessed by a natural group. Survey researchers are adept at creating groups and statistically grounding their relevance (as by factor analysis, scaling, or criteria variables) to make sure they are, in fact, groups that make meaningful differences even though they have been created: for example, teachers high, medium, and low on "apprehension"; or upper, middle, and lower class;

or local-cosmopolitan.[8] However, only a handful of survey researchers have used their skill to create multiple comparison subgroups for discovering theory. This would be a very worthwhile endeavor (see Chapter VIII on quantitative data).

The tactic of creating groups is equally applicable for sociologists who work with qualitative data. When using only interviews, for instance, a researcher surely can study comparison groups composed of respondents chosen in accordance with his emergent analytic framework. And historical documents, or other library materials, lend themselves wonderfully to the comparative method. Their use is perhaps even more efficient, since the researcher is saved much time and trouble in his search for comparison groups which are, after all, already concentrated in the library (see Chapter VII). As in field work, the researcher who uses library material can always select additional comparison groups after his analytic framework is well developed, in order to give himself additional confidence in its credibility. He will also—like the field worker who sometimes stumbles upon comparison groups and then makes proper use of them—occasionally profit from happy accidents that may occur when he is browsing along library shelves. And, again like the researcher who carefully chooses natural groups, the sociologist who creates groups should do so carefully according to the scales of generality that he desires to achieve.

As the sociologist shifts the degree of conceptual generality for which he aims, from discovering substantive to discovering formal theory, he must keep in mind the *class* of the groups he selects. For substantive theory, he can select, as the same substantive class, groups regardless of where he finds them. He may, thus, compare the "emergency ward" to all kinds of medical wards in all kinds of hospitals, both in the United States and abroad. But he may also conceive of the emergency ward as a subclass of a larger class of organizations, all designed to render immediate assistance in the event of accidents or break-

8. In fact, in backstage discussions about which comparative groups to create and choose in survey analysis, the answer frequently is: "Where the breaks in the distribution are convenient and save cases, and among these choose the ones that give the 'best findings.'" Selvin, however, has developed a systematic method of subgroup comparison in survey research that prevents the opportunistic use of "the best finding" criteria. See *The Effects of Leadership* (Glencoe, Ill.: Free Press, 1960).

downs. For example, fire, crime, the automobile, and even plumbing problems have all given rise to emergency organizations that are on 24-hour alert. In taking this approach to choosing dissimilar, substantive comparative groups, the analyst must be clear about his purpose. He may use groups of the more general class to illuminate his substantive theory of, say, emergency wards. He may wish to begin generating a formal theory of emergency organizations. He may desire a mixture of both: for instance, bringing out his substantive theory about emergency wards within a context of some formal categories about emergency organizations.[9]

On the other hand, when the sociologist's purpose is to discover formal theory, he will definitely select dissimilar, substantive groups from the larger class, while increasing his theory's scope. And he will also find himself comparing groups that seem to be non-comparable on the substantive level, but that on the formal level are conceptually comparable. Non-comparable on the substantive level here implies a stronger degree of apparent difference than does *dissimilar*. For example, while fire departments and emergency wards are substantially dissimilar, their conceptual comparability is still readily apparent. Since the basis of comparison between substantively non-comparable groups is not readily apparent, it must be explained on a higher conceptual level.

Thus, one could start developing a formal theory of social isolation by comparing four apparently unconnected monographs: *Blue Collar Marriage, The Taxi-Dance Hall, The Ghetto* and *The Hobo* (Komarovsky, Cressey, Wirth, Anderson).[10] All deal with facets of "social isolation," according to their authors. For another example, Goffman has compared apparently non-comparable groups when generating his formal theory of stigma. Thus, anyone who wishes to discover formal theory should be aware of the usefulness of comparisons made on high level conceptual categories among the seemingly non-comparable; he should actively seek this kind of comparison; do it with flexibility; and be able to interchange the apparently

9. Cf. Shils, *op. cit.,* p. 17.
10. Respectively, Mirra Komarovsky (New York: Random House, 1962); Paul Cressey (Chicago: University of Chicago Press, 1932); Louis Wirth (Chicago: University of Chicago Press, 1962 edition); and Nels Anderson (Chicago: University of Chicago Press, 1961 edition).

non-comparable comparison with the apparently comparable ones. The non-comparable type of group comparison can greatly aid him in transcending substantive descriptions of time and place as he tries to achieve a general, formal theory.[11]

Why Select Groups

This concern with the selection of groups for comparison raises the question: Why does the researcher's comparison of groups make the content of the data more theoretically relevant than when he merely selects and compares data? The answer is threefold. Comparison groups provide, as just noted, control over the two scales of generality: first, conceptual level, and second, population scope. Third, comparison groups also provide simultaneous maximization or minimization of both the differences and the similarities of data that bear on the categories being studied. *This control over similarities and differences is vital* for discovering categories, and for developing and relating their theoretical properties, all necessary for the further development of an emergent theory. By maximizing or minimizing differences among comparative groups, the sociologist can control the theoretical relevance of his data collection. Comparing as many differences and similarities in data as possible (as mentioned in Chapter II) tends to force the analyst to generate categories, their properties and their interrelations as he tries to understand his data (see Chapter V also).

Minimizing differences among comparison groups increases the possibility that the researcher will collect much similar data on a given category while he spots important differences not caught in earlier data collection. Similarities in data that bear on a category help verify its existence by verifying the data behind it.

The basic properties of a category also are brought out by similarities, and by a few important differences found when minimizing group differences. It is helpful to establish these properties before differences among groups are maximized. For

11. This statement is made in implicit opposition merely to "writing" one's theory in a general formal manner, on the basis of sheer conjecture or on the basis of one group, as is typical of journal articles.

example, the basic property of calculating the social loss of dying patients is their age, as was discovered by observation on geriatric and nursery wards. It was important to establish this property before going on to establish other properties of social loss by studying dying on other kinds of wards.[12]

Minimizing differences among comparison groups also helps establish a definite set of conditions under which a category exists, either to a particular degree or as a type—which in turn establishes a probability for theoretical prediction. For example, "open awareness contexts" about dying—where the patient and the staff are aware that he is dying—are expectable whenever patients are held "captive" in a government hospital (whether national, state, or county). "Captive" patients may be convicts, veterans, or research patients.[13]

The other approach, maximizing differences among comparison groups, increases the probability that the researcher will collect different and varied data bearing on a category, while yet finding strategic similarities among the groups. The similarities that occur, through many diverse kinds of groups, provides, of course, the most general uniformities of scope within his theory. As the analyst tries to understand the multitude of differences, he tends to develop the properties of categories speedily and densely and, in the end, to integrate them into a theory that possesses different levels of conceptual generality, thereby delimiting the theory's scope. The sociologist does not merely look for negative cases bearing on a category (as do others who generate theory); he searches for maximum differences among comparative groups in order to compare them on the basis of as many relevant diversities and similarities in the data as he can find.

When beginning his generation of a substantive theory, the sociologist establishes the basic categories and their properties by minimizing differences in comparative groups.[14] Once this

12. See Barney G. Glaser and Anselm L. Strauss, "The Social Loss of Dying Patients," *American Journal of Nursing*, Vol. 64, No. 6 (June, 1964).

13. See Glaser and Strauss, *Awareness of Dying, op. cit.*, Chapter 6.

14. Good substantive theory can result from the study of one group, if the analyst carefully sorts data into comparative subgroups. For example, see Evans-Pritchard, *Witchcraft, Oracles and Magic Among the Azande* (Oxford, England: Clarendon Press, 1937), and our discussion of this book in Chapter VI.

basic work is accomplished, however, he should turn to maximizing differences among comparison groups, in accordance with the kind of theory he wishes to develop (substantive or formal) and with the requirements of his emergent theory. When maximizing differences among comparative groups (thereby maximizing differences in data) he possesses a more powerful means for stimulating the generation of theoretical properties once his basic framework has emerged.[15] Maximizing brings out the widest possible coverage on ranges, continua, degrees, types, uniformities, variations, causes, conditions, consequences, probabilities of relationships, strategies, process, structural mechanisms, and so forth, all necessary for elaboration of the theory.

As the sociologist maximizes differences by changing the scope of his research—for example, by going to different organizations, regions, cities or nations—he discovers more startling differences in data. His attempts to understand how these differences fit in are likely to have important effects on both his research operations and the generality of scope of his theory. These differences from other organizations, regions, or nations will make him wonder where he could have found the same differences at original research sites. And how can he continue his theoretically focused research along this line when he returns to home base?

At the same time the scope of his theory is broadened, not qualified. For example, one of us once noted that in Malayan hospitals families work in caring for dying patients. This observation was interesting because up to this point we had considered the family member, in the United States, as either being treated as another patient (sedated, given rest) or just ignored as a nuisance. Reviewing our American data, though, we discovered that the family is used in several ways for the care of dying patients. We had failed to focus on this not-so-observable occurrence. Thus, we discovered a cross-national uniformity—not a difference—by noting abroad what we had missed in America. We then proceeded to study it at our home base, where we had more time for the inquiry. We had similar experiences when comparing hospitals in various regions of the United States with those closer to home, in San Francisco.

15. Shils, *op. cit.*, p. 25.

Chart 1 presents the basic consequences of minimizing and maximizing groups in generating theory.

CHART 1. CONSEQUENCES OF MINIMIZING AND MAXIMIZING DIFFERENCES IN COMPARISON GROUPS FOR GENERATING THEORY

Differences in Groups	Data on Category	
	Similar	Diverse
Minimized	Maximum similarity in data leads to: (1) Verifying usefulness of category; (2) Generating basic properties; and (3) Establishing set of conditions for a degree of category. These conditions can be used for prediction.	Spotting fundamental differences under which category and hypotheses vary.
Maximized	Spotting fundamental uniformities of greatest scope	Maximum diversity in data quickly forces: (1) Dense developing of property of categories; (2) Integrating of categories and properties; (3) Delimiting scope of theory.

How To Select Groups

Part of the sociologist's decision about which groups to select is the problem of *how* to go about choosing particular groups for theoretically relevant data collection. First, he must remember that he is an active sampler of theoretically relevant data, not an ethnogapher trying to get the fullest data on a group, with or without a preplanned research design. As an active sampler of data, he must continually analyze the data to see where the next theoretical question will take him. He must them systematically calculate where a given order of events is—or is not—likely to take place.[16] If ongoing events do not give him theoretical relevance, he must be prepared

16. See Merton's discussion of strategic research sites in Robert K. Merton, Leonard Broom, and Leonard S. Cottrell (Eds.), *Sociology Today* (New York: Basic Books, 1959), p. xxvi.

to manipulate events by words or actions in order to see what
will happen.

The following memo from our research for *Awareness of
Dying* describes how the active search for data occurs as the
researcher asks himself the next theoretically relevant question,
which, in turn, directs him to seek particular groups for study:

> Visits to the various medical services were scheduled as fol-
> lows: I wished first to look at services that minimized patient
> awareness (and so first looked at a premature baby service and
> then at a neurosurgical service where patients were frequently
> comatose). I wished next to look at dying in a situation where
> expectancy of staff and often of patients was great and dying was
> quick, so I observed on an Intensive Care Unit. Then I wished to
> observe on a service where staff expectations of terminality were
> great but where the patient's might or might not be, and where
> dying tended to be slow. So I looked next at a cancer service.
> I wished then to look at conditions where death was unexpected
> and rapid, and so looked at an emergency service. While we
> were looking at some different types of services, we also observed
> the above types of service at other types of hospitals. So our
> scheduling of types of service was directed by a general con-
> ceptual scheme—which included hypotheses about awareness,
> expectedness and rate of dying—as well as by a developing con-
> ceptual structure including matters not at first envisioned. Some-
> times we returned to services after the initial two or three or four
> weeks of continuous observation, in order to check upon items
> which needed checking or had been missed in the initial period.[17]

And in connection with cross-national comparisons, here is
another research memo which shows how groups are selected:

> The emphasis is upon extending the comparisons made in
> America in theoretically relevant ways. The probability of fruitful
> comparisons is increased very greatly by choosing different and
> widely contrasting countries. That is, the major unit of compari-
> son is the country, not the type of hospital. The other major unit

17. "Once the theoretical gap is identified, it leads almost as a matter
of course to further questions, each with its distinctive rationale," "The
objective typically requires a search for empirical materials through which
the problem can be investigated to good advantage." We have detailed
these general comments of Merton on developing theory by linking them
to comparative analysis and its specific strategies. (*Ibid.*, pp. xxiii-xxiv.) See
also Dalton's discussion of using the "next question technique" to guide his
comparative analysis of industrial organizations, in Melville Dalton, "Preconceptions and Methods in Men Who Manage," in Hammond, *op. cit.*

of comparison, as we have seen in our own hospitals, is the type of hospital service, since what ensues around the terminal patient depends on how he dies and under what circumstances. In each country, therefore, I shall attempt to maximize the kinds of dying situations which I would see. I know, for instance, that in some Asian countries many hospitals consist of only one large ward, and this means that I will have to visit hospitals in contrasting regions of the countries. But in the cities, even in Asia, the same hospital may have differing services; and, as in Malaya, there will be hospitals for Chinese and hospitals for mixed ethnic groups right within the same city.

The selection of hospitals and services at which I would observe overseas will be guided, as in the current terminal study, by the conceptual framework developed to date. I will want to observe at hospitals, to begin with, where [four important] structural conditions we have noted are different than in America. I will observe, where possible, in hospitals (or on wards) where all four conditions are maximally different from the usual American conditions; also where three are different, where two are different, and one. I shall also choose wards or services which will maximize some of the specific conditions studied in the United States: namely, wards where dying is predominantly expected by staff and others where dying is relatively unexpected; wards where patients tend to know they are dying, and ones where they do not; wards where dying tends to be slow, and wards where predominant mode of dying tends to be relatively rapid. I hope to observe on various of those wards patients who are of high as well as low social value, and will try to visit locales where conditions are such that very many patients tend to be of low social value, as well as where there would tend to be many patients of high social value.

Degree of Theoretical Sampling

When choosing groups for theoretical relevance, two strategic questions of degree of sampling arise: How many groups should one choose? To what degree should one collect data on a single group? Answering these questions requires discussions on theoretical saturation, "slice" of data, and depth of theoretical sampling.

Theoretical Saturation

As we have said, the sociologist trying to discover theory cannot state at the outset of his research how many groups he will sample during the entire study; he can only count up the groups at the end. Since data for various categories are usually collected from a single group—although data from a given group may be collected for only one category—the sociologist usually is engaged in collecting data from older groups, or returning to them, while simultaneously seeking new groups. Thus he continually is dealing with a multiplicity of groups, and a multiplicity of situations within each; while absorbed with generating theory he would find it hard to count all these groups. (This situation contrasts with that of the researcher whose study involves verification or description, in which people are distributed throughout various categories, and he, therefore, must state the number of groups that will be sampled, according to rules of evidence governing the collection of reliable data.)

Even during research focused on theory, however, the sociologist must continually judge how many groups he should sample for each theoretical point. The criterion for judging when to stop sampling the different groups pertinent to a category is the category's *theoretical saturation.* *Saturation* means that no additional data are being found whereby the sociologist can develop properties of the category. As he sees similar instances over and over again. the researcher becomes empirically confident that a category is saturated. He goes out of his way to look for groups that stretch diversity of data as far as possible, just to make certain that saturation is based on the widest possible range of data on the category.

One reaches theoretical saturation by joint collection and analysis of data. (See Chapter V for a discussion of saturation during analysis of data.) When one category is saturated, nothing remains but to go on to new groups for data on other categories, and attempt to saturate these new categories also. When saturation occurs, the analyst will usually find that some gap in his theory, especially in his major categories, is almost, if not completely filled. In trying to reach saturation he maximizes differences in his groups in order to maximize the varieties of data bearing on a category, and thereby develops as many diverse properties of the category as possible. The criteria for determining saturation, then, are a combination of the empirical limits of the data, the integration and density of the theory, and the analyst's theoretical sensitivity.

Saturation can never be attained by studying one incident in one group. What is gained by studying one group is at most the discovery of some basic categories and a few of their properties. From the study of similar groups (or subgroups within the first group), a few more categories and their properties are yielded. But this is only the beginning of a theory. Then the sociologist should try to saturate his categories by maximizing differences among groups. In the process, he generates his theory. For example, from studying one incident in one group we might discover that an important property of nursing students' perspectives about course work is their assessment of the differential importance of certain kinds of course work to the faculty; but this discovery tells us almost nothing. To find out such properties as when and how an assessment is made and shared, who is aware of given assessments, and with what consequences for the students, the faculty, the school, and the patients whom the students nurse, dozens and dozens of situations in many diverse groups must be observed and analyzed comparatively.[18]

Theoretical and Statistical Sampling

It is important to contrast theoretical sampling based on the saturation of categories with statistical (random) sampling. Their differences should be kept clearly in mind for both designing research and judging its credibility. Theoretical sampling is done in order to discover categories and their properties, and to suggest the interrelationships into a theory. Statistical sampling is done to obtain accurate evidence on distributions of people among categories to be used in descriptions or verifications. Thus, in each type of research the "adequate sample"

18. Fred Davis and Virginia Olesen, "Problems and Issues in Collegiate Nursing Education" in Fred Davis (Ed.), *The Nursing Profession* (New York: John Wiley and Sons, 1966), pp. 138-75.

that we should look for (as researchers and readers of research) is very different.

The adequate theoretical sample is judged on the basis of how widely and diversely the analyst chose his groups for saturating categories according to the type of theory he wished to develop. The adequate statistical sample, on the other hand, is judged on the basis of techniques of random and stratified sampling used in relation to the social structure of a group or groups sampled. The inadequate theoretical sample is easily spotted, since the theory associated with it is usually thin and not well integrated, and has too many obvious unexplained exceptions. The inadequate statistical sample is often more difficult to spot; usually it must be pointed out by specialists in methodology, since other researchers tend to accept technical sophistication uncritically.

The researcher who generates theory need not combine random sampling with theoretical sampling when setting forth relationships among categories and properties. These relationships are suggested as hypotheses pertinent to direction of relationship, not tested as descriptions of both direction and magnitude. Conventional theorizing claims generality of scope; that is, one assumes that if the relationship holds for one group under certain conditions, it will probably hold for other groups under the same conditions.[19] This assumption of persistence is subject only to being disproven—not proven—when other sociologists question its credibility. Only a reversal or disappearance of the relationship will be considered by sociologists as an important discovery, not the rediscovery of the same relationship in another group; since once discovered, the relationship is assumed to persist. Persistence helps to generalize scope but is usually considered uninteresting, since it requires no modification of the theory.

Furthermore, once discovered the relationship is assumed to persist in direction no matter how biased the previous sample of data was, or the next sample is. Only if the hypothesis is disproven do biases in the sample come under question. For generating theory these biases are treated as conditions changing the relationship, which should be woven into the analysis as

19. See discussion on this in Hans L. Zetterberg, *On Theory and Verification in Sociology* (Totowa, N.J.: Bedminster Press, 1963), pp. 52-56.

such. Thus, random sampling is not necessary for theoretical sampling, either to discover the relationship or check out its existence in other groups.[20] However, when the sociologist wishes also to describe the magnitude of relationship within a particular group, random sampling, or a highly systematic observation procedure done over a specified time is necessary. For example, after we discovered the positive relationship between the attention that nurses gave dying patients and the nurses' perceptions of a patient's social loss, we continually found this relationship throughout our research and were quick to note conditions altering its direction. But we could never state the precise magnitude of this relationship on, say, cancer wards, since our sampling was theoretical.

Another important difference between theoretical and statistical sampling is that the sociologist must learn when to stop using the former. Learning this skill takes time, analysis and flexibility, since making the theoretically sensitive judgment about saturaton is never precise. The researcher's judgment becomes confidently clear only toward the close of his joint collection and analysis, when considerable saturation of categories in many groups to the limits of his data has occurred, so that his theory is approaching stable integration and dense development of properties.

By contrast, in statistical sampling the sociologist must continue with data collection no matter how much saturation he perceives. In his case, the notion of saturation is irrelevant to the study. Even though he becomes aware of what his findings will be, and knows he is collecting the same thing over and

20. We have taken a position in direct opposition to Udy, who says: "Any research of any type whatsoever which seeks to make generalizations beyond the material studied involves problems of sampling. . . . [The researcher] is implicitly identifying a larger population, of which his cases purport to be a representative sample, and contending that certain relationships observed in his sample could not have occurred there by chance. It is simply not true that one can avoid sampling problems by proceeding in words instead of numbers or by avoiding the use of statistical techniques, though it is unfortunately true that by avoiding such methods one can often keep sampling problems from becoming explicit." Udy's gross, categorical position could be modified to compatibility with ours, we believe, if he thought rather in terms of diverse purposes of research and the degree to which each purpose requires a relationship to be described in terms of its various properties: existence, direction, magnitude, nature, and conditions, etc. In any event, a few lines later he then admits that "one cannot really solve them" (problems of representativeness). Udy, *op. cit.*, pp. 169-170.

over to the point of boredom, he must continue because the rules of accurate evidence require the fullest coverage to achieve the most accurate count. If the researcher wishes to diverge from his preplanned research design because of conceptual realizations and implicit analyses, he must hold his wish in abeyance or laboriously integrate his new approach into the research design, to allow a new preplanned attack on the total problem. He must not deviate from this new design either; eventually it leads him back into the same "bind." [21]

Slice of Data

In theoretical sampling, no one kind of data on a category nor technique for data collection is necessarily appropriate. Different kinds of data give the analyst different views or vantage points from which to understand a category and to develop its properties; these different views we have called *slices of data.* While the sociologist may use one technique of data collection primarily, theoretical sampling for saturation of a category allows a multi-faceted investigation, in which there are no limits to the techniques of data collection, the way they are used, or the types of data acquired.[22] One reason for this openness of inquiry is that, when obtaining data on different groups, the sociologist works under the diverse structural conditions of each group: schedules, restricted areas, work tempos, the different perspectives of people in different positions, and the availability of documents of different kinds. Clearly, to

21. For example, Udy says, "The coding operation proved to be very tedious 'dog work' in the worst sense of the terms. I . . . was now attempting to resist, rather than encourage flights of imagination. I had to accept the fact that there were gaps in the data about which I could do nothing" (*op. cit.*, pp. 178-79). To avoid this bind, many sociologists hire data collectors and coders in preplanned research for description and verification. Then, however, discoveries are made too late to effect changes in data collection. See the tug-of-war waged between Riesman and Watson on this bind: Riesman continually wanted to break out and Watson wanted to maintain tight control; David Riesman and Jeanne Watson, "The Sociability Project: A Chronicle of Frustration and Achievement," in Hammond, *op. cit.*, pp. 269-84.

22. For examples of multifaceted investigations, see in Hammond, *op. cit.*: the research chronicles of Renee Fox, "An American Sociologist in the Land of Belgian Research"; Dalton; and Seymour M. Lipset, "The Biography of a Research Project: Union Democracy."

succeed he must be flexible in his methods and in his means for collecting data from group to group.[23]

The result is, of course, a variety of slices of data that would be bewildering if we wished to evaluate them as accurate evidence for verifications. However, for generating theory this variety is highly beneficial, because it yields more information on categories than any one mode of knowing (technique of collection). This makes the research very exciting to the sociologist, providing motivation to keep him at his task. The different ways of knowing about a category virtually force him to generate properties as he tries to understand the differences between the various slices of data, in terms of the different conditions under which they were collected.[24] But it must be remembered that this comparative analysis of different slices of data should be based on the researcher's theoretical understanding of the category under diverse conditions, not on methodological differences and on standard problems of the diverse techniques he has used.

Among the many slices of data that may be collected, which one is the best to obtain? The answer is, of course, the collection technique that best can obtain the information desired, provided that conditions permit its use in some manner.[25] For an extreme example, Dalton had to bribe a secretary in order to see secret personnel records so that he could find out the ethnic composition of an executive hierarchy, rather than trying to guess its composition from names.[26]

Most often, however, the sociologist's strategy will be constrained by such structural conditions as who is available to

23. Compare the flexibility in ethics of Dalton, *op. cit.*, pp. 59-62, with the ethical problems of Riesman and Watson, *op. cit.*, pp. 260-69.

24. Lipset said he wished to test his theory of union democracy by a survey of the International Typographers' Union. What actually happened when he compared this new slice of data to the formed theory was not testing but coming to terms with differences. Thereby more theory on union democracy was generated. See Seymour M. Lipset in Hammond, *op. cit.*, pp. 107-119.

25. Thus, any discussion about whether survey data are better or worse than field data is usually meaningless. Often the researcher is forced to obtain only one kind—and when theory is the objective, both kinds are useful. Only under particular conditions of a group which allows both does the question arise: which method would give the best data on the information desired? The answer is technical, not doctrinaire.

26. Dalton, *op. cit.*, pp. 66 and 67.

be observed, talked with, overheard, interviewed, or surveyed, and at what times. He should realize that no matter what slices of data he is able to obtain, comparing their differences generates properties, and most any slice can yield the same necessary social-structural information. For example, no matter whom the sociologist observes or talks with in a situation where someone is dying (patient, nurse, doctor, chaplain or family member), he will soon know what type of awareness context is operating. Possibly his theory will receive considerable development from any information that happens his way; even subtantively "trivial" data can help, if it yields useful information on a relevant category. For example, one can gain useful data on the life styles of professionals by examining, for this group, a national market-research survey about meat consumption (done for the meat-packing industry). The data need not be important in themselves; only the category which they indicate must be theoretically relevant. Similarly, a down-to-earth article on illness and pain by a nurse or patient may yield very useful information to a researcher who is studying the management of pain in hospitals.

Another slice of data that should be used is the "anecdotal comparison." Through his own experiences, general knowledge, or reading, and the stories of others, the sociologist can gain data on other groups that offer useful comparisons. This kind of data can be trusted if the experience was "lived." Anecdotal comparisons are especially useful in starting research and developing core categories. The researcher can ask himself where else has he learned about the category and make quick comparisons to start to develop it and sensitize himself to its relevancies.

As everyone knows, different people in different positions may offer as "the facts" very different information about the same subject, and they vary that information considerably when talking to different people. Furthermore, the information itself may be continually changing as the group changes, and different documents on the same subject can be quite contradictory. Some sociologists see these circumstances as presenting an unbounding relativism of facts—no data is accurate. Since such a situation is unbearable to those who wish to verify or describe, they tend to claim that only their method can give the "accurate" evidence. Other methods that they might use only yield biased or impressionistic data, and so can be discounted.[27] Using this argument, they take only one slice or mode of knowing as giving the "facts." Since they do not seek other modes, they remain untroubled. For example, in one noted study of adolescents in high schools, only the adolescents were surveyed; and in a study of workers in a factory, only workers were observed and interviewed.[28]

But when different slices of data are submitted to comparative analysis, the result is *not* unbounding relativism. Instead, it is a proportioned view of the evidence, since, during comparison, biases of particular people and methods tend to reconcile themselves as the analyst discovers the underlying causes of variation. This continual correction of data by comparative analysis gives the sociologist confidence in the data upon which he is basing his theory, at the same time forcing him to generate the properties of his categories. The continual correction of data also makes the sociologist realize clearly an important point: when used elsewhere, theory generated from just one kind of data never fits, or works as well, as theory generated from diverse slices of data on the same category. The theory based on diverse data has taken into consideration more aspects of the substantive or formal area, and therefore can cope with more diversity in conditions and exceptions to hypotheses.

If the sociologist has two slices of data (such as field and survey data), but does not engage in comparative analysis, he will generate his theory from one mode of collection and ignore the other completely when it disproves his theory—although he may selectively use confirmatory pieces of the other data as supporting evidence Thus, when no comparative analysis is

27. For example, "The significance of the quantitative case study, then, is (1) that it stimulates the kind of theoretical insights that can be derived only from quantitative analysis as well as the kind that results from close observation of an empirical situation, and (2) that it provides more severe checks on these insights than an impressionistic study and thus somewhat increases the probably validity of conclusions." Peter Blau, "The Research Process in the Study of the Dynamics of Bureaucracy," in Hammond, *op. cit.*, p. 20.

28. Coleman, *op. cit.*; and see, for the study of workers, Donald Roy, "Efficiency and the Fix: Informal Intergroup Relations in a Piecework Machine Shop," *American Journal of Sociology*, 60 (1954), pp. 255-266.

done, different slices of data are seen as tests of each other, not as different modes of knowing that must be explained and integrated theoretically. The result is that, without comparative analysis, even men who generate theory tend to use and fall into the rhetoric of verification.[29] They miss out on the rich diversity of modes of knowing about their categories. And they fail to tell their readers of their other data, since they believe, quite wrongly, that it disproves their theory, when it would have actually enriched it immensely.

Depth of Theoretical Sampling

The *depth* of theoretical sampling refers to the amount of data collected on a group and on a category.[30] In studies of verification and description it is typical to collect as much data as possible on the "whole" group. Theoretical sampling, though, does not require the fullest possible coverage on the whole group except at the very beginning of research, when the main categories are emerging—and these tend to emerge very fast.[31] Theoretical sampling requires only .collecting data on categories, for the generation of properties and hypotheses.

Even this kind of selective collection of data, however, tends to result in much excess data, from which new and related categories emerge. For example, after a full day in the field, when the field worker is tired and jammed with dozens of incidents to report in his field notes, he need only dictate data about his categories. Going through his categories also helps him to remember data he may have forgotten during his full day. With these categories firmly in mind, directing his attention, the field worker can focus on remembering the details of his day's observations with the confidence that the notes will be implicitly

29. These same sociologists tend to be debunkers who try to dig up something out of their own reading to disprove the theory presented by their colleague. They do not understand they are merely offering a new slice of data that under comparative analysis would enrich his theory by providing or modifying properties and categories.

30. See the instructive discussion on "depth" by Udy, *op. cit.*, pp. 164-65.

31. For examples on the quick emergence of relevant categories see, Blanche Geer, "First Days in the Field," in Hammond, *op. cit.;* and Blau, *op. cit.*, pp. 33-34. Blau discovered the significance of the "consultation" pattern within a week after starting his field research.

guided by his categories. Any additional information he decides to note afterwards is "gravy" for theoretical consideration, not a required chore for the fullest coverage. Theoretical sampling, therefore, can save much time in note-taking.

It is not too difficult to compare as many as forty groups on the basis of a defined set of categories and hypotheses (not on the basis of the "whole" group), and when groups within groups are compared (e.g.. different and similar wards within different types of hospitals). These groups can be studied one at a time, or a number can be studied simultaneously. They can also be studied in quick succession, to check out major hypotheses before too much theory is built around them. Without theoretical sampling, the field worker, or the writer of a survey questionnaire, collects as much data as he can and hopes that this full coverage will "catch enough" that later will prove relevant. Probably, though, it will prove too thin a basis for a developed theory.[32] Theoretical sampling reduces the mass of data that otherwise would be collected on any single group. Indeed, without theoretical sampling for categories one could not sample multiple groups; he would be too bogged down trying to cover just one.

The depth to which a category should be sampled is another matter. The general idea is that the sociologist should sample a category until confident of its saturation, but there are qualifications. All categories are obviously not equally relevant, and so the depth of inquiry into each one should not be the same.[33] *Core* theoretical categories, those with the most explanatory power, should be saturated as completely as possible. Efforts to saturate less relevant categories should not be made at the cost of resources necessary for saturating the core categories. As his theory develops and becomes integrated, the sociologist learns which categories require the most and least complete saturation, and which ones can be dropped. Thus, the theory generates its own selectivity for its direction and depth of development.

In actual practice, even the saturation of core categories can be a problem. In field work especially, the tendency always is to begin collecting data for another category before enough

32. For example see Riesman and Watson, *op. cit.*, p. 295.
33. See Shils, *op. cit.*, p. 17.

has been collected on a previous one. The sociologist should continue to saturate all categories until it is clear which are core categories. If he does not, he risks ending up with a vast array of loosely integrated categories, none deeply developed. This results in a thin, unvalenced theory. Since stable integration of the theory requires dense property development of at least some core categories, it then becomes difficult to say which of the array are the core categories; that is, those most relevant for prediction and explanation.

Temporal Aspects of Theoretical Sampling

When generating theory through joint theoretical collection, coding, and analysis of data, the temporal aspects of the research are different from those characteristic of research where separate periods of work are designated for each aspect of the research. In the latter case, only brief or minor efforts, if any, are directed toward coding and analysis while data are collected. Research aimed at discovering theory, however, requires that all three procedures go on simultaneously to the fullest extent possible; for this, as we have said, is the underlying operation when generating theory. Indeed, it is impossible to engage in theoretical sampling without coding and analyzing at the same time.

Theoretical sampling can be done with previously collected research data, as in secondary analysis, but this effort requires a large mass of data to draw on in order to develop a theory of some density of categories and properties. The sociologist engages in theoretical sampling of the previously collected data, which amounts to collecting data from collected data. Also, he is bound to think of ways to make quick, brief data-collection forays into other groups, to find additional relevant comparative data. Therefore, in the end, theoretical sampling and data collection for discovering theory become simultaneous, whether the sociologist uses collected data or collects his own data, or both. How much time and money are available is important in deciding to what degree the data to be sampled will have been collected previously by the researcher or anyone else who compiles data.

All studies require respites from data collection for the relief and health of their personnel. Generating theory by joint collection, coding and analysis requires such respites for additional, obvious reasons. The sociologist must engage continually in some systematic coding (usually just jotting categories and properties on the margins of his field notes or other recorded data) and analytic memo writing (see Chapter V). He must be looking for emergent categories, reformulating them as their properties emerge, selectively pruning his list of categories while adding to the list as the core of his theory emerges, along with developing his hypotheses and integrating his theory—in order to guide his theoretical sampling at each step of the way. If he does not take respites for reflection and analysis, he cannot avoid collecting a large mass of data of dubious theoretical relevance.

Most generating of theory should be done in uninterrupted quiet, away from the field or the machine room. This is true especially during earlier stages of the project, when more time is needed for careful formulation. At later stages, the sociologist will find that analysis can proceed more easily during moments of data collection. When his categories are firmer in integration and development, he usually can spot what he is doing in theoretical terms while collecting data. At this time, he may observe in a few minutes all that he needs to know about a group with reference to a given theoretical point. However, actually generating theory at the moment of collecting data is never easy; usually it takes reflection afterward to discover what one has actually found. In addition, if one has colleagues on the same project, they all must have respites from data collection to discuss what they are doing and should do next. Such discussion is difficult or impossible in the field because they are either scattered in different places or cannot talk freely in other people's presence.

The sociologist eventually learns to pace the alternating tempo of his collecting, coding and analyzing in order to get each task done in appropriate measure, in accordance with the stage of his research and theory development. At the beginning, there is more collection than coding and analysis; the balance then gradually changes until near the end when the research involves mostly analysis, with brief collection and coding for picking up loose ends. To pace the alternating tempo of these three operations, the sociologist soon learns that analysis can be usefully accomplished at various times: immediately after leaving the field; during the evening between successive days of data collection; and during two- or three-day, or weekly, respites from data collection. However, the systematic formulation of the core structure of his theory may take considerable time, though it need not. In either event, the sociologist should be very flexible about timing his work. He should not be afraid to take, literally, months off his data collection, if necessary (and if possible), to think through his emergent theory before returning to the field.

The continual intermeshing of data collection and analysis bears directly on how the data collection is brought to a close. A researcher can always try to collect more data for checking hypotheses or for generating new properties, categories and hypotheses. When writing is done in or near the field, the temptation to go back is especially strong. These final searches for data tend to be for either specific confirmation (the researcher moving now with considerable sureness and speed) or elaboration (the researcher wishing to round out his work by exploring some area that was previously untouched or even unconsidered).[34] They can be strongly tempting if personal relations formed in the field are satisfying or if exciting new events are developing there. However, collection of additional data can be a waste of time for categories already saturated or for categories not of core value to the theory.[35] Sometimes there is a tendency to wait in the field just in case something new should happen, but often it does not—and the study is prolonged unnecessarily. This tendency may be related to the researcher's anxiety to "know everything," which is not necessary for theoretical saturation.

34. Cf. A. Strauss, L. Schatzman, R. Bucher, D. Ehrlich, and M. Sabshin, *Psychiatric Ideologies and Institutions* (New York: Free Press of Glencoe, 1964), Chapter 2. See also H. Becker, B. Geer, E. Hughes and A. Strauss, *Boys in White* (Chicago: University of Chicago Press, 1962) for interviews after field observation.

35. Though highly unlikely, there is, of course, the small chance that additional data can "explode" an otherwise finished analytic framework and cause the researcher to spend months or years before he is satisfied enough to publish. This hazard is not confined to work with qualitative data, but is especially characteristic of it.

The tempo of the research is difficult to know beforehand, because it is largely contingent on the tempo of the emerging theory, which may come quickly at some points and at others involve long periods of gestation. This difficulty raises a problem: in presenting proposals for research grants, how does the sociologist who intends to generate theory anticipate the amount of time necessary, for data collection and for the whole project? This is a question that review boards want answered—but it is difficult to answer for studies focused on generating theory, while relatively easy for those devoted to verification and description, which require preplanned schedules.

Because the sociologist who wishes to generate theory cannot state beforehand how many groups he will study and to what degree he will study each one, he cannot say how much time his project will take. But he can state the type of theory, substantive or formal, that he wishes to generate, and give the geographical areas where he will study certain kinds of groups. Specifying the kinds of groups will indicate the range of types necessary to achieve the desired scope and conceptual generality and to maximize differences for developing properties. In field and survey research, rough estimates can be given of how many large units (such as number of cities, regions, and countries) will be sampled. In library research, the sociologist can talk of the different caches of material to be used (see Chapter VII). From these descriptions, he can estimate the time necessary for completion of his project, allowing ample time at least for the data collection, and realizing that the final theoretical analysis and writing can continue for years.

Detailed breakdowns of the timing of research (number of situations to be observed in one group, hours of observation, numbers and positions of people to be interviewed or surveyed, amount of time necessary for respites) are also difficult to give in a research proposal designed for discovering theory, since they depend on the directions the emerging theory takes, and on the temporal open-endedness of theoretical sampling. However, after describing the kinds of groups to be studied, the researcher can sometimes describe structural conditions that surely will affect the detailed timing of his project.

For example, when and how often do situations for routine sampling occur (what shifts, lunches or staff meetings)? What are the best hours, days of the week, or times of the year to meet the people to be sampled, or to get the kind of data necessary? What kinds of encapsulated periods of data collection are there, such as training periods, seasons, job periods (as time for building a house in order to study subcontractors), or periods of waiting for unscheduled situations to occur (as with suicides)? How long does it take to follow the course of action in situations occurring over time (such as recovering from polio)? The researcher might find it worthwhile to explore his groups briefly for some of these structual contingencies that affect timing before he writes his anticipated timing of research into a proposal. Since the core theory would begin to appear during even this exploratory period, he might gain a clearer visualization of how long he will need to fill out the theory. Colleagues who have had experiences in similar research and/or groups can also help in judging temporal contingencies.

Finally, another time-consuming aspect of data collection is establishing rapport with the people who are to be interviewed or observed. To establish rapport quickly is, of course, sometimes difficult. Particularly in field studies on one group in depth, the sociologist may spend weeks or even months getting people to allow him to study them at will. Theoretical sampling could also require this amount of time too, though establishing rapport is often not necessary. In later stages of the research, when sampling many comparative groups quickly for data on a few categories, the sociologist may obtain his data in a few minutes or half a day without the people he talks with, overhears or observes recognizing his purpose. He may obtain his data before being shooed off the premises for interfering with current activities; and he may obtain his data clandestinely in order to get it quickly, without explanations, or to be allowed to obtain it at all.

In field studies. theoretical sampling usually requires reading documents, interviewing, and observing at the same time, since all slices of data are relevant. There is little, if any, systematic interviewing of a sample of respondents, or interviewing that excludes observation. At the beginning of the research, interviews usually consist of open-ended conversations during which respondents are allowed to talk with no imposed limitations of time. Often the researcher sits back and listens while the respondents tell their stories. Later, when interviews and observations are directed by the emerging theory, he can ask direct questions bearing on his categories. These can be answered sufficiently and fairly quickly. Thus, the time for any one interview grows shorter as the number of interviews increases, because the researcher now questions many people, in different positions and different groups, about the same topics. Although the time taken by most interviews decreases as the theory develops, the sociologist still cannot state how long all his interviews will take because a new category might emerge at any time; this emergence will call for lengthy open-ended conversations and prolonged observations within some groups. Also, theoretical sampling aimed at following an incident or observing over a period of time requires sequential interviews, with no clear notion of when the sequence will be terminated.

Conclusion

Theoretical sampling, then, by providing constant direction to research, gives the sociologist momentum, purpose and confidence in his enterprise. He develops strong confidence in his categories, since they have emerged from the data and are constantly being selectively reformulated by them.[36] The categories, therefore, will fit the data, be understood both to sociologists and to laymen who are knowledgeable in the area, and make the theory usable for theoretical advance as well as for practical application. The sociologist will find that theoretical sampling, as an active, purposeful, searching way of collecting data, is exciting, invigorating and vital. This point is especially important when one considers the boring, dull, and stultifying effects on creativity of the methods involving separate and routine data collection, coding and analysis which are used frequently in descriptive and verificatory studies. Conventional field

36. Theoretical sampling would have avoided the dilemma facing Watson and Riesman (op. cit.) in their study of sociability. Watson feared the loss of her detailed, preconceived code when starting to collect data, since Riesman lacked confidence in it and wanted to change it completely. If they had undertaken an active theoretical search for categories that worked and fit, then the preconceived code could have been selectively reformulated with the approval and confidence of both researchers.

research is also exciting work but, as we have detailed, it lacks the more extensive commitment to discovery of theory displayed by research utilizing theoretical sampling.

One final and important point: since each researcher is likely to encounter special conditions in his research, he will inevitably add to the discussion of theoretical sampling as outlined in this chapter. We would scarcely wish to limit this type of comparative analysis to what we can say about it, from either our own research or our knowledge of others' research. We have merely opened up the topic. The motto should be: the more studies are based on theoretical sampling, the more effective should future theoretical sampling and comparative analyses become—provided researchers write about their strategies and techniques.

IV

From Substantive to Formal Theory

Since substantive theory is grounded in research on one particular substantive area (work, juvenile delinquency, medical education, mental health), it might be taken to apply only to that specific area. A theory at such a conceptual level, however may have important general implications and relevance, and become almost automatically a springboard or stepping stone to the development of a grounded formal theory.[1]

As we remarked in Chapter II, substantive theory is a strategic link in the formulation and generation of grounded formal theory. We believe that although formal theory can be generated directly from data, it is most desirable, and usually necessary, to start the formal theory from a substantive one. The latter not only provides a stimulus to a "good" idea, but it also gives an initial direction in developing relevant categories and properties and in choosing possible modes of integration. Indeed, it is difficult to find a grounded formal theory that was not in some way stimulated by a substantive theory. Often the sub-

1. For example, one author of this book received the following note from a colleague: "Thanks very much for your article on comparative failure in science. The notion of comparative failure would seem to have application in many areas of life." Other colleagues wrote letters detailing the relevance of "comparative failure" to religion, marriage, social class, and political behavior. Others phoned to give their ideas about comparative failure, and still others sent theory and research references. Though not using this term, these references provided immediate material for a comparative analysis that would facilitate generating a formal theory of comparative failure.

stantive and formal theories are formulated by different authors. Sometimes in formal theory the substantive theory is implicit, having been developed previously by the author or another writer.

In this chapter we shall only begin the discussion of the processes by which a substantive theory is advanced to a formal one. We should emphasize that, since our experience and knowledge are least extensive in this area, most of our discussion will be concerned with general rules, positions, and examples of initial efforts at generating formal theory. More specific procedures await the time when enough sociologists will have generated grounded formal theory that their procedures can be codified. Although we lack many specific examples, we feel certain of our general position on the ways that formal theory should be generated. Near the end of the chapter, we shall discuss the closely related questions: "Why go on to formal theory?" and "What are its uses?"

Generating Formal Theory

One-Area Formal Theory

There are at least two "rewriting" techniques for advancing a substantive to a formal theory that is grounded in only one substantive area. The sociologist can simply omit substantive words, phrases or adjectives: instead of saying "temporal aspects of *dying* as a nonscheduled status passage" he would say "temporal aspects of nonscheduled status passage." He can also rewrite a substantive theory up a notch: instead of writing about how doctors and nurses give medical attention to dying patients according to the patient's social value, he can talk of how professional services are distributed according to the social value of clients.[2] By applying these rewriting techniques to a substantive theory, the sociologist can change the focus of attention from substantive to formal concerns. He writes a one-area formal theory on the basis of a substantive theory; he does not generate the formal theory directly from the data.

2. See Barney G. Glaser and Anselm L. Strauss, "The Social Loss of Dying Patients," *American Journal of Nursing*, Vol. 64, No. 6 (June, 1964).

A quick perusal of any sociological journal will demonstrate that almost all sociologists believe this *is* the way to write formal theory! For example, Selvin and Hagstrom recently have published an article entitled, "Two Dimensions of Cohesiveness in Small Groups," [3] but this article does not offer the grounded formal theory its title implies, only a grounded substantive theory (about college women) written up a notch. At the close of the paper, some comparative speculation is offered about broader implications; there is no comparative research or analysis to establish formal theory.

Such rewriting techniques applied to a substantive theory produce only an adequate start toward formal theory, not an adequate formal theory itself. Probably the researchers are, as is typical, responding to the substantive stimulation with some general implications. All they have done is to raise the conceptual level of their work mechanically; they have not raised it through comparative understanding. They have done nothing to broaden the scope of their theory on the formal level by comparative investigation of different substantive areas. They have not escaped the time and place of their substantive research, though their formal writing of the theory may lead readers into thinking so. A classic example of this type of theory writing is Merton and Kitt's theory of reference group behavior.[4] We can only wonder what such theories might have looked like if their authors had done the comparative analyses implied by their writing.

Another danger of the rewriting technique as used on a single substantive area is that, for the reader, it tends to dissociate the data from the formal theory. When the theory is very abstract, it becomes hard to see how it came from the data of the study, since the formal theory now renders the data without a substantive theory intervening.

Also, the formal theory cannot fit or work very well when written from only one substantive area (and usually only one case of the area), because it cannot really be developed sufficiently to take into account all the contingencies and qualifications that will be met in the diverse substantive areas to which

3. *Sociometry* (March, 1965).
4. Robert K. Merton, *Social Theory and Social Structure* (New York: Free Press of Glencoe, 1959), pp. 225-80.

it will be applied. All that happens is that it will be modified by other theories through the comparative method, since by itself it is too sparsely developed to use in making trustworthy predictions and explanations. Thus the one-area formal theory becomes, in actuality, treated as a substantive theory to be generalized by comparative analysis.[5]

Multi-Area Formal Theory

When advancing a substantive theory to a formal one, the comparative analysis of groups is still the most powerful method for generating core categories and their properties and formulating a theory that fits and works. The rewriting techniques are subsumed in the process. The logic used in discovering substantive theory, which provided an efficient guide to selecting multiple groups of one substantive area, also will provide a guide for obtaining more data from many kinds of substantive areas, in order to generate formal theory. While the process of comparative analysis is the same for generating either substantive or formal theory, it becomes harder to generate the latter because of its more abstract level and the wider range of research required. Yet the task can be done by one sociologist or a few collaborators. It need not be relegated to the distant future when the division of labor within sociology will have built the wall of formal theory from the research bricks of a multitude of sociologists. There are never enough bricks and there are too few good synthesizers who wish to search out the bricks and thus put the wall together.[6] These worthy people are usually too busy working on their own data!

Two examples from our own work will suggest how one can begin to generate formal theory through comparative analysis. As we have discussed in a recent article, "awareness contexts" are not confined to situations in which people are dying, but

5. For example, see Donald Roy, "Work Satisfaction and Social Reward in Quota Achievement," *American Sociological Review*, 18 (1953), pp. 507-14. For further discussion see Barney G. Glaser and Anselm L. Strauss, "Awareness Contexts and Social Interaction," *American Sociological Review*, 29 (1964), p. 676.

6. C. Wright Mills, *The Sociological Imagination* (New York: Grove Press, 1959), p. 65 and *passim*.

are found generally in all kinds of social interaction.[7] Consequently, if we wish to develop a *formal* theory of awareness contexts, we are automatically led to analyzing data from many substantive areas. Here is how this might be done starting with our substantive theory of awareness contexts (in dying):

Awareness contexts. Situations where awareness contexts exist are, for instance, clowning at circuses, buying and selling cars, hustling in pool halls, comparative bidding, the passing of Negroes as whites, spying as a usual practice carried out by nations, and the mutual suspicion of prisoners of war in Chinese prison camps.

Quick scrutiny of these situations (as well as our earlier preliminary analysis of differences between some of them and the dying situation) suggests several categories in terms of which they can be usefully compared. The signs or indicators of an interactant's status may vary in *visibility* to the other interactants. Different *numbers of interactants* can be involved (two, three, or more). Different *numbers of groups* can be represented by the interactants. The *ratios of insiders and outsiders* present during the interaction may vary (one patient and dozens of staff members; five cons and one mark; one Negro, five "wise" people who know his secret, and millions of white and Negro persons who do not). The positions of interactants may also vary *hierarchically* (same or different level of the hierarchy). And of course the *stakes* of the interaction may vary tremendously.

Comparisons of each category for diverse substantive groups ✓ quickly leads to the development of properties and the formulation of associated hypotheses. Suppose that one focuses, for instance, upon the identifying signs of status. Some signs are physical (skin color), some are behavioral (speech or gesture), some are marks of skill (the agility of the card shark), some are insignia (uniforms and clothing), and so on. For any given interactional situation, certain signs of status may be thought of as *primary* and others as *secondary*: in America, skin color is the primary indicator of "Negro" just as genitalia are of respective sex. The secondary signs—those that strongly suggest

7. Glaser and Strauss, "Awareness Contexts and Social Interaction," *op. cit.*, pp. 669-679.

status, especially when found in conjunction with primary signs—would be, for "Negro," "kinky hair" and perhaps "southern-style speech"; and, for sex, clothing, hair style, and gesture. The visibility of such signs depends on learned ability to recognize them; for instance, many people have never learned to recognize homosexuals, and others would not know an American Indian if they saw one.

Understandably, some interactants may not even recognize the signs of their own status; for instance, the dying person may be kept unaware of his own position (closed awareness context). Signs can be manipulated, both crudely and subtly. For instance, they may simply be removed from vision, as when stigmata are concealed. They can be disguised, as when kinky hair is straightened or, as John Griffin did when passing for Negro, skin color is changed temporarily with chemicals.[8] Signs can also be suppressed, as when an interactant chooses not to indicate that he is really an American spy, or when a Japanese-American visiting Japan speaks Japanese at a department store so as not to be recognized as a "rich American." All these tactics, of course, are aimed toward minimizing potential recognition by other interactants.

Counter-tactics consist of eliciting important "give-away" signs, to avoid having to wait for signs and hoping to recognize them. Some counter-tactics for recognizing persons who are suppressing their identity depend on "passing" as a member of their group (an FBI man posing as a Communist), or on getting information from others within the group. Persons of similar status may use conventional signs to further recognition; the deliberate use of these signs will vary, depending on whether outsiders are present or absent, and whether they are "wise" (sympathetic to insiders) or not.[9] Usually there are places where the gathered insiders can forgo their efforts to disguise or suppress identifying signs. But they may need (as with drug addicts) counter-tactics to avoid betrayal even in such secluded places.

It is worth emphasizing that identifying signs sometimes need to be rectified—as when a customer in a store is mistaken for a salesman, or a man mistaken for a thief must prove his

8. John H. Griffin, *Black Like Me* (New York: Signet Books, 1962).
9. See Erving Goffman, *Stigma* (New York: Prentice-Hall, 1963).

innocence to bystanders, or even to police and later to a court of law. Sometimes identifying signs are "rectified" falsely! The new signs are believed and accepted, even though the original indications were really true. In "mutual pretense" situations, the dying patient in some sense rectifies the notion that he is dying by acting very much alive; given the ambiguity of most signs, other people act up to his false rectification, until the signs are either so unambiguous that the game is hard to play, or until he drops the pretense and admits his real situation.[10] A subjective and subtle variation occurs when an interactant's status is rejected and he himself begins to doubt who he is, as in Nazi Germany when gentiles with faint Jewish lineage came to doubt their true identities because their claims to be non-Jewish were denied.

Such comparisons of diverse groups in terms of identifying "signs" quickly lead to both useful properties and hypotheses about this facet of a formal theory of awareness context. Just as in the development of substantive theory, the hypotheses will be concerned with such matters as tactics and counter-tactics, as well as with their structural conditions, their consequences, and so on. But it is important to understand that this kind of inquiry can be furthered immensely by systematic analysis, not only of a single category but of *combinations* of categories: signs and stakes, for instance; or signs, stakes, ratios of insiders-outsiders, and numbers of group representatives present at the interaction. This kind of analysis becomes increasingly richer, because it leads the researcher to ask "Where can I find another comparison group that differs in one more specified respect?" When he finds that group, its examination leads him to further generation and qualification of this theory. By such means, exceedingly complex and well-grounded formal theory can be developed. It is precisely by such means that a substantive theory of awareness contexts can be extended upward in conceptual generality and outward in scope. In doing so, many more useful types of awareness contexts would be generated and related to interactants' behavior.

Status passages. Our second example is the initial generation of a formal theory of status passages, prompted by our substan-

10. See Glaser and Strauss, *Awareness of Dying* (Chicago: Aldine Publishing Company, 1965), Footnote 4, p. 279.

tive theory on the status passage involved in dying.[11] We have written about the "nonscheduled status passage" of dying; several other dimensions (properties) of status passage also arose from our study. One of these is whether or not a status passage follows an institutionally prescribed sequence of transitional statuses. For instance, many ethnographic descriptions of growing up and aging, and many descriptions of organizational careers, delineate prescribed passages. (Such passages may or may not be precisely scheduled.)

"Transitional status" is a concept denoting time in terms of the social structure. It is a social system's tactic for keeping a person in passage between two statuses for a period of time. He is put in a transitional status, or sequence of them, that determines the period of time that he will be in a status passage. Thus the transitional status of "initiate" will, in a particular case, carry with it the given amount of time it will take to make a non-member a member—a civilian is made a soldier by spending a given number of weeks as a basic trainee; an adolescent spends a number of years 'in training" to be an adult.

A third dimension of status passage is the degree to which it is regulated; that is, to what degree there are institutionalized operations for getting an occupant in and out of beginning, transitional, and end statuses and for keeping others informed of the passage. Rites of passages are instances of such regulated operations. It is notable in our studies of dying patients that the nonscheduled status passage involved both fairly regulated and fairly unregulated temporal elements. One regulated aspect is that at certain points in the passage the doctor must announce the death to a family member. But less regulated is the typical problem: when (if ever) does the physician tell the patient that he is dying? The regulated and unregulated elements of the nonscheduled status passage together generate one structural condition leading to differential definitions among parties to the passage.

Further dimensions of status passages include to what degree the passage is considered undesirable; whether or not it is inevitable; and how clear are the relevant transitional statuses and the beginning and end statuses of the passage itself. Dying

11. Glaser and Strauss, "Temporal Aspects of Dying as a Non-Scheduled Status Passage," *American Journal of Sociology* (July, 1965), pp. 48-59.

in hospitals can be located by all these structural dimensions in the following way: the status passage is nonscheduled, nonprescribed, undesirable, and, after a point, inevitable. The passage is sometimes regulated but sometimes not; and sometimes relatively unambiguous but (except for its end status) sometimes not.

The next step is to study different types of status passage in order to begin generating a formal theory. Various combinations of the above dimensions provide ways of typing different status passages as well as some of the conditions under which the passage is managed. Differences between two sets of these conditions will, therefore, tend to explain why two types of status passages are managed differently.

For example, in the United States the engagement status passage (between the statuses of being single and married) is usually institutionally nonscheduled, like dying, though unlike dying it is desirable to the parties involved. Because it is a status they have chosen, the status occupants themselves determine when they are in passage, what the transitional statuses will be, and for how long a period they will be in each one. In contrast, couples involved in personally undesirable or forced engagements, such as sometimes found in Europe and Japan, especially among the upper class, do not control their own transition.

A status passage that contrasts with both the engagement and dying is the defendant status passage, which links the statuses of citizen and prisoner. It is scheduled and undesirable. Commitment to a state mental hospital can be regarded as an instance of the defendant passage. In contrast to dying, while the legalized legitimator of the passage is a judge, the unofficial legitimator can be, in fact, a lawyer, a general practitioner, a psychiatrist, the family, or the "defendant" himself. Thus, anyone who would be an unofficial legitimator must develop tactics to make both his claim as such "stick" and his definition of the defendant's sanity status accepted by the court. Comparative analysis of the characteristic tactics in this situation with those used during engagement or dying passages can be useful for developing a formal theory.

Also, useful comparisons between the recovery and dying status passage are provided by a study of the polio patients who recover from their acute attacks of polio but who suffer varying degrees of muscular impairment.[12] This particular kind of recovery passage is non-institutionally scheduled or prescribed, undesirable, and, after a point, inevitable. One difference with dying is that the end status—where the passage will lead—is frequently unclear. The doctor is uncertain about the degree to which the patient will regain use of the affected muscles. As a result, the doctor as legitimator is often very chary with information to family and patient, both in the hospital and after discharge (even though after a time he may form a clear idea of where the patient will end up). This lack of clear announcements about the end status stimulates the patient and family to engage in vigorous searches for cues which might define just how much better the patient can be expected to get.

In Davis's account of the polio recovery there is very little information or analysis concerning the coordination of people's behavior that is obtained by defining statuses correctly. The reason is easy to find: while our study was focused upon medical personnel in the hospital, his study—especially in later phases of the passage to "getting better"—focused largely upon the family outside the hospital. The medical personnel would not be so concerned with coordinating a passage outside their organizational jurisdiction.

The above examples are taken from our research; however, as we noted earlier, anyone can begin generating formal theory directly from published theory. For instance, he might systematically extend Erving Goffman's "On Cooling the Mark Out." [13] In this useful paper, Goffman focused on the type of status demotion that reflects on the incapacity of the demoted person. "Cooling out" means demoting him while simultaneously taking measures to minimize those of his reactions that would be most destructive to the institutional setting where the demotion occurs. Goffman's theory of "cooling out" encompasses such matters as when this process occurs, what typical tactics are used in cooling out, and what happens when the demoted person refuses to be cooled out. The theory is built on Goffman's

12. Fred Davis, *Passage Through Crisis* (Indianapolis: Bobbs-Merrill, 1963).

13. *Psychiatry,* 15 (1952), pp. 451-63.

reflections about various kinds of institutional settings (*e.g.*, bureaucratic, small establishments) and situations (courtship, demotion).

An examination of his paper quickly shows that, in fact, Goffman begins by pointing to comparison groups that he does not later build systematically into his comparative analysis. He uses these initial comparisons to set his own point of view squarely before the reader (quite like Cressey in *The Taxi-Dance Hall*).[14] Thus, "losing a role" may occur through promotion, abdication or demotion. Likewise, demotion may or may not involve reflection of the person's capacities. Each of these comparisons, in fact, can be built into the emerging theory to give it much more scope and depth. Even if demotion alone is focused on, Goffman has offered useful cues for extending his analysis. Thus, what happens when demoters and demoted both agree he has been demoted, as over against when they define him as demoted but he does not? What about the reverse situation? What about when demoters (and bystanders) do not agree among themselves? And when they are differentially above or below him in status? And when there are variable dimensions of "awareness context"—whether "open," "closed" or "suspicion"—concerning agreement or disagreement? Also, what about the distance that he is demoted? And when more than one person is demoted simultaneously? Other cues for theoretical sampling are offered in passing by Goffman. He remarks that criminal gangs sometimes can afford not to cool out the client, but department stores necessarily must be concerned. The implications of that important point—including when each party can or cannot afford to cool out—are not followed through. We are told also, through a passing remark, that agents who cool out may themselves react (as with guilt) to their actions. But what different kinds of agents, under what conditions, react similarly or differently? Also, if we scrutinize what we are offered in the way of tactics for cooling out or situations where it typically occurs, then we find lists of tactics and situations that are related in the analysis only rather loosely to different types of organizations or situations. Systematic comparison of organizations—either through field research or, quite feasibly,

14. See our commentary on this common practice in Chapter III.

through secondary analysis of published substantive research—will quickly begin to densify the emergent formal theory.[15]

This kind of scrutiny and illustrative extension of Goffman's theory suggests that an important strategy in generating formal theory through theoretical sampling is to begin with someone else's formal theory. That theory may be developed less abstractly than Goffman's, and may be tied much more closely to firsthand research.[16] The strategy consists of asking, first of all, what comparisons the author has forgotten or "thrown away" because of his initial focus; second, what comparisons he has suggested in passing but has not followed up; third, what comparisons are suggested directly by his analysis; and fourth, what comparisons are suggested by one's own reflections on the theory. As these analyses feed into the development of another theory, further comparisons—directed by that theory—will occur to the analyst, just as if he were thinking about his own data. This strategy not only permits the efficient generation of grounded theory, but allows speedy incorporation and transcendence of other sociologists' theories.

Direct Formulation of Formal Theory

Formal theory formulated directly from comparative data on many substantive areas is hard to find, as we have noted earlier, since stimulation and guidance, even if unacknowledged, have usually come from a substantive theory. However, it is possible to formulate formal theory directly. The core categories can emerge in the sociologist's mind from his reading, life experiences, research and scholarship. He may begin immediately to generate a formal theory by comparative analysis, without making any substantive formulations from one area; though

15. For extension of Goffman's work, along these lines, see Barney G. Glaser, "Stable Careers of Comparative Failures," Chapter 10 in *Organizational Scientists* (Indianapolis: Bobbs-Merrill, 1964); Fred Goldner, "Demotion in Industrial Management," *American Sociological Review*, 30 (1965), pp. 714-24; N. Martin and A. Strauss, "Patterns of Mobility Within Industrial Organizations," *Journal Business*, 29 (1956), pp. 101-10; and Douglas Moore, "Demotion," *Social Problems*, 9 (1962), pp. 213-20.

16. For instance, one may begin generating formal theory from Fred Davis' paper on "Deviance Disavowal," *Social Problems*, 9 (1961), pp. 120-32. Cf. our comments on his paper in "Awareness Contexts and Social Interaction," *American Sociological Review*, 29 (1964), pp. 669-79.

before he is through, he will have many fledgling substantive theories in his memos from his comparisons of substantive areas. The procedures are essentially the same as those suggested directly above.

This approach takes considerable discipline because several dangers arise when the guidance of a substantive theory is missing. The sociologist must make certain through pilot tests that the formal categories are relevant to data. In other words, do the categories fit and work? Are they clearly indicated by data, and do they explain, predict, and interpret anything of significance? If not, the categories are useless even if they "feel right" to the researcher; the theory may sound "nice and neat" but no one will really know what to do with it.[17]

The sociologist must also be wary of using the rhetoric and models of the neat, clear, logico-deductive formal theories as a substitute for data. Looking around for data can be a very difficult task when they bear on an abstract category like "anticipatory succession" or "person-set."[18] The sociologist faced with this problem may slip into the rhetoric of another formal theory, thus giving up the search for data that would help him generate a way of thinking about his theory, a model for integrating it, and a set of properties for it that is pertinent to data. In short, he abandons generating a grounded formal theory in favor of borrowing the ways of logico-deductive formal theorists.

For example, the authors of the theories on anticipatory succession and person-sets ran their attempts through the rhetoric of Merton's "anomie" adaptations, in order not to run out of ideas. This tactic has also been used with Parsons's patterned variables and his theory on functional requisites of an organization.[19] Since the borrowers of theory so often lack empirical

17. For an example of a formal theory that sounds "nice" and "neat" but appears "useless" to us—because its relevance as an explanation of anything or its dubious fit to the real world has not been demonstrated but simply assumed out-of-hand—see Peter Blau, *Exchange and Power in Social Life* (New York: John Wiley and Sons, 1964).

18. See Bernard Levenson, "Bureaucratic Succession," in Amitai Etzioni (Ed.), *Complex Organizations* (New York: Holt, Rinehart and Winston, 1961), pp. 362-75, and David Catlovitz, *Student Faculty Relations in a Medical School* (Ann Arbor, Mich.: University Microfilms, Inc., 1960), Appendix.

19. See, for example, Neil J. Smelser, *Social Change in the Industrial Revolution* (Chicago: University of Chicago Press, 1959), Chapters I, II, and III.

referents, the borrowing is never done by asking the following question of logico-deductive theory: How do I know this theory is relevant to the data that my formal theory purports to handle, and that it will help formulate my theory? This question is easier to ask and answer with grounded formal theory.

Another danger to beware of when directly generating formal theory from data is the tendency to slip from the true generation of formal theory to the simple ordering of a mass of data under a logically worked-out set of categories. The relative case of being logical with abstractness means that logic dominates the theory; the result is a growing love of one's "nice, neat" speculations, which one feels must be correct because they sound so logical. The data are then forcibly ordered by the conceptual framework, not used to generate properties and categories, and so have no disciplining effect on how the theory turns out. Again the result is not a grounded formal theory, but merely an orderly, "postal clerk" approach to sorting out facts.[20]

On to Formal Theory?

Most sociologists unquestionably tend to avoid the formulation of *grounded* formal theory; they stay principally at the substantive level. In addition to the inherently greater difficulties in working with high level abstractions, and in feeling confident about broader generalities, we believe there are several other reasons for this avoidance.

First of all, a researcher tends to know one or two substantive areas well, and feels increasingly comfortable as he learns more about them over the years. The internal satisfactions and securities of such specialization are abetted by the further rewards of mature expertise in a specialized field, rewards that emanate from colleagues and the wider public.[21] Furthermore, sociologists learn very early the dictum that there is a great difference between a dilettante and a true "pro." The latter knows his data inside and out. This conviction tends to keep ✓

20. See Smelser, *op. cit.,* Chapter II: "Some Empty Theoretical Boxes," and Chapter III: "Filling the Boxes." See also Smelser, *Collective Behavior* (New York: Free Press of Glencoe, 1963).

21. Cf. Fred Reif and Anselm L. Strauss, "The Impact of Rapid Discovery Upon the Scientist's Career," *Social Problems* (1965), pp. 297-311.

sociologists from researching more widely, and certainly from working more abstractly, because they feel they must amass and comprehend great amounts of data before they can safely claim "findings."

Another reason for avoiding the generation of formal theory is its supposed depersonalizating effect. Formal theory is viewed as too abstract, too divorced from people and everyday life to seem real. Many sociologists resist and distrust the separation of formal theory from the time and place of specific social structures. They see conceptual level and scope of the theory as too unbounded, and the parsimony of its terms too limiting. Thus, although sociologists know a formal theory can help in a substantive area of interest for which they have no theory, nor much data, nor time for research, they do not actually trust its applicability and powers of explanation and prediction. One colleague wrote us, apropos his own area of specialization: "Also I suppose I am sufficiently offended by the airy assertions that pass as sociological theory to want no part of it." This colleague had just published a remarkably plausible substantive theory, but wished to go no further in generalizing it to a formal theory.

Other colleagues have told us that the future of sociology rests on theories of substantive areas (period!) and so proceed to generate them. This task is, of course, important for sociology's future, but so is formal theory—there will not always be a substantive theory to help those sociologists who need a relevant theory, say, for use in consultation or lectures, but who have neither time nor inclination to generate a theory from their own research.

The depersonalization of formal theory is most apparent in logico-deductive theories, for it is truly difficult to relate them to the real world. Depersonalization is minimized and minimal in grounded formal theory because this theory is based on the data from many substantive areas, and may lean heavily on a substantive theory for only one area. It is not really far removed from the real world. Those colleagues who do not see much future for formal theories are thinking almost exclusively of the logico-deductive ones. We are confident that many will change their minds if they focus rather on grounded formal theory and its two links with data: many substantive areas and a substantive theory. A good example of grounded formal theory may be found in Becker's *Outsiders;* he carefully generates a formal theory about the social control and creation of deviance from the comparative analysis of his substantive theories on musicians and marijuana users.[22]

Uses of Formal Theory

Insofar as the sociologist does concern himself with formal theory, currently he tends to handle it in several alternative ways. First, he may set out to verify, in a given substantive area, some small portion of one or more formal theories, often derived from prominent theorists. Such verification studies are legion.

A second approach is to study with comparative research materials an important body of theoretical writing, as when Robert Blauner systematically scrutinized a number of industries with respect to their degree of "alienation." [23] This type of research is typically confined to careful variation and qualification of the central guiding theory, checking it under diverse conditions (see Chapter VI). This approach tends to block chances for development of new theory based on the comparative analysis, except insofar as the old theory seems to require qualification. It uses comparative analysis conventionally, to show and explain variations in an established general theory. In contrast, our use of comparative analysis generates and generalizes a new theory; variations and explanations became part of the process, *not* the product.

A third approach is to apply several formal theories to a substantive area that the sociologist already knows well, in an effort to give his materials greater meaning. He does this as a post-hoc enterprise in research after the data is collected; but sometimes the formal theories direct portions, at least, of his data collection. The sociologist also does this to order and prepare lectures.

Probably the most widespread use of formal theory, how-

22. H. Becker, *Outsiders* (New York: Free Press of Glencoe, 1962).
23. Robert Blauner, *Alienation and Freedom* (Chicago: University of Chicago Press, 1964).

ever, is this: when initiating specific researches a sociologist begins with a loose conceptual framework of formal ideas, hunches, notions, concepts, and hypotheses about the substantive area under consideration.[24] This framework is often linked with and biased toward the researcher's graduate training in formal theory under a particular professor (Parsonians from Harvard, Mertonians from Columbia), as well as with his further experiences since graduation. Examples of this use of formal theory abound. However, the characteristic difficulties it can present when the formal theory is ungrounded are well illustrated in the following review (by Strauss) of William A. Rushing's *The Psychiatric Professions: Power, Conflict and Adaptation in a Psychiatric Hospital Staff:*

> Designed primarily for sociologists and secondarily for people who are interested in psychiatric hospitals, this book can be read on two distinct levels: theoretical and descriptive. A sociologist can, indeed, engage in a very useful exercise by giving himself three separate readings. He can read the book first for its theory, then again for its description, and finally reread it for its descriptions but asking himself what is disappointing in the description because the theory is disappointing in some regard. This is how I read the book.
>
> Rushing spent a number of months observing and interviewing professionals in a university (teaching) psychiatric hospital. Like other commentators on psychiatric hospitals, he was impressed by the general lack of clear-cut consensus about professional roles in the mental hospital setting. So he takes as a central thesis that the "modern mental hospital" is not "yet" fully institutionalized but is "in process of institutionalization." His problem is how to analyze this process, with particular focus on its social psychological aspects (the impact of the establishment on individuals who work there). For this analysis, he finds conventional role theory too static: its forte is to illuminate relatively institutionalized structures rather than those that are not very institutionalized. Role theory therefore needs supplementary concepts. Among the key concepts—derived, I gather, mainly from Thibaut, Homans, Merton and Parsons—are power (and power strategies), influence, cost (and cost inducing, preventing, reducing, strategies), relative deprivation, reference group, and instrumental versus expressive activities.
>
> Using qualitative analysis, abetted by frequent quotes from his fieldnotes and interviews, Rushing discusses chapter by chap-

---

24. See Blau's and Udy's approach for examples, in Philip Hammond (Ed.), *Sociologists at Work* (New York: Basic Books, 1964).

ter the social positions, plights and strategies of various auxiliary personnel in the hospital: notably, social workers, recreational workers, clinical psychologists, and psychiatric nurses. The discussion turns around a systematic and step by step presentation of hypotheses, with qualitative evidence bearing upon them. Two quotes from the concluding chapter will convey the kinds of hypotheses which he presents: "the typology of power strategies: implementing cost-inducing, structural cost-reducing, and maintaining cost-preventing. . . . We hypothesized that this typology is related to the institutionalization process: the character of the particular power strategy—its function for the actor— depends upon the degree to which social relationships have been institutionalized" (page 241).

The descriptive material offered throughout the book is ordered by the theoretical requirements of each chapter. Anyone who has observed psychiatric hospitals closely—including state hospitals where the winds of current doctrine happen to blow even softly—will recognize many features either explicitly discussed by Rushing or implicitly touched upon by his descriptions and by his interviewees' remarks. The book teems with illustrations of the ambiguity associated with auxiliary personnel's tasks, of conflict among these personnel and between them and the psychiatrists, of strategies for getting work done and professional interests accomplished.

Nevertheless my response to the book is that it is not successful in portraying—through joined description and analysis— a hospital that is very much "in process." I lay the blame on an unwillingness to abandon conventional role theory for something bolder, something more suited to, as Rushing aptly regards it, the non-institutionalized hospital. Rushing's assumption is that these hospitals are moving toward institutionalization—which is probably incorrect, and if so still raises questions as to the most fruitful ways of studying their institutionalization. Careful as is Rushing's development of social psychological theory, it suffers from the all too customary effort to fit combined bits of logical formal theory to a substantive area. Not much, I suspect, is really added to the formal theories other than indicating how portions of them can be applied in this particular substantive area. If I am incorrect in that assertion, then at least the book fails to indicate how those formal theories (bearing on power, influence, cost, reference groups, relative deprivation) were modified, qualified or extended.

As for the relationships among professionals in the hospital: immersed as I have been in similar hospital settings, I miss in his account a quality of ongoing development of relationships. He portrays very well the conflict and tension among personnel and touches occasionally upon outcome of conflict and tension; but there is conveyed hardly any sense of institutional or professional development. He has not especially caught development in his descriptions, which are relatively static, or in his theorizing, which is essentially non-processual. While the book is very useful for its descriptive materials and detailed quotes, I believe it is also useful as an object lesson about a type of prevalent research style in the use of logical formal theory.[25]

The several uses of formal theory discussed in this quotation are enterprises quite different from the generation of grounded formal theory, accomplished through systematic study of multiple comparison groups and substantive theories. Perhaps the closest relative to such formulation is the kind of essay writing established many years ago by Georg Simmel, and nurtured by such contemporaries as Erving Goffman and David Riesman, in which the essayist—with or without systematic data before him —develops a series of general propositions of relatively high abstraction. Such writing can be criticized as being, at best, full of insights and, at worst, as pure speculation. (Some "insights" may later be "tested" by more rigorously minded sociologists.) From our viewpoint, such writing is exceedingly valuable, but as theory it lacks both integration of well-defined concepts and sufficiently credible grounding in careful comparative research.

The more prestigious style of logico-deductive, systematic "grand theorizing" is, in the hands of its most brilliant practitioners, more than merely esthetically satisfying: it also gives impetus to considerable useful, precise verification of hypotheses. But it provides no directive—any more than it did a century ago when Comte and Spencer were its spokesmen—to closing that embarrassingly noticeable gap between highly abstract theory and the multitude of miniscule substantive studies so characteristic of current sociology.[26] It should be evident that we put greater faith in grounded formal theory to close that gap, for it readily fits "what's going on" in everyday situations. Possibly the main benefit yielded by grand theories is their use of abstract models (mathematical, process, system, functional, interdependences, equilibrium, etc.). The integration of formal

25. The review was published in *Social Forces* (Chapel Hill: The University of North Carolina Press, 1964).

26. The gap was already embarrassingly noticeable in 1940 when Herbert Blumer commented on it. See "The Problem of the Concept in Social Psychology," *American Journal of Sociology*, 45 (1940), pp. 709-19.

theory often requires more guidance from such explicit models than substantive theory does, because of a greater level of abstraction. However, as we stated in Chapter II, the integration of a formal theory can begin very usefully with the emerging integration scheme that was used for the substantive theory that actually stimulated the formal theory's generation.

Because grounded formal theory fits and works, we see its use in research and teaching as more trustworthy than logico-deductive theory, for the simple reason that the latter often requires forcing of data into categories of dubious relevance to the data's meaning. Grounded formal theory is also more trustworthy for sensitizing the researcher to the generation of new substantive theory and for helping him to formulate it.

Grounded formal theory is thus also highly useful in predictions and explanations when we are consulted about substantive areas where we have no theory, and no time or inclination to develop one. Explanations and predictions from logico-deductive formal theory are used mainly where they will do no harm; that is, in the classroom, as "tacked-on" explanations of accomplished research (as mentioned in Chapter I), and as hypotheses (prediction) in the service of the perennial testing of parts of a formal theory with the eternal hope that it can be modified to fit reality.

Grounded formal theory is more trustworthy for consultations because both laymen and sociologists can readily see how its predictions and explanations fit the realities of the situation. This is strategically important. While in research, predicting and explaining have few real risks (the researcher merely modifies the theory according to his findings), a layman does not trust a prediction of what will happen in his situation unless he can readily see how it applies. Similarly, he will not accept a theoretical explanation unless he can readily see how it explains his situation, and gives him a sound basis for corrections and future predictions. Grounded formal theory, like substantive theory, earns the trust of laymen and sociologists alike. Both consultant and consultee must have this trust in order to work together (see Chapter X).

As yet there is not much of this type of consultation in sociology. Seldom is such a general theorist (if you can find one) called in for consultation by other sociologists, laymen, organizations or governments. Most consultants are well known for their research and everyday experience in a particular area, and perhaps for a portion of their substantive theory if they have generated some. The transferability of formal theories to diverse substantive areas is seldom done in sociological consultation because most formal theories are ungrounded, and therefore not trusted by either sociologists or laymen when they face "real life circumstances."

Theoretical consultation is an area of sociological work that would be suitable for many sociologists, but cannot really be opened up until there are many more grounded formal theories. Then, for example, a general theorist, not only the well-known researchers, could be called in for consultation about juvenile delinquency because he is especially skilled at applying grounded formal theory to substantive areas. Sociology cannot reach this stage of development if we continue to plod on with grand logical theorizing and miniscule verifications. But this stage can be reached through the generation of grounded substantive and formal theories. Whether a substantive problem is theoretical or practical, and whether extensive research is called for or not, general theorists skilled at applying grounded formal theories are needed as consultants for making cogent predictions and explanations, and for helping decide the course of action for research or practical action.

V

The Constant Comparative Method
of Qualitative Analysis*

Currently, the general approaches to the analysis of qualitative data are these:

1. If the analyst wishes to convert qualitative data into
crudely quantifiable form so that he can provisionally test a
hypothesis, he codes the data first and then analyzes it. He
makes an effort to code "all relevant data [that] can be brought
to bear on a point," and then systematically assembles, assesses
and analyzes these data in a fashion that will "constitute proof
for a given proposition." [1]

2. If the analyst wishes only to generate theoretical ideas—
new categories and their properties, hypotheses and interrelated
hypotheses—he cannot be confined to the practice of coding
first and then analyzing the data since, in generating theory, he
is constantly redesigning and reintegrating his theoretical notions
as he reviews his material.[2] Analysis after the coding operation

---

* We wish to thank the editors of *Social Problems* for permission to
publish this paper as Chapter V. See Barney G. Glaser, *Social Problems,*
12 (1965), pp. 436-45.

1. Howard S. Becker and Blanche Geer, "The Analysis of Qualitative
Field Data" in Richard N. Adams and Jack J. Preiss (Eds.), *Human
Organization Research* (Homewood, Ill.: Dorsey Press, Inc., 1960), pp.
279-89. See also Howard S. Becker, "Problems of Inference and Proof in
Participant Observation," *American Sociological Review,* (December, 1958),
pp. 652-60; and Bernard Berelson, *Content Analysis* (Glencoe, Ill.: Free
Press, 1952), Chapter III, and p. 16.

2. Constantly redesigning the analysis is a well-known normal tendency
in qualitative research (no matter what the approach to analysis), which
occurs throughout the whole research experience from initial data collec-

would not only unnecessarily delay and interfere with his purpose, but the explicit coding itself often seems an unnecessary, burdensome task. As a result, the analyst merely inspects his data for new properties of his theoretical categories, and writes memos on these properties.

We wish to suggest a third approach to the analysis of qualitative data—one that combines, by an analytic procedure of constant comparison, the explicit coding procedure of the first approach and the style of theory development of the second. The purpose of the constant comparative method of joint coding and analysis is to generate theory more systematically, than allowed by the second approach, by using explicit coding and analytic procedures. While more systematic than the second approach, this method does not adhere completely to the first, which hinders the development of theory because it is designed for provisional testing, not discovering, of hypotheses.[3] This method of comparative analysis is to be used jointly with theoretical sampling, whether for collecting new data or on previously collected or compiled qualitative data.

Systematizing the second approach (inspecting data and

---

tion through coding to final analysis and writing. The tendency has been noted in Becker and Geer, *op. cit.*, p. 270, Berelson, *op. cit.*, p. 125; and for an excellent example of how it goes on, see Robert K. Merton, *Social Theory and Social Structure* (New York: Free Press of Glencoe, 1957), pp. 390-92. However, this tendency may have to be suppressed in favor of the purpose of the first approach; but in the second approach and the approach presented here, the tendency is used purposefully as an analytic strategy.

3. Our other purpose in presenting the constant comparative method may be indicated by a direct quotation from Robert K. Merton—a statement he made in connection with his own qualitative analysis of locals and cosmopolitans as community influentials: "This part of our report, then, is a bid to the sociological fraternity for the practice of incorporating in publications a detailed account of the ways in which qualitative analyses *actually* developed. Only when a considerable body of such reports are available will it be possible to *codify* methods of qualitative analysis with something of the clarity with which quantitative methods have been articulated." *Op. cit.*, p. 390. This is, of course, also the basic position of Paul F. Lazarsfeld. See Allen H. Barton and Paul F. Lazarsfeld, "Some Functions of Qualitative Analysis in Social Research," in Seymour M. Lipset and Neil J. Smelser (Eds.), *Sociology: the Progress of a Decade* (Englewood Cliffs, N.J.: Prentice-Hall, 1961). It is the position that has stimulated the work of Becker and Geer, and of Berelson, cited in Footnote 1.

redesigning a developing theory) by this method does not supplant the skills and sensitivities required in generating theory. Rather, the constant comparative method is designed to aid the analyst, who possesses these abilities, in generating a theory that is integrated, consistent, plausible, close to the data—and at the same time is in a form clear enough to be readily, if only partially, operationalized for testing in quantitative research. Still dependent on the skills and sensitivities of the analyst, the constant comparative method is not designed (as methods of quantitative analysis are) to guarantee that two analysts working independently with the same data will achieve the same results; it is designed to allow, with discipline, for some of the vagueness and flexibility that aid the creative generation of theory.

If a researcher using the first approach (coding all data first) wishes to discover some or all of the hypotheses to be tested, typically he makes his discoveries by using the second approach of inspection and memo-writing along with explicit coding. By contrast, the constant comparative method cannot be used for both provisional testing and discovering theory: in theoretical sampling, the data collected are not extensive enough and, because of theoretical saturation, are not coded extensively enough to yield provisional tests, as they are in the first approach. They are coded only enough to generate, hence to suggest, theory. Partial testing of theory, when necessary, is left to more rigorous approaches (sometimes qualitative but usually quantitative). These come later in the scientific enterprise (see Chapter X).

The first approach also differs in another way from the constant comparative method. It is usually concerned with a few hypotheses couched at the same level of generality, while our method is concerned with many hypotheses synthesized at different levels of generality. The reason for this difference between methods is that the first approach must keep the theory tractable so that it can be provisionally tested in the same presentation. Of course, the analyst using this approach might, after proving or disproving his hypotheses, attempt to explain his findings with more general ideas suggested by his data, thus achieving some synthesis at different levels of generality.

A fourth general approach to qualitative analysis is "analytic induction," which combines the first and second approaches in a manner different from the constant comparative method.[4] Analytic induction has been concerned with generating and proving an integrated, limited, precise, universally applicable theory of causes accounting for a specific behavior (e.g., drug addiction, embezzlement). In line with the first approach, it tests a limited number of hypotheses with all available data, consisting of numbers of clearly defined and carefully selected cases of the phenomena. Following the second approach, the theory is generated by the reformulation of hypotheses and redefinition of the phenomena forced by constantly confronting the theory with negative cases, cases which do not confirm the current formulation.

In contrast to analytic induction, the constant comparative method is concerned with generating and plausibly suggesting (but not provisionally testing) many categories, properties, and hypotheses about general problems (e.g., the distribution of services according to the social value of clients). Some of these properties may be causes, as in analytic induction, but unlike analytic induction others are conditions, consequences, dimensions, types, processes, etc. In both approaches, these properties should result in an integrated theory. Further, no attempt is made by the constant comparative method to ascertain either the universality or the proof of suggested causes or other properties. Since no proof is involved, the constant comparative method in contrast to analytic induction requires only saturation of data—not consideration of all available data, nor are the data restricted to one kind of clearly defined case. The constant comparative method, unlike analytic induction, is more likely to be applied in the same study to any kind of qualitative information, including observations, interviews, documents, articles, books, and so forth. As a consequence, the constant comparisons required by both methods differ in breadth of purpose, extent of comparing, and what data and ideas are compared.

Clearly the purposes of both these methods for generating theory supplement each other, as well as the first and second

4. See Alfred R. Lindesmith, *Opiate Addiction* (Bloomington: Principia, 1947), pp. 12-14; Donald R. Cressey, *Other People's Money* (New York: Free Press of Glencoe, 1953), p. 16 and *passim;* and Florian Znaniecki, *The Method of Sociology* (New York: Farrar and Rinehart, 1934), pp. 249-331.

approaches. All four methods provide different alternatives to qualitative analysis. Table I locates the use of these approaches to qualitative analysis and provides a scheme for locating additional approaches according to their purposes. The general idea of the constant comparative method can also be used for generating theory in quantitative research. Then one compares findings within subgroups and with external groups (see Chapter VIII).

TABLE I. USE OF APPROACHES TO QUALITATIVE ANALYSIS

Generating Theory	Provisional Testing of Theory	
	Yes	No
Yes	Combining inspection for hypotheses (2) along with coding for test, then analyzing data (1)	Inspection for hypotheses (2)
	Analytic induction (4)	Constant comparative method (3)
No	Coding for test, then analyzing data (1)	Ethnographic description

The Constant Comparative Method

We shall describe in four stages the constant comparative method: (1) comparing incidents applicable to each category, (2) integrating categories and their properties, (3) delimiting the theory, and (4) writing the theory. Although this method of generating theory is a continuously growing process —each stage after a time is transformed into the next—earlier stages do remain in operation simultaneously throughout the analysis and each provides continuous development to its successive stage until the analysis is terminated.

1. *Comparing incidents applicable to each category.* The analyst starts by coding each incident in his data into as many categories of analysis as possible, as categories emerge or as data emerge that fit an existing category. For example, the category of "social loss" of dying patients emerged quickly from comparisons of nurses' responses to the potential deaths of their patients. Each relevant response involved the nurse's appraisal

of the degree of loss that her patient would be to his family, his occupation, or society: "He was so young," "He was to be a doctor," "She had a full life," or "What will the children and her husband do without her?" [5]

Coding need consist only of noting categories on margins, but can be done more elaborately (e.g., on cards). It should keep track of the comparison group in which the incident occurs. To this procedure we add the basic, defining rule for the constant comparative method: *while coding an incident for a category, compare it with the previous incidents in the same and different groups coded in the same category.* For example, as the analyst codes an incident in which a nurse responds to the potential "social loss" of a dying patient, he also compares this incident, before further coding, with others previously coded in the same category. Since coding qualitative data requires study of each incident, this comparison can often be based on memory. Usually there is no need to refer to the actual note on every previous incident for each comparison.

This constant comparison of the incidents very soon starts to generate theoretical properties of the category. The analyst starts thinking in terms of the full range of types or continua of the category, its dimensions, the conditions under which it is pronounced or minimized, its major consequences, its relation to other categories, and its other properties. For example, while constantly comparing incidents on how nurses respond to the social loss of dying patients, we realized that some patients are perceived as a high social loss and others as a low social loss, and that patient care tends to vary positively with degree of social loss. It was also apparent that some social attributes that nurses combine to establish a degree of social loss are seen immediately (age, ethnic group, social class), while some are learned after time is spent with the patient (occupational worth, marital, status, education). This observation led us to the realization that perceived social loss can change as new attributes of the patients are learned. It also became apparent, from studying the comparison groups, under what conditions (types of wards and hospitals) we would find clusters of patients with different degrees of social loss.

5. Illustrations will refer to Barney G. Glaser and Anselm L. Strauss, "The Social Loss of Dying Patients," *American Journal of Nursing*, 64 (June, 1964), pp. 119-121.

As categories and their properties emerge, the analyst will discover two kinds: those that he has constructed himself (such as "social loss" or 'calculation" of social loss); and those that have been abstracted from the language of the research situation. (For example, "composure" was derived from nurses' statements like "I was afraid of losing my composure when the family started crying over their child.") As his theory develops, the analyst will notice that the concepts abstracted from the substantive situation will tend to be current labels in use for the actual processes and behaviors that are to be explained, while the concepts constructed by the analyst will tend to be the explanations.[6] For example, a nurse's perception of the social loss of a dying patient will affect (an explanation) how she maintains her composure (a behavior) in his presence.

After coding for a category perhaps three or four times, the analyst will find conflicts in the emphases of his thinking. He will be musing over theoretical notions and, at the same time, trying to concentrate on his study of the next incident, to determine the alternate ways by which it should be coded and compared. At this point, the second rule of the constant comparative method is: *stop coding and record a memo on your ideas.* This rule is designed to tap the initial freshness of the analyst's theoretical notions and to relieve the conflict in his thoughts. In doing so, the analyst should take as much time as necessary to reflect and carry his thinking to its most logical (grounded in the data, not speculative) conclusions. It is important to emphasize that for joint coding and analysis there can be no scheduled routine covering the amount to be coded per day, as there is in predesigned research. The analyst may spend hours on one page or he may code twenty pages in a half hour, depending on the relevance of the material, saturation of categories, emergence of new categories, stage of formulation of theory, and of course the mood of the analyst, since this method takes his personal sensitivity into consideration. These factors are in a continual process of change.

If one is working on a research team, it is also a good idea to discuss theoretical notions with one or more teammates. Teammates can help bring out points missed, add points they

6. Thus we have studies of delinquency, justice, "becoming," stigma, consultation, consolation, contraception, etc.; these usually become the variables or processes to be described and explained.

have run across in their own coding and data collection, and crosscheck his points. They, too, begin to compare the analyst's notions with their own ideas and knowledge of the data; this comparison generates additional theoretical ideas. With clearer ideas on the emerging theory systematically recorded, the analyst then returns to the data for more coding and constant comparison.

From the point of view of generating theory it is often useful to write memos on, as well as code, the copy of one's field notes. Memo writing on the field note provides an immediate illustration for an idea. Also, since an incident can be coded for several categories, this tactic forces the analyst to use an incident as an illustration only once, for the most important among the many properties of diverse categories that it indicates. He must look elsewhere in his notes for illustrations for his other properties and categories. This corrects the tendency to use the same illustration over and over for different properties.

The generation of theory requires that the analyst take apart the story within his data. Therefore when he rearranges his memos and field notes for writing up his theory, he sufficiently "fractures" his story at the same time that he saves apt illustrations for each idea (see Step 4). At just this point in his writing, breaking down and out of the story is necessary for clear integration of the theory.

2. *Integrating categories and their properties.* This process starts out in a small way; memos and possible conferences are short. But as the coding continues, the constant comparative units change from comparison of incident with incident to comparison of incident with properties of the category that resulted from initial comparisons of incidents. For example, in comparing incident with incident we discovered the property that nurses constantly recalculate a patent's social loss as they learn more about him. From then on, each incident bearing on "calculation" was compared with "accumulated knowledge on calculating"—not with all other incidents involving calculation. Thus, once we found that age was the most important characteristic in calculating social loss, we could discern how a patient's age affected the nurses' recalculation of social loss as they found out more about his education. We found that education was most influential in calculations of the social loss of a middle-aged

adult, since for a person of this age, education was considered to be of most social worth. This example also shows that constant comparison causes the accumulated knowledge pertaining to a property of the category to readily start to become integrated; that is, related in many different ways, resulting in a unified whole.

In addition, the diverse properties themselves start to become integrated. Thus, we soon found that the calculating and recalculating of social loss by nurses was related to their development of a social loss "story" about the patient. When asked about a dying patient, nurses would tell what amounted to a story about him. The ingredients of this story consisted of a continual balancing out of social loss factors as the nurses learned more about the patient. Both the calculus of social loss and the social loss story were related to the nurse's strategies for coping with the upsetting impact on her professional composure of, say, a dying patient with a high social loss (*e.g.*, a mother with two children). This example further shows that the category becomes integrated with other categories of analysis: the social loss of the dying patient is related to how nurses maintain professonal composure while attending his dying.[7] Thus the theory develops, as different categories and their properties tend to become integrated through constant comparisons that force the analyst to make some related theoretical sense of each comparison.

If the data are collected by theoretical sampling at the same time that they are analyzed (as we suggest should be done), then integration of the theory is more likely to emerge by itself. By joint collection and analysis, the sociologist is tapping to the fullest extent the in vivo patterns of integration in the data itself; questions guide the collection of data to fill in gaps and to extend the theory—and this also is an integrative strategy. Emergence of integration schemes also occurs in analyses that are separate from data collection, but more contrivance may be necessary when the data run thin and no more can be collected. (Other aspects of integration have been discussed in Chapter II.)

3. *Delimiting the theory.* As the theory develops, various

7. See Glaser and Strauss, "Awareness and the Nurse's Composure," in Chapter 13 in *Awareness of Dying* (Chicago: Aldine Publishing Co., 1965).

delimiting features of the constant comparative method begin to curb what could otherwise become an overwhelming task. Delimiting occurs at two levels: the theory and the categories. First, the theory solidifies, in the sense that major modifications become fewer and fewer as the analyst compares the next incidents of a category to its properties. Later modifications are mainly on the order of clarifying the logic, taking out non-relevant properties, integrating elaborating details of properties into the major outline of interrelated categories and—most important—reduction.

By reduction we mean that the analyst may discover underlying uniformities in the original set of categories or their properties, and can then formulate the theory with a smaller set of higher level concepts. This delimits its terminology and text. Here is an illustration which shows the integration of more details into the theory and some consequent reduction: We decided to elaborate our theory by adding detailed strategies used by the nurses to maintain professional composure while taking care of patients with varying degrees of social loss. We discovered that the rationales which nurses used, when talking among themselves, could all be considered "loss rationales." The underlying uniformity was that all these rationales indicated why the patient, given his degree of social loss, would, if he lived, now be socially worthless; in spite of the social loss, he would be better off dead. For example, he would have brain damage, or be in constant, unendurable pain, or have no chance for a normal life.

Through further reduction of terminology we were also discovering that our theory could be generalized so that it pertained to the care of all patients (not just dying ones) by all staff (not just nurses). On the level of formal theory, it could even be generalized as a theory of how the social values of professionals affect the distribution of their services to clients; for example, how they decide who among many waiting clients should next receive a service, and what calibre of service he should be given.

Thus, with reduction of terminology and consequent generalizing, forced by constant comparisons (some comparisons can at this point be based on the literature of other professional areas), the analyst starts to achieve two major requirements of theory: (1) *parsimony* of variables and formulation, and (2) *scope* in the applicability of the theory to a wide range of situations,[8] while keeping a close correspondence of theory and data.

The second level for delimiting the theory is a reduction in the original list of categories for coding. As the theory grows, becomes reduced, and increasingly works better for ordering a mass of qualitative data, the analyst becomes committed to it. His commitment now allows him to cut down the original list of categories for collecting and coding data, according to the present boundaries of his theory. In turn, his consideration, coding, and analyzing of incidents can become more select and focused. He can devote more time to the constant comparison of incidents clearly applicable to this smaller set of categories.

Another factor, which still further delimits the list of categories, is that they become *theoretically saturated*. After an analyst has coded incidents for the same category a number of times, he learns to see quickly whether or not the next applicable incident points to a new aspect. If yes, then the incident is coded and compared. If no, the incident is not coded, since it only adds bulk to the coded data and nothing to the theory.[9] For example, after we had established age as the base line for calculating social loss, no longer did we need to code incidents referring to age for calculating social loss. However, if we came across a case where age did not appear to be the base line (a negative case), the case was coded and then compared. In the case of an 85-year-old dying woman who was considered a great social loss, we discovered that her "wonderful personality" outweighed her age as the most important factor for calculating her social loss. In addition, the amount of data the analyst needs to code is considerably reduced when the data are obtained by theoretical sampling; thus he saves time in studying his data for coding.

8. Merton, *op. cit.*, p. 260.
9. If the analyst's purpose, besides developing theory, is also to count incidents for a category to establish provisional proofs, then he must code the incident. Furthermore, Merton has made the additional point, in correspondence, that to count for establishing provisional proofs may also feed back to developing the theory, since frequency and cross-tabulation of frequencies can also generate new theoretical ideas. See Berelson on the conditions under which one can justify time-consuming, careful counting; *op. cit.*, pp. 128-34. See Becker and Geer for a new method of counting the frequency of incidents; *op. cit.*, pp. 283-87.

Theoretical saturation of categories also can be employed as a strategy in coping with another problem: new categories will emerge after hundreds of pages of coding, and the question is whether or not to go back and re-code all previously coded pages. The answer for large studies is "no." The analyst should start to code for the new category where it emerges, and continue for a few hundred pages of coding, or until the remaining (or additionally collected) data have been coded, to see whether the new category has become theoretically saturated. If it has, then it is unnecessary to go back, either to the field or the notes, because theoretical saturation suggests that what has been missed will probably have little modifying effect on the theory. If the category does not saturate, then the analyst needs to go back and try to saturate it, provided it is central to the theory.

Theoretical saturation can help solve still another problem concerning categories. If the analyst has collected his own data, then from time to time he will remember other incidents that he observed or heard but did not record. What does he do now? If the unrecorded incident applies to an established category, after comparison it can either be ignored because the category is saturated; or, if it indicates a new property of the category, it can be added to the next memo and thus integrated into the theory. If the remembered incident generates a new category, both incident and category can be included in a memo directed toward their place in the theory. This incident alone may be enough data if the category is minor. However, if it becomes central to the theory, the memo becomes a directive for further coding of the field notes, and for returning to the field or library to collect more data.

The universe of data that the constant comparative method uses is based on the reduction of the theory and the delimitation and saturation of categories. Thus, the collected universe of data is first delimitated and then, if necessary, carefully extended by a return to data collection according to the requirements of theoretical sampling. Research resources are economized by this theoretical delimiting of the possible universe of data, since working within limits forces the analyst to spend his time and effort only on data relevant to his categories. In large field studies, with long lists of possibly useful categories and thousands of pages of notes embodying thousands of incidents, each of which could be coded a multitude of ways, theoretical criteria are very necessary for paring down an otherwise monstrous task to fit the available resources of personnel, time, and money. Without theoretical criteria, delimiting a universe of collected data, if done at all, can become very arbitrary and less likely to yield an integrated product; the analyst is also more likely to waste time on what may later prove to be irrelevant incidents and categories.

4. *Writing theory.* At this stage in the process of qualitative analysis, the analyst possesses coded data, a series of memos, and a theory. The discussions in his memos provide the content behind the categories, which become the major themes of the theory later presented in papers or books. For example, the major themes (section titles) for our paper on social loss were "calculating social loss," "the patient's social loss story," and "the impact of social loss on the nurse's professional composure."

When the researcher is convinced that his analytic framework forms a systematic substantive theory, that it is a reasonably accurate statement of the matters studied, and that it is couched in a form that others going into the same field could use—then he can publish his results with confidence. To start writing one's theory, it is first necessary to collate the memos on each category, which is easily accomplished since the memos have been written about categories. Thus, we brought together all memos on calculating social loss for summarizing and, perhaps, further analyzing before writing about it. One can return to the coded data when necessary to validate a suggested point, pinpoint data behind a hypothesis or gaps in the theory, and provide illustrations.[10]

Properties of the Theory

Using the constant comparative method makes probable the achievement of a complex theory that corresponds closely to

10. On "pinpointing" see Anselm Strauss, Leonard Schatzman, Rue Bucher, Danuta Ehrlich and Melvin Shabshin, *Psychiatric Ideologies and Institutions* (New York: Free Press of Glencoe, 1964), Chapter 2, "Logic, Techniques and Strategies of Team Fieldwork."

the data, since the constant comparisons force the analyst to consider much diversity in the data. By *diversity* we mean that each incident is compared with other incidents, or with properties of a category, in terms of as many similarities and differences as possible. This mode of comparing is in contrast to coding for crude proofs; such coding only establishes whether an incident indicates the few properties of the category that are being counted.

The constant comparison of incidents in this manner tends to result in the creation of a "developmental" theory.[11] Although this method can also be used to generate static theories, it especially facilitates the generation of theories of process, sequence, and change pertaining to organizations, positions, and social interaction. But whether the theory itself is static or developmental, its generation, by this method and by theoretical sampling, is continually in process. In comparing incidents, the analyst learns to see his categories in terms of both their internal development and their changing relations to other categories. For example, as the nurse learns more about the patient, her calculations of social loss change; and these recalculations change her social loss stories, her loss rationales and her care of the patient.

This is an inductive method of theory development. To make theoretical sense of so much diversity in his data, the analyst is forced to develop ideas on a level of generality higher in conceptual abstraction than the qualitative material being analyzed. He is forced to bring out underlying uniformities and diversities, and to use more abstract concepts to account for differences in the data. To master his data, he is forced to engage in reduction of terminology. If the analyst starts with raw data, he will end up initially with a substantive theory: a theory for the substantive area on which he has done research (for example, patient care or gang behavior). If he starts with the findings drawn from many studies pertaining to an abstract sociological category, he will end up with a formal theory per-

11. Recent calls for more developmental, as opposed to static, theories have been made by Wilbert Moore, "Predicting Discontinuities in Social Change," *American Sociological Review* 29 (1964), p. 322; Howard S. Becker, *Outsiders* (New York: Free Press of Glencoe, 1962), pp. 22-25; and Barney G. Glaser and Anselm Strauss, "Awareness Contexts and Social Interaction," *op. cit.*

taining to a conceptual area (such as stigma, deviance, lower class, status congruency, organizational careers, or reference groups).[12] To be sure, as we described in Chapter IV, the level of generality of a substantive theory can be raised to a formal theory. (Our theory of dying patients' social loss could be raised to the level of how professional people give service to clients according to their respective social value.) This move to formal theory requires additional analysis of one's substantive theory, and the analyst should, as stated in the previous chapter, include material from other studies, with the same formal theoretical import, however diverse their substantive content.[13] The point is that the analyst should be aware of the level of generality from which he starts in relation to the level at which he wishes to end.

The constant comparative method can yield either discussional or propositional theory. The analyst may wish to cover many properties of a category in his discussion or to write formal propositions about a category. The former type of presentation is often sufficiently useful at the exploratory stage of theory development, and can easily be translated into propositions by the reader if he requires a formal hypothesis. For example, two related categories of dying are the patient's social loss and the amount of attention he receives from nurses. This can easily be restated as a proposition: patients considered a high social loss, as compared with those considered a low social loss, will tend to receive more attention from nurses.

12. For an example, see Barney G. Glaser, *Organizational Careers* (Chicago: Aldine Publishing Co., 1967).

13. ". . . the development of any one of these coherent analytic perspectives is not likely to come from those who restrict their interest exclusively to one substantive area." From Erving Goffman, *Stigma: Notes on the Management of Spoiled Identity* (Englewood Cliffs, N.J.: Prentice-Hall, 1963), p. 147. See also Reinhard Bendix, "Concepts and Generalizations in Comparative Sociological Studies," *American Sociological Review*, 28 (1963), pp. 532-39.

VI

Clarifying and Assessing
Comparative Studies

Throughout this book we advocate a general comparative method for generating grounded theory. But since there are various types of work that go by the name of "comparative method" (as discussed briefly in Chapter III), this chapter explores how various uses of comparative method can be distinguished and their value for generating theory can be assessed. First, we shall offer an "accounting scheme" that should be helpful both for locating and assessing the comparative analysis used or advocated in any publication, and for making clear distinctions between it and our general mode of analysis.

We begin by outlining the accounting scheme and then discuss a number of publications by sociologists and social anthropologists who have variously used comparative methods.

An Accounting Scheme

In 1955, in a survey of "Comparisons in Cultural Anthropology," Oscar Lewis noted the "ever-increasing concern of anthropologists with problems of theory and method, and the accumulation of great masses of data which cry out for systematic comparative analysis." [1] Comparative analysis, in other words, thrives on the need to theorize. Lewis also remarked on

1. *Yearbook of Anthropology* (New York: Wenner-Gren Foundation for Anthropological Research, 1955), pp. 259-92; quote on p. 260.

anthropologists' lack of agreement about what comparative analysis, or method, was. Ten years later, Fred Eggan, in his paper on "Comparative Method in Anthropology," also remarked that "at this late date we should be able to utilize 'the comparative method' as a general cover term, realizing that there are important distinctions within it." [2] Though sociologists also advocate and use comparisons, they are not always aware that such analyses may include a range of quite different operations.[3]

We can recognize the particular mode of analysis presented in any given publication by applying a checklist of questions (suggested by our previous discussion, especially in Chapter II).

1. Is the author's main emphasis upon *verifying* or *generating* theory?

2. Is he more interested in *substantive* or *formal* theory?

3. What is the *scope* of theory used in the publication?

4. To what degree is the theory *grounded*?

5. How *dense* in conceptual detail is the theory?

6. What *kinds of data* are used, and in what capacity, in relation to the theory?

7. To what degree is the theory *integrated*?

8. How much *clarity* does the author reveal about the type of theory that he uses?

Of course these are not the only queries one could direct at comparative analyses, but let us see how useful they can be. For convenience, we call this checklist of guiding questions an accounting scheme, since it will allow assessments to be made of each publication in terms of the generation of theory.

Because our basic distinction is between the verification and the generation of theory, we begin our scrutiny of various writings with some that fall on the verification side, and then discuss others that are more generative. We shall touch on the other guiding questions when discussing each publication, but shall emphasize those particular questions that highlight whether comparative analysis was used maximally or minimally to gen-

2. In Melford Spiro (Ed.), *Context and Meaning in Cultural Anthropology* (New York: Free Press of Glencoe, 1965), pp. 357-72; quote on p. 359.

3. Edward Shils, "On the Comparative Study of the New States," in C. Geertz, Ed.), *Old Societies and New States* (New York: Free Press of Glencoe, 1963), pp. 1-26.

erate grounded theory. Its relevance for that topic will be précised in a concluding, or prefacing, "summary" sentence.

Comparisons for Verification

We begin with two research publications in which verification is much more prominent than the development or generation of theory. Both publications are concerned mainly with existing rather than emergent theory, but are rather different from each other.

Guy Swanson: *The Birth of the Gods* [4]

In his preface, Swanson notes that "These studies were undertaken because I wanted to discuss the social organization of religion and ethics with my students and could find little in the way of tested explanations for the basic phenomena." There are several key words in his sentence: he is concerned with *basic phenomena*—in this instance religion's nature and origins; he is also concerned with the various *explanations* of those phenomena; and those dual concerns are directly linked with his interest in *tested explanations* (verification).

"From what experiences," Swanson asks at the outset, "do the ideas of the supernatural and its myriad forms arise?" Since "verifiable answers" to such a broad question are "almost impossible to obtain," Swanson poses several more specific questions, "each of which contributes toward solving the more general problem." These questions pertain to "monotheistic deity, polytheistic gods, ancestral spirits, reincarnation, the immanence of the soul, the prevalence of witchcraft, and the notion of gods who concern themselves with human moral problems." Swanson's own explanations for each belief "will be tested against information from fifty primitive and ancient societies" (p. 2).

Several points about Swanson's approach are especially important for us. First, the various explanations that he wishes to test are derived from both popular and scholarly literature. Second, he states that the "most elaborate attempt to confront

4. Ann Arbor: University of Michigan Press, 1960.

the contents of supernatural experiences and construct a theory adequate to them is that of . . . Durkheim" (p. 14). This explanation is the main source for Swanson's work. Durkheim's position is "plausible" but leaves much "to be desired" (p. 17). Third, Swanson does not merely operationalize Durkheim's position on the supernatural; rather he is stimulated by it to develop a number of related hypotheses of his own, bearing on the beliefs he plans to explore. Fourth, he sets about testing each hypothesis, with clarity of purpose and an evident attempt to make his procedures clear. Fifth, the sources of his data are publications about a sample of societies. Sixth, the gathering of data from reading these publications is directed by the hypotheses and designed to test them. Seventh, the verification is done with great awareness and care: there is coding of indicators, attempt to examine negative instances, and so on. Finally, evidence is examined for its pertinence to alternative explanations; that is, those which were not developed by Swanson himself.

In this study, comparative method is almost wholly in the service of verification. Specifically, comparisons are made among societies according to association of various relevant items, like the relation of sovereign kinships to the activity of ancestral spirits or the number of superior gods. What about comparisons made in the service of emerging theory? Very little new theory arises here. What theory emerges is almost wholly in the form of follow-through on imperfect associations or arises through careful analyses of negative cases; that is, when a society behaves differently than predicted. Any emergent theory is distinctly minor in bulk and import compared with the original theory. Swanson, however, is eager to test the new hypotheses whenever he has sufficient resources available.

What does the remainder of our accounting scheme tell about Swanson's use of comparative method? Like many sociologists, he addresses himself in a few closing pages to the relation between his substantive study and larger sociological issues (the "place of the theory in the study of social organization"). The study otherwise is focused wholly on substantive theory, although theory of considerable scope. The theory is *logically derived from Durkheim's theory*, rather than grounded in data; the function of data is principally to *test* theory. A great number of categories are developed, so the theory is fairly dense in "conceptual detail." The theory is exceptionally well integrated in one sense: the major substantive question about the supernatural is broken into seven questions and closely linked hypotheses about each are formulated. One additional point is raised by our accounting scheme: how much clarity about the type of theoretical formulation does the author of this monograph reveal? The answer is that he evidences great awareness of his purposes, and of what his theory is, where it comes from, and what he wishes to accomplish with it.

If one were to coin a single phrase to summarize Swanson's use of comparative method, and to contrast it with other uses discussed below, it might be this: *Make comparisons among an* ✓ *array (of societies) to verify well-specified derived theory, using relatively fixed categories.*

Robert Blauner: *Alienation and Freedom* [5]

A similar summarizing statement about Blauner's book might be this: *Make comparisons among an array (of industries) to verify aspects of a general body of received theory*—existing theory received from one's elders—*using relatively fixed categories.* In his preface, Blauner states clearly his basic assumption: the "idea that the alienation can be used scientifically— rather than polemically—to elucidate the complex realities of present-day industrial society." Alienation is one of the pervasive perspectives inherited from earlier generations; nevertheless it "has inspired fruitless polemics more often than serious scientific research" (p. 4). Most writers accept too oversimplified a notion of alienation and its consequences. Blauner, struck by "the existence of critically different types of work environments within modern industry," wished to see whether these environments "result in large variations in the form and intensity of alienation" (p. 4). Using the language of verification, he sums up that the "present investigation is an attempt to demonstrate and to explain the uneven distribution of alienation among factory workers in American industry."

But "no simple definition of alienation can do justice to the many intellectual confusions which have engaged this concept

5. Chicago: University of Chicago Press, 1964.

as a central explanatory idea." So Blauner, thinking of its sociological dimensions, needed to decide how he was going to
specify and operationalize alienation (p. 15). After scrutinizing
the literature, he decided upon four dimensions: meaningless-
ness, isolation, self-estrangement, and fragmentations in man's
experience (pp. 32-33).

His use of comparative method involves a comparison of
four factory industries (printing, textiles, automobiles, and
chemicals). Why these particular industries were chosen is
not made clear. Because of Blauner's focus upon industrial diversity, the reader must assume that the choice was meant to maximize that diversity. There are four variables—technology, division of labor, social organization, and economic structure—
which vary from industry to industry. Therefore, "these four
variables are the key underlying elements in comparative industrial analysis. Their unique constellation in a specific use
imparts to an individual industry its distinctive character and
results in a work environment that is somewhat special in its
impact on the blue-collar labor force" (pp. 10-11).

The data bearing on these industries were drawn from a
variety of sources. Quantitative data came from a job-attitude
study, carried out some years ago by Elmo Roper for *Fortune*
(blue-collar workers in 16 factory industries). Blauner also
analyzed industrial case studies and previously published accounts of his four industries. He interviewed 21 blue-collar
workers in one chemical plant; he also used a questionnaire
survey of this plant that had been made by a colleague. Since
different matters about each industry caught the attention of the
researchers who originally made these studies, the four industries were not always identical, nor were the discussions of each
one always exactly comparable. Nevertheless, each of Blauner's
analyses does center on the four principal dimensions of alienation, plus the four industry variables.

Blauner's conclusion is that his

> comparative analyses of these four industrial settings . . . show
> that an employee's industry decides the nature of the work he
> performs . . . and affects the meaning which that work has for
> him. It greatly influences the extent to which he is free in his
> work life and the extent to which he is controlled by technology
> or supervision. It also influences his opportunity for personal

growth and development . . . even affects the kind of social personality he develops, since an industrial environment tends to breed a distinctive social type.

A corollary is that there is no simple answer to whether the contemporary factory worker is alienated: "Each dimension of alienation . . . varies in form and intensity according to the industrial setting" (p. 166) "The method of comparative industrial analysis therefore illustrates the diversity and pluralism within modern manufacturing, highlights the unequal distribution of alienation and freedom among the factory labor force, and exposes the causal factors underlying these variations" (p. 166).

In his last chapter, Blauner abandons industry-by-industry analysis and attempts to "summarize some of the findings of the investigation." His discussion turns around some basic trends in industry, especially as they bear on the dimensions of alienation. His four industries serve as illustrations of what has happened already, and what may happen in the future, since they are at different stages in following these trends.

What do our directed questions tell us about this study? Clearly, Blauner, impressed by the general body of alienation theory, wished to verify one qualified version of it (alienation varies by work environment). His emphasis is so completely on verification that almost no *new* theory emerges from the study, except for his closing discussion of possible trends. Even that is less a matter of theory than of empirical fact and prediction.

The monograph treats a formal theory, though in relation to substantive areas of industry and work. The theory's scope is quite wide. To what degree is it "grounded" theory? Blauner used a received theory (alienation), which he then operationalized according to pertinent dimensions. By the end of the study, therefore, his specific and qualified version of alienation theory is grounded on careful analysis of data. Next, how dense in conceptual detail is his theory? Because the study is organized around four dimensions of alienation and four variables varying from industry to industry, one expects—and finds—a relative richness of conceptual detail. In fact, in the analysis of each industry differential as well as similar categories are used. (If there is any emergent theory in the study, it is embodied in the discussion of these differential categories.)

Another question is how well the theory is integrated. The answer varies—as it emerges from the discussion of each industry, the theory is relatively well integrated at the general level of the four dimensions of alienation. In the general discussion of American industry as a whole, the theory is probably less well integrated. The integration of varying lower levels of abstraction, even in the analyses of specific industries, is fairly successful.

Two more questions remain. The first pertains to data: diverse kinds were used for verificatory purposes and employed self-consciously to maximize diversity of industrial environment and alienation effects. Second: how much clarity is shown about the type of theoretical formulation? Here the answer is not as straightforward as with the Swanson monograph. Blauner is certainly aware that he is specifying and qualifying theory about alienation, and that the level of abstraction entailed in his major generalizations is quite high. But, judging from the style of his discussion, about both specific industries and American industry as a whole, he is much less clear about the relations of lower and higher level generalizations.

One final remark may be useful in understanding Blauner's handling of comparative method and of theory. He is not nearly as scientistic as many verifiers (Swanson, for instance). His approach to his received theory is more reverent than questioning—not asking "Does it work; is it right?" but admiring its illumination of the contemporary social scene. As he says in his last paragraph, "Finally, I have attempted to demonstrate the usefulness of the alienation perspective in clarifying our understanding of the complexities of the modern social world" (p. 187). Noting that alienation can be expressed systematically so as to raise "important analytical, as well as sociopolitical, questions," he hopes to have shown that these questions can be "partially answered through empirical research" (especially comparative research). But the questions are still answered "without eliminating the human value orientation that has informed the historical usage of this body of thought, for the moral power inherent in the alienation tradition has been its view of man as potentiality." His closing lines again emphasize "a strain between empirical tough-mindedness and human relevance in social research." In short: Verify (and qualify) this great body of received theory—with every expectation of its relative accuracy. Fortunate indeed are we for our perceptive ancestors!

Assumed Verification Plus Limited Generation

Some comparative analyses are made in the service of theories that are accepted as so correct and so useful that researchers wish merely to contribute to them in minor ways. The hallmark of this style of research is a language that emphasizes "clarification" or "elaboration" of the *received* theory (or system of theory). The researcher may also emphasize, and even overemphasize, that he is validating his derived hypotheses; but he never really questions his received theory. His aim unquestionably is to generate new categories and hypotheses, but he does this *only* within the limits of the original theoretical framework. Excellent examples of this genre are two books, one published by Robert Redfield in 1941, and the other by E. N. Eisenstadt in 1956. Both were addressed at essentially the same great, received body of social theory, dealing with contrasts between primitive and modern societies.

Robert Redfield: *The Folk Culture of Yucatan* [6]

Contrasts between folk and urban, primitive and modern, sacred and secular, custom and contract, and other analogous pairs are among our inheritances from past social theorists. The men who have written about the theme represented by those paired comparisons include Henry Maine, Lewis Morgan, Ferdinand Tonnies, and Emile Durkheim. These men are named by Robert Redfield as his intellectual ancestors, in a book that represented his own attempt to think about and study the great traditional sociological theme. Throughout his career, Redfield was interested in one or another of this theme's variants; his book on Yucatan represents an early, and systematic, attack on the differences between folk and urban cultures.

6. Chicago: University of Chicago Press, 1941.

In this "impressive comparative study," Redfield struck on the idea of studying four Yucatan communities—a city, a town, a peasant village, and a tribal village—along a continuum from "folk" to "urban." [7] Through extensive fieldwork in each community, he wished, as noted in the opening lines of his preface, "to do two things at once: to summarize a great many particular facts about a particular people at a certain time and also to declare or to suggest some general notions about the nature of society and culture" (p. ix). A few pages later, he summarizes, "The chief objective of this investigation is, then, to define differences in the nature of isolated homogeneous society, on the one hand, and mobile heterogeneous society, on the other, so far as these kinds of societies are represented in Yucatan" (p. 17). He makes clear that although he will describe particular communities, "the account of the contrasts is made in general terms" so that "questions of more general interest will arise out of consideration of these materials."

These quotes suggest that Redfield was less interested in ethnographic detail than in the "big questions" raised by his predecessors. They also suggest a certain ambiguity as to whether he was engaged in verification or, as he says, in "clarifying" received theory about the transitions from folk to urban societies.

Redfield summarizes the results of his comparative analysis in his last chapter, "The Folk Culture and Civilization." His "most general conclusion," is that the four communities do represent the folk-urban continuum postulated before he began the actual study. He also reached other conclusions which, from our viewpoint, represent emergent hypotheses developed within the limiting framework of received theory. Some of these new hypotheses are frankly speculative; others he felt were more grounded.

For instance, after summing up his comparisons of the Yucatan towns, Redfield addresses himself to the more general questions of whether "all long-isolated, homogeneous societies" are "sacred, collectivistic, and characterized by well-organized cultures" (p. 356). Studies of primitive societies suggest this is so. Comparison of them with our own society also suggests an affirmative answer. However, one further comparison, taken

7. The judgment is Fred Eggan's, *op. cit.*, p. 368.

from ethnographic work by Sol Tax in Guatemalan communities, appeared to Redfield as a modification of the basic proposition of this question. The Guatemalan research suggests the qualification that: "There are long-isolated, non-literate, homogeneous, culturally well-organized local communities in relative equilibrium . . . characterized by predominance of secular and impersonal behavior and sanctions and by individualism with relative unimportance of kinship institutions." Redfield regarded this negative case as a challenge that necessitated deepening his basic theoretical framework. For him, it raised the question of "how these Guatemalan societies come to be (if they are) secular and individualistic, while being culturally well organized and homogeneous." That question could not be answered without further historical knowledge, but Redfield suggests several alternative hypotheses, all frankly speculative.

If we now summarize this study according to our accounting scheme, what should be concluded? Redfield's main intent was to develop new hypotheses within the framework of received theory; he wished also to use his Yucatan material to verify aspects of the theory. His field work comparisons were in the service of both these goals.

This research was addressed, of course, to formal theory of great scope. The substantive theory, though, is not much developed, unless one reads Redfield's ethnography as more than dense empirical detail, grounded by careful field work in particular Yucatan communities. The conceptual density—at either substantive or formal levels—is not very great. Relatively few new categories or properties are developed. The high-level theorizing is well integrated, both by the logic of Redfield's reasoning and through his presentation of analyses. Again, the integration is done well withn the limits of received theory.

Finally, how clear was Redfield about the type of theoretical formulations he was making? About this, judgments are likely to vary. It seems to us that Redfield's own ambiguity about his work is reflected in his repeated statements that conclusions are "tentative," and in his opening remarks that his study is both "a report" about Yucatan communities and "a book" about "some general notions about the nature of society and culture." It may be, he says, that a report and a book cannot be combined, but he has put them together because "every plausible means should be tried in strengthening our shaky bridges between general propositions . . . and such special knowledge as we have of particular societies" (p. ix). We would judge from this that Redfield primarily was interested in developing general theory, but felt the necessity of grounding his analyses in careful field work. Understanding his major purpose more clearly might have served it better, and might also have allowed him to jump the limits of the original theoretical framework— or at least extended it more. In his last writings he managed to do this.[8] A summarizing statement about the comparative method used in the earlier book is: *Make comparisons among an array (of villages) primarily to develop new hypotheses within the framework of a general body of received theory, and secondarily to verify its minor aspects.*

S. N. Eisenstadt: *From Generation to Generation* [9]

While Redfield is tentative and exploratory in style, Eisenstadt's frankly exploratory research is couched in a more assertive language of "to analyze," "to validate," "to verify," "to show," "to specify conditions." Eisenstadt addresses the same great body of received theory but several important changes have taken place in the 15 years between the two books. First: this research, published in 1956, reflects the acknowledged influence of the Parsons-Shils functionalism. Second: the major variable comes directly from Parsons (particularistic versus universalistic societies). Third: a specific issue is addressed, namely, "to analyze the various social phenomena known as age groups, youth movements, etc., and to ascertain whether it is possible to specify the social conditions under which they arise or the types of societies in which they occur" (p. 15). And fourth: there is a self-conscious and ingenious use of a multitude of comparisons, both to verify initial major hypotheses and to develop associated ones. Eisenstadt says that he wished on the basis of comparisons to "test the hypotheses on which this study is based, validate and elaborate them" (p. 15). All his elaboration, as we shall see, is well within the limits of the function-

8. Cf. *The Little Community* (Chicago: University of Chicago Press, 1955).

9. New York: Free Press of Glencoe, 1956.

alist version of the older dichotomy of primitive-modern societies.

Eisenstadt's basic problem "is to find what conditions of the social system favor or, alternately, prevent the emergence of age groups, what kinds of groups can be age-homogeneous, and what their functions are within the social system" (p. 36). He begins his presentation with what he calls "a broad hypothesis" (or "broad, overall hypotheses"), comprising several parts: for instance, age as the basis for role allocation is most important in societies that are particularistic, diffuse and ascriptive; age-homogeneous groups tend to arise in societies in which family or kinship units cannot ensure, or hinder, the members' attainment of full social status.

To validate and elaborate such hypotheses, Eisenstadt utilizes ethnographic and historical materials bearing on a number of primitive and historic societies, as well as extensive documentary materials on youth groups and movements. He gives his "general criteria of comparison" (p. 62), which consist of a number of criteria for membership in age groups, the internal structure of age groups, and the place of these groups within social systems (pp. 57-58). He uses these criteria first to find differences and similarities among his societies, especially in terms of his basic distinction between "particularistic" and "modern" societies. Then, in a gradually evolving and complex presentation, he presents analyses based on a great variety of comparisons, which are directed by emergent analyses and hypotheses, which in turn are associated with new "variables" (such as stratification, achievement, and specialization).

Eisenstadt is careful to look for both similarities and differences, and makes explanations of differences essential to his inquiry. His choice of certain comparisons (two societies or more) often rests on the expectation of finding differences, which will bring out differential conditions to account for different age groups and their functions. Sometimes he comments that "no exceptions" were found; sometimes an exception is interpreted as apparent rather than genuine. Comparisons are presented in considerable discursive detail; and although the same basic group of societies is used repeatedly, new instances are occasionally used as comparisons.

A quick look at Eisenstadt's book will show that he repeatedly claims to have "validated" (even "fully validated") his hypotheses; evidently he is much concerned with verification. At the same time, he is concerned with "elaborating" initial hypotheses; that is, with generating new hypotheses derived from his original ones. His original hypotheses derive from Parsonian functionalism, as do certain problems (for instance, the functions of age groups for "integrating" the social system"). We may conclude that Eisenstadt in this study displays proper reverence for received theory, but wishes to extend its usefulness to age groups. In turn, of course, what is learned about this substantive area will be channeled back into a general knowledge of social systems.

Eisenstadt has thoroughly accepted the received theory. Not only has it set his problems and suggested most of his major hypotheses; the "big" theory has also helped him to generate categories applicable to age groups and to discover their properties. Furthermore, although his comparisons are ingenious, varied, and multitudinous, they are governed by Parsonian theory and its derivative hypotheses—and not, so far as we can determine, by his data. *The great complexity of comparative analysis turns out to be "manufactured" complexity of theoretical organization, rather than a genuinely "understood" complexity of the world of events.* In the same way that survey researchers ingeniously cross-tabulate their quantitative data and then report positive results, Eisenstadt has determined his comparison groups through relatively standard derivations from received theory, done a kind of cross-tabulation (analysis), and then reported his results.

Like survey researchers, he also tends to report in great detail every operation that worked: forecasting, reporting, explaining, discussing, summarizing, and then moving on to the next point. This style tells us something about the kind of integration achieved, which might be termed "discursive developmental"— merely the continuing discussion of cumulative analyses. Integration also is based on the guiding functionalist framework. Integration of various levels of analysis can be quite tight, because hypotheses are derived from the initial theory and divergencies as well as similarities have been compared for societies and age groups. The conceptual detail is also dense, for generally the same reasons.

Despite an honest attempt to explain occasional exceptions,

this style of research did not really allow the researcher to challenge the pre-formed theoretical scheme that guided his operations from the outset. It is not surprising that he found no exceptions and could "analyze" what seemed to be exceptions; reverence for a pre-existing theory blocks out opportunity to select potentially destructive comparisons. Eisenstadt's systematic comparisons of divergencies were conducted only within the limits of the initial theory and derived hypotheses, both of which he wished to elaborate. If he had really wished to test them—certainly if he had wished to challenge them—he would have instituted an equally ingenious search for genuinely qualifying comparison groups.

Perhaps one example will be sufficient. Eisenstadt assumes that "social system," "society," and sometimes even "nation" are equivalent. In discussing the possible integrational functions of age groups, therefore, he never institutes a real search for age groups outside the framework of this somewhat mystical conception of a unified society. What about multi-ethnic nations, like Malaya and India? What about age groups in religious sects? And despite a brief discussion of young revolutionaries, there is no real examination of their relations with older, equally alienated adults. Eisenstadt only glancingly refers to those relations, since his major point about young revolutionaries is their break with their elders.

The remaining question raised by our accounting scheme is the degree of clarity shown by its author about its type of theoretical formulation. Eisenstadt certainly understands the general relation between his formulations and functional-social system theory, as well as the interrelations among his varied hypotheses. However, we believe that he has not clearly understood how his theoretical formulations pertain to his data. He attacks an open world of phenomena with relatively closed theory, assuming that the theory is open to revision by his data. We have suggested that it is not. This is why he continually claims validation of his hypotheses when they seem to have been inadequately tested. He is open to this judgment precisely because—unlike Blauner or Redfield—he has generated, and with care, many new hypotheses. A summarizing statement about his comparative method might be: *Make comparisons among an array (of societies, age groups) both to test received theory and to generate hypotheses deduced from it, using relatively fixed categories.*

Organizing Data Versus Generating Theory

Before we discuss comparisons that are made principally to generate theory, it will be useful to consider a style of analysis that is easily mistaken for such comparisons.

Richard LaPiere: *Collective Behavior* [10]

Illustrative of this style is a book published in 1938 by LaPiere. (This book is still a very stimulating source for anyone interested in that substantive area.) In his preface, LaPiere remarks on the impressive mass of data that had accumulated about "the social interactions in which the individual develops . . . and . . . manifests his personality." But the data are "often conflicting, unrelated and incomplete." So LaPiere brought these data together and supplemented them with materials drawn from a variety of sources: newspapers, magazines, fiction, and nonfiction. His remaining aim was to build, from this aggregate of data, "a tentative frame of reference for further study."

After a few introductory chapters, each succeeding one deals with a different form of behavior: institutional, conventional, regimental, formal, congenial, audience, public, exchange, political, panic, fanatical. The chapters are grouped logically under major sections, titled: Cultural Types of Interaction, Recreational Types of Interaction, Control Types, and Escape Types. Something like comparison among chapters is achieved by using relatively uniform rubrics under which data and discussion are grouped. The standard rubrics are: origin and function, ideologies, membership, overt and covert aspects of interaction, leadership (some chapters omit or add others). But the reader must supply his own comparisons, as there is little cross-reference among the chapters.

Using our checklist of questions, what can we say about

10. New York: McGraw-Hill, 1938.

LaPiere's use of his comparisons? What emerges from his comparative handling of a great mass of data is a comprehensive and organized scheme for making sense of them. He develops a great many hypotheses, although he presents them frequently as statements rather than as propositions in a formal theory. A great many categories are explored and handled integratively through the organizational scheme. But the scheme governs the total outcome. Also, in contrast to true generation of theory, whatever comparisons LaPiere has made are hidden, though he must have made some comparisons to arrive at his standard rubrics. Even so, they would not represent a genuine interplay, back and forth between data and theory, with comparison groups chosen to maximize the generation of theory. LaPiere does not seem to understand that he has developed an organizing strategy rather than a theory. His approach may be summarized as: *Make comparisons among an array (of social interactions) to build a frame of reference that will encompass the data.*

Comparisons for Generation

We turn next to various modes of comparative analysis that have been employed principally for generating theory. Listed in the order of their discussion, the publications to which we now apply our accounting scheme are intended to illustrate: generation despite a bias toward verification (Morris Janowitz), logical generation combined with illustrative verification (Erving Goffman), generation restricted to the search for regularities (Tomatsu Shibutani and Kian Kwan), generation by a combination of logico-deductive theory and grounded inquiry (Amitai Etzioni), generation grounded in limited comparison groups (Clifford Gertz), generation grounded in internal comparisons (E. Evans-Pritchard) and insightful generation with minimal integration (Robert Park, Georg Simmel). We end with an instance of generated theory that is well grounded but insufficiently integrated (Anselm Strauss *et al.*).

Morris Janowitz: *The Military*
in the Political Development of New Nations [11]

Morris Janowitz's theory about the military's influence on the political development of new nations is an excellent example of a generated substantive theory that is harmed by a researcher's bias toward verification. In the style of verification, he preselects groups of new nations on the basis of their common features, excluding nations that are fundamentally different. This procedure is entirely proper for verifying propositions, but in generating theory (which he does), nations should not be judged on the basis of similarities and differences *until* the necessary theoretical analysis has been accomplished—to find out if common features are actually so common and fundamental differences so fundamental. As we have noted in Chapter III, preselecting groups on this basis is unnecessary and even hinders the generation of a theory. The groups should be chosen as the development of the theory directs.

Still following the verification approach, Janowitz preconceived what his theory would look like: "comparative analysis deals with variations in the extent and form of military involvement in domestic politics from country to country." Since he goes on to generate a theory, however, "extent and form" are but two of the many different kinds of theoretical ideas that might have emerged from his analysis. For example, he also deals with functions, preconditions, mechanisms, and career processes. Indeed, of the entire armamentarium of types of theoretical ideas, how could he possibly know what would be the most relevant, or what might emerge until he had accomplished his theoretical analysis?

Janowitz also preconceives three models of "civil-military" relations as the ones relevant to his remaining analysis. Again, these may be useful models for verification, but they hinder an emergent theoretical analysis of the actual civil-military relations within new nations. Janowitz in fact develops these models by making a comparative analysis of new and old nations—thus generating theory. But this does not mean that these models can then be directly applied in comparative analysis among new

11. Chicago: University of Chicago Press, 1964.

nations, which he also starts out to do. The three models must be compared, and they may or may not apply to the chosen focus on new nations. (It would have been interesting to note how, in civil-military relations the Latin American nations would fit these models and suggest others.)

Finally, Janowitz is firmly in the grip of the rhetoric and method of verification when he states toward the end of his first chapter: "The following illustrative propositions about internal organization are offered to help explain the patterns of political behavior of the military in new nations as compared with industrialized nations on the basis of available data." Here his vacillation between the methods of verification *and* generation is clear. He wishes to have propositions because of his emphasis on verification and so he preconceives some; yet at the same time he realizes that a theory from which such propositions should be derived has yet to be generated. So he calls the propositions "illustrative" and speaks of them as helping to explain—a theoretical job. At the close of Chapter I he clearly states that his aim is to explore these propositions, not test them. Thus, he frees himself for generating while still keeping the trappings of verification.

In the remainder of his book Janowitz generates a remarkable theory of civil-military relations within new nations, on the basis of a comparative analysis of nations, using many different slices of data on each one. His substantive theory has a clearly defined scope; it is sufficiently dense; it seems to work and fit his data. But because of his bias toward verification in laying out his approach, the theory lacks integration in the density of theoretical properties. He can talk of consequences, conditions and mechanisms all in one paragraph, with no realization of them *as* theoretical properties, since he is concentrating on "exploring his propositions." Thus he lacks the clarity of focus necessary for integrating the properties of his theory, because he is not clear about the type of formulation. He clearly wants to generate theory, and does, and is only confounded, not really stopped, by wishing to use the format of verification. His approach may be summarized as: *Make comparisons among an array (of societies, military organizations) principally to generate theory, using preselected categories based on the logic of verification.*

Erving Goffman: *The Presentation of Self* [12] and *Stigma* [13]

Since the publication of *The Presentation of Self in Every-day Life,* Erving Goffman has been widely regarded as a man who could develop effective, or at least stimulating, theory. His perspectives and concepts have become part of the standard vocabulary of sociology. Since Goffman has employed a type of comparative analysis, his work merits discussion here. An examination of his recent *Stigma,* supplemented by occasional references to *The Presentation of Self,* will supply the material for our commentary.

Goffman's prefaces leave no question that his books are directed at the development of theoretical frameworks beyond the study of given substantive areas. In *Stigma,* he notes that numerous good studies about stigmas have accumulated; he wishes to show "how this material can be economically described within a single conceptual scheme." In *The Presentation of Self,* he begins, "I mean this report to serve as a sort of a handbook detailing one sociological perspective from which social life can be studied, especially the kind . . . organized within the physical confines of a building or plant." He also refers to that particular perspective as a model and a framework.

Goffman is among the most prolific inventors of concepts in sociology, and both books are justifiedly notable for their new concepts. These are integral to the development of his theoretical frameworks. He says of his *Stigma* framework: "This task will allow me to formulate and use a special set of concepts."

Goffman typically begins his books by presenting his theoretical framework. From this he builds upward and outward, "in logical steps." He introduces categories one after the other, and simultaneously develops this framework by discussing their referents and the relationships among them. For instance, in *Stigma* we are introduced quickly to stigma itself, then to virtual and actual social identity, and other categories, also to relevant properties, conditions, processes, tactics, actors, and consequences.

---

12. Edinburgh, Scotland: Edinburgh University Press, 1956, and New York: Doubleday, 1959.
13. Englewood Cliffs, N.J.: Prentice Hall, 1963.

An important question, from our point of view, is exactly how Goffman's illustrations function, since they are a species of comparison. He gives a clue in the preface to his first book: "The illustrative materials used in this study are of mixed status: some are taken from respectable researches where qualified generalizations are given concerning reliably recorded regularities; some are taken from informal memoirs written by colourful people; many fall in between. The justification for this approach (as I take to be the justification for Simmel's also) is that the illustrations together fit into a coherent framework that ties together bits of experience the reader has already had and provides the student with a guide worth testing in case-studies of institutional life."

What is he saying? First, that the comparative materials function in the service of formal theory. Second (although more implicit), that they will help the reader understand the framework better. Presumably they do this both by clarifying the concepts they illustrate and by helping to build up a cumulative perspective.

For many readers, the illustrations probably function as a means of persuasion, whether or not Goffman intends this effect. They make the theory appear both potentially useful or effective, and truthful and accurate; they seem convincing evidence that "things are so." The very proliferation of footnoted sources and commentaries, plus the variety of time and place drawn upon for illustration, can be translated into an implicit language of verification. Despite Goffman's clear announcements of his intention to construct theoretical frameworks, sometimes one senses a genuine tension in his writing between the theorizing *and* his desire to describe the reality of an empirical world.[14]

While developing his framework by introducing and discussing categories, Goffman illustrates copiously with these comparative materials. Because Goffman's pages are dense with illustration and conceptualization, they have a closely packed texture. Readers sometimes may weary of too many illustra-

14. One reader has wondered in conversation with us: Does Goffman's "Total Institutions" represent a model or a description of many if not most mental hospitals, or is it really a description mainly of St. Elizabeth's Hospital where Goffman did most of the field work for his paper on total institutions?

tions, too many concepts (reviewers sometimes criticize Goffman for this), but they cannot help recognizing that a theoretical framework is being developed densely and carefully,
step by step.

However, Goffman rarely presents an analysis of an exception or a negative instance. His many illustrations are not used
to show differences but to illuminate properties, conditions, tactics and consequences. Probably, when Goffman is working out
his frameworks, his examination of diverse sources does stimulate
generation of categories, properties, tactics, hypotheses, and so
on. But he does not present those operations. Neither does he
build diverse comparisons into his presented analyses to add
rich and integrated density of conceptual detail.

How, then, are his theoretical frameworks integrated? Each
is integrated mainly through a step-by-step development of the
framework itself, including detailing the relationships among
major and minor categories, conditions, consequences, and tactics. After reading one of Goffman's presentations and compre-
hending the total framework, it is entirely possible to begin
again, and re-experience the *logical* integration, this time more
vividly than at first reading. On the other hand, closer scrutiny
of its logic may disappoint the reader. He may wonder why
certain discussions are inserted at given points. He may not
understand why some discussions are broken off so soon, or why
they move along to the next specific concept or relationship.
This has been our experience, even when we have provisionally
accepted the general framework and the assumptions on which
it rests.

Although relatively abstract levels of Goffman's theoretical
frameworks may be integrated satisfactorily, there is little integration among different levels of abstraction. One reason, of
course, is that Goffman does not systematically incorporate diversity, synthesized at many levels of generalization as possible.
Diversity gets built in sporadically or as a stimulus to development of a logical analysis. While the comparisons are rooted in
data, they seem chosen principally by circumstance. *Circum-
stantial sampling* leads to much less satisfactory integration
than would theoretical sampling. We conclude it is doubtful
whether Goffman clearly recognizes the type of theory that he
develops. His use of comparative method may be summarized

as: *Make comparisons of an array (of diverse phenomena) to illustrate theory generated and integrated mainly by a kind of internal logic.* To some degree his theory is grounded but to what degree, and how, is difficult to know.

Shibutani and Kwan: *Ethnic Stratification: A Comparative Approach* 15

Recently Tomatsu Shibutani and Kian Kwan have attempted to order systematically, through an explicit comparative method, the data of race and ethnic relations. They remark that an extensive literature has accumulated on their subject and that "we have tried to bring some of this material together into an orderly scheme." They, however, offer more than an organizational scheme; they offer a "theoretical scheme" which "will give direction to research by providing useful concepts and specific hypotheses" (p. vi). They claim only provisional status for their theoretical scheme, but in such a chaotic field, even provisonial theory can be very useful. Hence they are not much concerned with verification as such, although they have attempted verification by "simple enumeration"—"the collection of confirmatory cases and a diligent search for negative ones" (p. vi). Nevertheless, the reader is presented with explicitly formulated propositions, "for otherwise they cannot be tested" in future investigations.

For the main outlines of their theoretical framework, the authors are much indebted to three social theorists. Park supplied a good deal of the substantive core of the framework, with very essential additions from the social psychology of George H. Mead. The ideas of Charles Cooley also are essential to at least one crucial aspect of the theoretical framework. The authors also draw on standard sociological concepts and perspectives. They develop a variety of hypotheses, some of major importance in the total theory. Comparative materials are taken from two principal sources. The first is a great variety of scholarly studies in many fields. The second source is *The New York Times,* used for materials bearing on recent world events. Other nonspecialized writing is used rather sparingly.

These comparative materials are used in the service of one

15. New York: Macmillan, 1965.

specific type of theoretical formulation, discussed early in the book under the heading "Comparative Study of Stratification" (p. 20). The authors note that "scientific inquiry rests upon the assumption that there are regularities in the occurrences of nature—that things happen over and over in a sufficiently similar manner to permit the operations to be described in abstract terms." In sum, these are "generalizations" that are testable "through empirical evidence." They involve "regularities," "resemblances," "similarities." They are formulated in abstract terms.

Shibutani and Kwan note that many scholars have questioned whether a scientific study of race and ethnic relations is possible, since each historical situation seems unique. Historians especially "argue . . . that such generalizations fail to take into account the distinctive qualities of each event" although its uniqueness must be taken into account in explaining it. The authors answer that "Many historical occurrences display sufficient similarity to warrant our treating them as representatives of a class of events." Shibutani here is following the traditional distinction—put forth, for example, by Park and Burgess who got it from German scholars—between history as the study of the unique event and sociology as the study of general processes. But where most sociologists who accept this distinction would turn wholly to contemporary data, Shibutani and Kwan propose a method that is both *historical* and *comparative*." They will draw materials from everywhere and anywhere, regardless of place or time, and subject them to comparative analysis.

The focus on regularities governs their search for data. They look for confirmatory evidence and for exceptions with equal care. The focus on regularities also governs the use of comparative materials in the actual discussion itself. The data function mainly as illustrations, as the authors themselves understand very well; illustration throughout the book is copious, interesting and, in Blumer's 1939 terminology, "illuminating." The authors are careful to use illustrations that show varied and diverse manifestations of given regularities, using them with great knowledgeability and flexibility. But the *diversity* is rarely, if ever, used either to generate new hypotheses, or systematically to develop suspected aspects of old hypotheses. Diversity functions rather to illustrate (although conceivably it may have generated some theory when the overall framework was first being developed).

Other consequences result from this use of comparative method. Although there is a richness of illustrative detail, it is not translated into useful new categories. Most categories, in fact, seem to derive from the general theoretical framework or from major hypotheses that are elaborated either from it or its directly supporting data. The method also affects integration of the theory. There is excellent integration both in logical sense (the scheme is worked out with consistency), and in the sense that many minor propositions (about conditions, consequences and processes) are related to the major propositions. However, many illustrations embodying conditions, consequences, processes, strategies, and processes are left unintegrated. Although these illustrations lend great richness to the account, they do so by underlining and supporting a given proposition (frequently set forth at the beginning of one or more illustrations, and then summarized at the close). Their richness is not necessarily or usually made an integral part of the theory.

The question remains, do the authors recognize the type of theoretical formulation they are using? Certainly they understood clearly their search for regularities, which they intended to relate systematically in an overall scheme. The confusion is in identifying regularities with similarities. Of course, Shibutani and Kwan also are interested in differential patterns that stem from differential conditions—and discover many—but a focus on similarity and resemblance, to the exclusion of an explicit focus on difference, eliminates one potentially fruitful aspect of an otherwise admirably conducted inquiry. We may summarize the use of comparative method by these authors as: *Make comparisons of an array (of diverse phenomena) principally to generate theory, using categories mainly derived from or suggested by a set of existing theories.* The theory consists mainly of generalizations that involve "*regularities.*" [16]

16. In his recent *Improvised News: A Sociological Study of Rumor* (Indianapolis: Bobbs-Merrill, 1966), Shibutani has used comparative analyses for discovering and densifying his theory, not for illustrating it. In fact, as we read his excellent monograph, he has used four separate modes for densifying his theory; taken together, these illustrate both the strengths and weaknesses of his comparative approach. First and foremost, he has shown the relevance of a tremendous body of research that ordinarily

Amitai Etzioni: *A Comparative Analysis of Complex Organizations* [17]

Etzioni's book is an interesting combination of logico-deductive and grounded generation of theory. He generated as much grounded theory as he could within the limits of the task that he set himself; but at the same time he was firmly committed to logical deduction of a formal theory and the forcing of data to fit it.

Three familiar sociological strategies for research and generation of theory give his book its logico-deductive aspect. First, his entire project is preconceived, thus limiting the possibilities that the grounded aspect of his theory will emerge on its own. For example, "We are concerned primarily with the relationship between compliance and each variable introduced and only in a limited way with the relationship among these variables" (p. xvii). This preconceived limitation prevents the reader from ever really knowing whether the core variable of compliance provides the most relevant relationships, because the complexity of all relationships by which "compliance" is surrounded is never shown. To preconceive relevance is to force data, not

---

would seem of little relevance to rumor. (Much of the research has been done by psychologists.) He does this either by drawing direct connections, or by reinterpreting findings so as to bring them into conjunction with the phenomenon of rumor. Shibutani also makes his theory more diverse by occasional reinterpretation of competing theory, so that relevant segments are integrated into his own (for example, "wish-fulfillment" explanations of rumor content).

Third, he has incorporated relevant segments of supporting theory, such as George H. Mead's and John Dewey's on perspectives and consensus, and of more specific substantive theories, such as Robert Park's on news and Gustav LeBon's on crowd contagion. These supporting theory segments in fact function as integrating elements in the final well-integrated theory. Fourth—and of most importance to us here—some densification of theory is achieved by virtue of comparative analyses: for instance, he specifies the varying conditions under which rumors may disappear. Our principal disappointment with Shibutani's comparative analyses are that they are sunk into the running narrative of the text, rather than highlighted; and they are not nearly extensive enough. The main reason why his comparative analyses are "deficient," we believe, is that he is unduly interested in countering individualistic theories of rumor with a sociological theory. He would have generated an even denser and more integrated theory—and felt freer to claim plausibility for it—had he pushed his theoretical sampling and comparative analyses much further.

17. Glencoe, Ill.: Free Press, 1961.

to discover from data what really works as a relevant explanation.

Second, preconception of his whole project leads Etzioni to logically deducing his core variable—compliance structures —chiefly from a multitude of other logico-deductive classifications. This is a traditional approach, but one that immediately squelches any chances for theoretical formulation to emerge from data, and consequently to fit them. This approach further leads Etzioni to force all his data—especially his classification of organizations—into his compliance scheme. We cannot see any emergence of fit to his data, for they are merely classified and put in appropriate places for further analysis. Thus again we lose sight of the possible relevance of his entire enterprise. Etzioni has, however, created a sophisticated compliance model: clear, integrated and plausible. We can only wonder at the possibly more impressive results had he turned this sophistication to discovering his model from the data. We are confident his results would have modified Weber's views of organizations even more profoundly.

Third, Etzioni's use of comparative analysis is very limiting in terms of generating theory from data. He understands clearly that his endeavor breaks the boundaries of current thought and goes beyond theories based on single cases, but he fails to take this breakthrough very far because, in the logico-deductive tradition, he predesigns a very limiting, traditional comparative analysis. He establishes only *one* comparative category—compliance (with several properties)—assuring us that the category is a "central element of organizational structure" and "distinguishes organizations." Since his method does not automatically show relevance, we have only his word for it.

Constraining the comparative analysis still further, he then classifies organizations according to compliance structures. This restriction of his comparative analysis by a logical scheme forces him to say that he will "show the fruitfulness of this approach and classification for organizational analysis." He feels he must justify the fit and relevance of a logico-deductive scheme—a negative task compared to being able to say something like, "now we can generate some organizational theory on compliance." Had his core variable been grounded and had he allowed himself the full flexibility of comparative analysis, he could have "taken off," confident of generating a worthwhile, relevant theory.

Fortunately, despite the unanswered questions of fit and relevance concerning compliance structures, Etzioni *has* generated grounded theory from "published and unpublished research" and any other slices of data that came his way. Within the limitations of preconceived scope and scheme for his theory, he has actually developed from data a well-integrated, dense, clear theory formulated at many levels of generality. He only forces propositions after giving the data an opportunity to suggest theory and finding it unsuccessful. Whenever his grounded basis runs out, he fills it in with conjecture in the logico-deductive tradition. We learn much from how he generates theory from the voluminous amount of published research that he has covered: he provides excellent guidelines for how to bring this research together to generate theory. His approach may be summarized as: *Make comparisons of an array (of diverse phenomena) to generate theory, principally using categories derived from existing theory.*

Clifford Geertz: *Peddlers and Princes* [18]

This book raises two problems for our discusssion: first, the consequences of posing an avowedly generative inquiry too directly at qualifying a big theory; second, the consequences of limiting comparison groups.

He introduces this exploratory study with: "Though it may be true that, as an economic process, development is a dramatic, revolutionary change, as a broadly social process it fairly clearly is not." In such "pretake-off" societies as Indonesia, two analytic tasks need to be done. First, what changes toward modernization are taking place? Second, "what . . . constellation of social and cultural forces . . . must be realized for development to start" and to break out "from the no man's land" where neither the traditional nor the modern is dominant? In general, anthropologists have studied the first problem and economists the second, but "a really effective theory of economic growth" will evolve only when the two approaches "are joined in a single framework of analysis."

18. Chicago: University of Chicago Press, 1963.

Geertz compares economic development in two towns, one in each region, focusing on what each case study (based on field work) reveals about social and cultural patterns relevant to economic development. Each town is discussed separately; but they are also contrasted for similarities and differences. Occasional references, mainly involving similarities, are made to order societies.

In his summary chapter, Geertz begins by arguing against a view (footnoted to Parsons and located as a source in Max Weber's concept of rationalization) that associates industrialization with an almost total change in traditional values and social structure. As Geertz notes, this conception of change "is implicit in the dichotomous typological terms it seems inevitably to invoke: *gemeinschaft* vs. *gesellschaft;* traditional vs. modern; folk vs. urban; universalistic-specific vs. particularistic-diffuse." Such highly generalized concepts obscure "the very differences we want to investigate in the hope of eventually arriving at some more solidly founded general regularities" about economic take-off. This is why his comparisons of field data on two towns which have very different social-cultural patterns are relevant "to more general theoretical issues." They can "introduce greater flexibility into our notions of what sort of economic structures are compatible with what sort of non-economic ones within a given social system" (pp. 143-46). Such comparisons provide "a more realistic and differentiated typology" and so move the general inquiry forward. Only "through an extended series of intensive comparative investigations of different varieties of developmental process . . . can we achieve the conceptual isolation of such regularities" (p. 147).

Finally, Geertz is interested in generating theory that involves both regularities and diversities. So he asks next, "What specific sociological generalizations about the dynamics of development, then, can we hazard on the basis of the limited, two-case comparative analysis here conducted?" (p. 147). He gives his answer in terms of six "tentative hypotheses," such as: "Innovative economic leadership (entrepreneurship) occurs in a fairly well defined and socially homogeneous group" and "This innovative group has crystallized out of a larger traditional group which has a very long history of extra-village status and interlocal orientation" (pp. 147-48). Each proposition is discussed very briefly, doubtless on the assumption that the case studies have already supplied sufficient illustrative detail.

At the end of his book, Geertz notes the important point that such studies as his "not only isolate some of the common factors and instances of development, but they also demonstrate the variety of forms which growth, as a unified process can take." Hence, a "longer series of Indonesian cases" would have two important consequences: "deeper understanding of development as a generalized abstract process," and "a more profound appreciation of a tremendous diversity of concrete social and culture contexts within which that generalized process can be embedded" (p. 153).

An important question for our own inquiry is: Why did Geertz use these two specific comparison groups? And why did he use only two groups? We do not actually know from the book itself whether Geertz's field trips to Java and Bali were only directed at problems of economic development; nor do we know whether he had good field data on other towns in the area that he might have utilized. What we do know with assurance is that he believed—and accurately so—that his two comparisons would sufficiently challenge a prevailing conception of economic development as well as giving rise to important generalizations about development. His closing statements clearly indicate an awareness that future comparisons will yield more extensive theory. He has been satisfied, therefore, with only the beginnings of a theoretical formulation—because he felt that this was enough to show the deficiencies of a prevailing conception of development.

The conclusion we draw is that if Geertz had not been so concerned with countering an established conception, he might *not* have been content with only two comparison groups. Quite possibly he had data on more towns, but thought the data not ample enough for generating more propositions. If so, a footnote to the paragraph introducing his propositions is significant; he notes that they are not wholly inductive, but based on knowledge of relevant social science literature and "on a general familiarity with the developmental processes in Indonesia, the underdeveloped world, and the premodern West generally" (p. 147).

However, he did not explicitly use this general familiarity

to add to his array of six propositions by using, or searching for, other comparison groups—even though he may have already had all the necessary information.

If he had, his theoretical framework would have been enlarged in scope, and improved in its conceptual density, which is now really quite thin. In both regards, we need only note his revealing footnote to the second proposition, that "One of the interesting questions this study raises, but because of the weakness of the state tradition in Modjoukuto and of the bazaar tradition in Tabanan cannot answer, is what occurs when both of these are found in vigorous form in the same town. Cursory knowledge of the small Javanese city of Jogjakarta, where this occurs, suggests that entrepreneurial groups may then emerge from both of these horizontal traditions, leading to a much more complex dynamic picture than that found in either of our towns" (p. 149). It is no accident that such commentary embroiders the main study. He was willing to generate theory, but stopped himself because he took the opposition's view too seriously; and also because, as an anthropologist, he could perhaps not quite let go of the propensity not to generalize without great ethnographic detail about the society. Density and integration of empirical fact must be the basis of dense and integrated theory. We might add that his ethnographic discussions of each town are integrated in accordance with his general interest in economic development, but his set of six tentative hypotheses has little integration except as it plausibly relates to his main interest. His approach may be summarized as: *Make comparisons of an array (of towns, social structures) to generate theory, with categories limited by use of only two major comparison groups.*

E. E. Evans-Pritchard: *Witchcraft, Oracles and Magic among the Azande* [19]

This famous monograph has been reprinted three times since its publication in 1937. In it, Evans-Pritchard clearly formulated a substantive theory about magic. According to Max Gluckman, subsequent research with other African tribes "has confirmed

19. New York: Oxford University Press, 1937.

this analysis entirely." [20] The monograph has also continued to stimulate a considerable amount of research, by which Evans-Pritchard's theoretical formulations have been both extended and deepened.

Its lasting value is one reason why his monograph interests us. More important, however, is that the original study was confirmed to a single society, yet, as in *most* field work, an implicit comparative method was used. We say "implicit" because, though comparisons were made with great skill and care, Evans-Pritchard certainly did not conceive of his research as "comparative." In reviewing his and related work on magic we shall focus on two points: how comparative analyses used on a single case can generate theory, and how these internal comparisons could be made even more effectively.

Although theories of magic and witchcraft abounded in the literature when Evans-Pritchard published his monograph, he made no reference to them. We can only suppose that he assumed scholars would know those alternative theories. Evans-Pritchard briefly describes Azande social organization, and then begins a parallel development of empirical description and substantive theory. His descriptions are either necessary background material or illustrations invariably related to the developing theory. Gluckman's summary of the theory is so useful that we quote it here:

> [Evans-Pritchard] eschews all psychological interpretation of witchcraft. He analyzes how the Azande perceive fully the empirical causes of the misfortunes that befall them, but they explain "why" a particular man suffers a particular misfortune at a particular time and place by ascribing it to the malevolence of a witch. Beliefs in witchcraft thus aroused explain the particularity of misfortunes. The sufferer seeks the responsible witch by putting the names of those whom he considers to be his personal enemies to oracular devices or persons. He seeks the witch among his enemies because the Azande believe that, though witchcraft is a constitutional, inherited quality, its evil "soul" is set to work by anti-social feelings like envy, spite, jealousy, anger, and hatred. A man may have witchcraft in him, but if he does not have these feelings, the witchcraft remains "cool" and harms no one. Witchcraft beliefs thus contain a philosophy of morality, as well as a theory of "causation," and this involves

20. *Custom and Conflict* (Oxford, England: Basil Blackwell, 1956), p. 82.

the beliefs in the total system of social control. Evans-Pritchard shows that when a man accuses a personal enemy of harming him, he is not "cheating," but is acting by a logic arising from a system of beliefs and . . . social relations. He states that witchcraft accusations are not made within the Azande vengeance-group of agnates, since witchcraft is inherited within this group. Accusations are made against other neighbors with whom a man has relations provoking the anti-social feelings, but accusations are also excluded against social superiors. He discusses the manner in which a man charges another with witchcraft, and how the accused reacts. He has a full analysis of how oracles and witch-doctors operate, and he shows how magical procedures to protect a man against witchcraft or to punish a witch close the circle. In the course of this analysis, Evans-Pritchard considers the relation of witchcraft to other types of mystical causes of misfortunes while all these causes are excluded as explanations of moral misdemeanors. He considers also how individuals operate the system of beliefs, and how the system itself is so constructed that it appears to accord with reality and is insulated against apparently contradicting evidence by secondary elaborations of belief and the limited perspective which any one man has on the setting of witchcraft accusations and magical operations.[21]

If one thinks about the theory described in this summary, it is evident that Evans-Pritchard's analysis of his field data on a single case included a range of internal comparisons. These comparisons can be seen immediately if they are posed as questions: Who could be accused and who could not? When was magic invoked and when was it not? Who used sorcery and who used magic? Who used good magic and who used bad magic? We can see that Evans-Pritchard was continually comparing one group of actors, events or behaviors with others. There is evidence in his monograph that he, like any field researcher, searched out comparison groups when his hypotheses called for confirmation, and pounced upon qualifying comparative data when he recognized their relevance to his developing hypotheses.

One striking characteristic of this monograph is how the theory emerges *from* the data. Evans-Pritchard understood perfectly how to generate theory from data, rather than allowing his inquiry to be controlled, or guided, by received or derived

21. *Closed Systems and Open Minds* (Chicago: Aldine Publishing Co., 1964), pp. 242-43.

theories. Doubtless his reactions to alternate theories of magic and witchcraft affected some of his field operations; but the very numbers of original categories, their properties, and relationships—and the degree of integration achieved by cumulative analyses—evinces how grounded in data his theory is. It is grounded—and extensive in scope—precisely because he used comparison carefully and skillfully.

Could he have made his theory even more extensive, perhaps even more integrated and conceptually denser, if he had explicitly used comparisons? (That is, if he had "pushed his comparative method further.") An answer may be suggested by the directions taken by researchers who followed up on Evans-Pritchard's theory.

According to Gluckman,

> They have assumed a large part of his analysis, and have then proceeded to investigate more fully a new range of problems . . . : who is and who is not accused of witchcraft in relation to the ascription of misfortune to other mystical agents, and how the incidence of accusations in a particular society is related to other constituents of the social system.[22]

Gluckman notes that M. G. Marwick,[23] studying the Cewa, had discussed "the conditions and social contexts in which competition is aggravated into conflict, so that believers can no longer apply the rationality of judicial procedures to their disputes and struggles, but invoke divination to validate accusations of witchcraft which facilitate and justify the rupturing of social relations." Marwick thus made "a considerable advance on parts of Evans-Pritchard's analysis."

V. W. Turner [24] "advances this theory even further" by analyzing judicial action, ritual practices, and accusations of witchcraft among the Ndembu. "Judicial mechanisms," writes Turner, "Tend to be invoked to redress conflict, where the conflict is overt, and . . . involve rational investigation into the motives and behavior of the contending parties. Ritual mechanisms tend to be utilized at a deeper level" when misfortunes are ascribed to mysterious forces and to disturbances in social relationships.

22. *Ibid.*, p. 243.
23. *Ibid.*, p. 250.
24. *Ibid.*, pp. 250-51.

Such disturbances occur when two or more social principles conflict so that rational inquiry cannot decide between or among them.

A final instance of building on Evans-Pritchard's work is Epstein's [25] thesis—using Zulu data—that accusations of witchcraft may sometimes solve, as well as precipitate, quarrels arising "between men from the conflict between allegiances to different and contradictory social principles." They do this by allowing "new relationships to be set up, and new types of friendship to be established."

Such extensions in scope and detail of Evans-Pritchard's theory have been accomplished by anthropologists who have also, in the main, each studied single societies. A good argument could be made that only by such additional intensive case studies can such a theory be extended. After all, this is one type of comparative method (which might be termed "serial" or "successive" comparison, because comparisons are added one at a time). That argument has the ring of truth, and is, essentially, the method suggested to anthropologists by Radcliffe-Brown. Theories frequently are extended and qualified in just this way—a researcher may even study quite another phenomenon than magic and witchcraft, but discover that his data bears on such a theory as Evans-Pritchard's. If his analysis is then made relevant to the theory, it too constitutes comparison.

But the important question is whether Evans-Pritchard himself (using him as only an example) could have increased the scope and detail of his theory without leaving the Azande. We believe that he could have, by making more and better—and always theoretically controlled—comparisons. To do this probably would have required more explicit awareness of what his comparisons could accomplish. Although Evans-Pritchard might never have arrived at some of the specific hypotheses and related comparisons conceived of by later researchers, he might have generated some even better ones.

Our question also raises another issue pertaining to the prevalence and undisputable usefulness of case studies. Many case studies merely embroider major theories, adding very little or nothing to them. Some fail to generate anything new, if the researcher solves his explanatory problems by merely relating

25. *Ibid.*, pp. 100-01.

his findings back to a major theory. Other case studies can generate considerable theory by using a major theory as a springboard. But, as we have often remarked in this book, this latter strategy frequently works to hamper or cripple the innovative capacities of the researcher. He finds himself "dotting *i*'s" in the base theory, rather than really working from it.

Another tradition exists, especially in field work: namely, to initiate the research using only a very general framework with no intention of using a given theory. The assumption is that one's data will be sufficiently rich to stimulate the generation of good theory. If this new theory can be joined with received theory, well and good; if not, then it can stand by itself. In a sense, this is what Evans-Pritchard did—or perhaps his theory became one more alternative theory of magic. The crucial point is that this rather free style of research lends itself to generation of theory; but we would argue that for maximum results this strategy also requires *explicit* comparisons.

In his recent paper on "The Comparative Method in Social Anthropology," Evans-Pritchard himself has unintentionally explained why he has not taken the next step and made his comparative analyses more useful to theory by enlarging their scope.[26] He begins by reviewing the decades of failure attendant on earlier anthropologists' attempts to make broad generalizations based on deficient data—culminating with the more recent work of George Murdock. Evans-Pritchard explicitly affirms his belief in the great value of studying differences as well as universals:

> The more the universality claimed, not only the more tenuous does the causal interpretation become but the more it loses also its sociological content. I would like to place emphasis on the importance for, social anthropology, as a comparative discipline, of differences, because it could be held that in the past the tendency has often been to place the stress on similarities. . . .

He advocates, along with Shapera, Eggan and others, "intensive comparative investigation on a limited scale as being most likely to lead to initial results of value. These have been "more re-

26. In *The Position of Women in Primitive Societies, and Other Essays in Social Anthropology* (New York: Free Press of Glencoe, 1965), pp. 13-36, especially p. 25 and pp. 28-31.

warding than large-scale statistical" comparative studies. He admits "there is a danger that the subject may well fall apart into a succession of isolated ethnographic studies, and were this to happen there might be no place for social anthropology as a distinctive scientific discipline."

Then—in a passage that is meaningful for us—he notes that his own book about witchcraft among the Azande can, and has been, checked by other anthropologists, through studies of other societies, so that "it will be possible to say whether some of my conclusions are likely to hold as general ones while others are valid only for Azande society or for some societies and not others." Evans-Pritchard seemingly perceives only that each anthropologist—in good command of his own particular cache of data—must check on the generalizations of other anthropologists and thus, step by step, build a comparative anthropology. "I do not see," he says, "what other procedure can be adopted." The message of our book is that there *is* another procedure for discovering the kind of grounded theory that he advocates. We may summarize his approach to comparative method then as: *Make comparisons of an array (of acts and social structures) characteristic of a single case—one array at a time—to generate grounded theory.* If your conclusions happen to bear on theory generated by others, then (he adds in the later publication) you may qualify or support that latter theory.

Robert Park: *Race and Culture* [27] and Georg Simmel: *The Sociology of Georg Simmel* [28]

The writings of Park and Simmel, those two hardy perennials of sociology, are much read, as the saying goes, "for stimulation." Stimulation for what? Presumably for ideas or loosely expressed hypotheses that can now be more rigorously expressed and then checked by contemporary methods of verification. As is widely recognized, the pages written by Park and Simmel sparkle with insightful ideas and are addressed to phenomena of enduring importance.

We wish to discuss their writing briefly, in terms of our accounting scheme, to emphasize a style of theorizing and

27. Glencoe, Ill.: The Free Press, 1950.
28. Glencoe, Ill.: The Free Press, 1950.

of comparative analysis that is still used today (by David Riesman, for instance). The generation of theory by Park and Simmel was based largely on data yielded by personal experience, on casual but not undirected observation, as well as on reading of wide scope. In consequence, when we read these men, we experience a kind of simultaneous double exposure to ideas of high abstraction closely linked with an immediately recognizable world. At the same time, we recognize also that their theory lacks integration—a matter to which they paid little attention and of which they were probably quite unaware.

For our purposes it is unnecessary to discuss both men in detail. What we say for Park will fit, with some modification, for Simmel; so we shall mainly touch upon Park's mode of generating theory. In an autobiographical note written near the close of his life, Park remarked that he traced his interest in sociology to reading Goethe's *Faust*.[29] "Faust was tired of books and wanted to see the world—the world of men." Park plunged quickly into the world of men after college, becoming a reporter; except for a short period as a graduate student, he never left it. He traveled widely, commenting in his autobiographical note, "I expect that I have actually covered more ground, tramping about in cities in different parts of the world, than any other living man." Characteristically he also immediately adds, "Out of all this I gained, among other things, a conception of the city, the community, and the region, not as a geographical phenomenon merely but as a kind of social organism." In other words, he was always transmuting impressions into general ideas. Later at the University of Chicago he imbued several generations of students with the value of first-hand observation (interviewing and field work)—an appreciation based on his own personal experiences as a reporter and traveler, and on seven years of face-to-face investigation of Negro life in the South.

Park was always striking off big ideas, generalizations, about social life. Rooted in personal observations and wide reading, these also rested upon a method of implicit comparisons. His concepts of marginality and the marginal man could not have been coined, nor their properties outlined, without at least

29. *Op. cit.*, pp. v-ix.

implicit—and often explicit—comparisons among social situations widely scattered in time and place. Park's major hypothesis about a race relations cycle is another instance of how he formulated high-level theory on the basis of mulling over (nowadays we would say "analysis of") comparative materials from throughout the world.[30] He was interested in accurate ideas, but never seemed much concerned with developing any methods of verification. Probably it is safe to say that even the famous studies done by students under his direction were less of interest to him for what they proved than for their further stimulation of his thoughts about cities, race relations, and society in general.

Simmel was more systematic. But many of the same things could be said about him. Perhaps he drew more upon scholarly studies for his materials, but he used them and his personal observations in much the same implicitly comparative fashion. Even a cursory examination of Simmel's more famous essays makes this evident. Probably he was more self-conscious about his theoretical aims than Park; in at least one place he says explicitly that, while later generations will need to develop better methods for checking theoretical formulations, today's task of developing significant theory cannot wait.[31]

What strikes us about the writings of both men is not only that they are stimulating, but that they reveal how their authors were above all generators of theory. How did they do this? We have already remarked that they loved doing it, remained in close touch with their data, and were dedicated to generating theory of great scope. They were also vitally interested in substantive theory, although almost always linking it either directly or indirectly with formal theory. They were highly inventive discoverers of categories and properties, and prolific generators of hypotheses—pecisely why many later sociologists find them so stimulating. Their comparisons were sometimes explicit, but their overall use of comparative method tended to be implicit. Above all its use tended to be unsystematic, in the sense that the search for comparison groups was not stretched to the limit for the development of theory. Their use of comparison groups was much more flexible than displayed by many later social scientists, including those who think of comparative

30. Park, *ibid.*, pp. 138-151.
31. Simmel, *op. cit.*

method in terms of fixed samples of units or items used in making comparisons.

Integration of theory is the point in the writings of Simmel or Park where they are most vulnerable. The essay form, which both men enjoyed using, is a wonderful—and nowadays a much undervalued—vehicle for transmitting excitingly relevant hypotheses at various levels of abstraction, along with related categories and properties; but use of the essay also usually reflects a less than satisfying integration in the author's formulation of theory. Sometimes the essay form is eagerly and effectively used for the very license that it permits. Its use by Park and Simmel reflects more their reactions against grand theory of their day and their personal dispositions to make sensible, if theoretically oriented, statements about important social events, relations, and processes. We may summarize their use of comparative materials as: *Make comparisons of an array (of diverse phenomena), to generate grounded theory, based on data yielded by personal observation, personal experience, and wide reading about the phenomena under study.*

Anselm Strauss *et al.*: *Psychiatric Ideologies and Institutions* [32]

Since we have outlined in some detail how theory can be generated by using theoretical sampling, we shall not give a case study that employs the method. Instead, we shall conclude our placement and assessment of comparative analyses with a discussion of a grounded theory that falls short on only one major count: its integration. The publication in question was written by one of the authors of the present book before our conceptions of theoretical sampling became as explicit as they now are.

The starting point of the earlier research was an observation: not all psychiatrists seemed to share the same beliefs about the etiology or treatment of mental illness. A previous investigator had suggested two professional "psychiatric ideologies" (psychotherapeutic and milieu-therapeutic), but at least one more position seemed widely shared (somato-therapeutic). These terms refer to conceptions of etiology and treatment

32. Anselm Strauss, Leonard Schatzman, Rue Bucher, Danuta Ehrlich and Melvin Sabshin (New York: Free Press of Glencoe, 1964).

respectively emphasizing the mind, the social environment, and the body. The general problems to be investigated were whether different ideologies did exist among the various psychiatric professionals (psychiatrists, psychologists, nurses, social workers) and their lay assistants, and how these ideologies affected their work in mental hospitals.

A comparative method was quickly hit upon. Field work would be done in one private hospital and in one state hospital. The first was nationally known as being psychoanalytically oriented, although some staff members seemed somatically oriented. The state hospital had a number of experimental acute wards, each operating with relative autonomy under a chief. Five wards were chosen because their chiefs seemed to represent a range of psychiatric ideologies. Field work was done also on various chronic wards, to maximize the chances of comparing chronic wards (without professional ideology because managed by aides) with acute wards (with ideologies), as well as to determine the influence of the hospital setting in general on each major kind of ward and on different types of chronic wards.

Field work was begun first at the private hospital and directed initially only by the frameworks of ideas known as the "sociology of work" and "symbolic interactionism." Another guiding notion was that the researchers should keep their eyes on "ideology." As categories, hypotheses, and so on, emerged— as they did, quickly and continually—they directed the further collection of data. They directed what kinds of comparative items would be sought, and where.

The chronic wards of the state hospital were studied next, and then the acute wards, one by one. Meanwhile, some field work was maintained at the private hospital. The theoretical framework continued to emerge; so much so, that visits were made to specific wards even after the conclusion of the alloted periods for study there. In general, our discussions in the present book about theoretical sampling, and the generation and the integration of theory, adequately characterize the course of the research reported in *Psychiatric Ideologies*.

Judged by the accounting scheme used for the other publications discussed in this chapter, *Psychiatric Ideologies* now looks to us as follows: Its emphasis is very much on generating theory, although the authors, like most field researchers, also had their eyes on presenting a credible account of the empirical world. (Some confusion about these aims is reflected in the chapter on methodology.) Their interest in generating theory is reflected in explicit attempts to develop formal as well as substantive theory, athough not equally in all chapters. Both types of theory are of considerable scope, as the concluding chapter reflects. The comparative field data are in the service of each type of theory. Because of the interplay of data and theory, the monograph has great conceptual detail, at varying levels of abstraction.

The monograph seems deficient principally in its integration of theory. Although in its concluding chapter, a number of related propositions are developed and discussed—which probably add to the readers' sense of integration as well as contributing to the actual integration—an examination of the volume shows that much more integration could have been achieved had the investigators been more aware of the need for it. There could have been a more systematic development of properties and relationships among properties, as well as further generation of categories and hypotheses directed toward integrating the various levels and segments of the final theoretical formulation. The approach used in this research can be summarized as: *identical with that advocated in these pages. Because the approach was not, however, as explicit as outlined here, the grounded theory was less than fully satisfactory in its integration.*

PART II:
THE FLEXIBLE
USE OF DATA

VII

New Sources for
Qualitative Data

This chapter points out a way that sociologists can greatly
extend the range of qualitative data servceable for generating
theory, and with relatively little expenditure of time, money,
and effort. Principally what is required are some imagination,
some ingenuity and, most of all, a considerable shift in attitude
toward qualitative materials themselves. One basic technique in
this effort is the comparative method discussed in Chapters III
and V, which can greatly enhance the discovery and analysis
of relevant qualitative data drawn from documentary sources.
*Then a calculated assessment of two major kinds of qualitative
data—field and documentary—is necessary in planning and
carrying out specific researches.*

It is probably safe to assert that most sociologists live their
intellectual lives in a world populàted principally by other
social scientists and their works. The literature they read, take
seriously, and master is the literature of social science. For
their special purposes, most documents produced by others—
letters, biographies, autobiographies, memoirs, speeches, novels
and a multitude of nonfiction forms—tend to be regarded as
irrelevant except for a few restricted purposes. Certainly this
considerable array of qualitative materials (including things as
far afield as deeds, jokes, photographs and city plans) is not
nearly so much used in researches for generating theory as are
interviews and observations.

Certain uses of these various documentary qualitative materials have been established. First, they may be used, especially in early days of the research, to help the researcher understand the substantive area he has decided to study. They may help him formulate his earliest hypotheses. For instance, he reads standard and popular works about, say, Japan, or wherever else he is going to work. Or he may read everything he can find on medicine in Sweden, or trade unions in Italy. In writing up his finished research, he may use these sources as additional reference points, even as secondary data. Even more likely, he will introduce the information in an opening chapter as a prelude to his analysis of his own data, giving the reader a simplified backdrop for the work. General literature is used, then, mainly for informing rather than as data for analysis.

Second, these qualitative sources are used for descriptive analysis, as in research on, say, entrepreneurship or political parties in France. This is in the tradition of political science and history, but has been given a sociological orientation. This second use of qualitative data is, of course, widespread and exceedingly helpful.

Third, special and highly empirical studies are made, as when the contents of novels or newspaper columns are studied for what they reflect of an era, a class, or the changing tastes of the country. (Nonfiction seems most used by sociologists who are interested in popular culture.) A variant of the special study is the sociologist's reconstruction of the history of some group or institution, as in stratification studies. Typically both of these kinds of research are much less focused on developing theory than on checking previous theory or getting sound empirical findings.

The extremely limited range of qualitative materials used by sociologists is largely due to the focus on verification. For many, if not most, researchers, qualitative data is virtually synonymous with field work and interviews, combined with whatever "background" documents may be necessary for putting the research in context. Possibly, sociologists' preference for using data produced by themselves, or scholars like themselves, is due to the traditional stance, at least in America, against confusing history—conceived as a humanistic field—with social science. The emphasis on using fieldwork and interviews may also rest on a feeling of wanting to see the concrete situation and informants in person. Since most sociologists work with contemporary materials, this desire can easily be satisfied.

And so some sociologists undoubtedly have never seriously considered the library as a source of real data for their work. Others distrust their own competencies in discovering and working with library materials as primary data. The well-trained sociologist may brave the rigors of the field or confront the most recalcitrant interviewees, but quail before the library.

But sociologists need to be as skilled and ingenious in using documentary materials as in doing field work. These materials are as potentially valuable for generating theory as our observations and interviews. We need to be as effective as historians in the library, but with inquiry directed to our own purposes. If need be, we should be as knowledgeable about literary materials as literary critics and other men of letters; but again without abandoning special sociological purposes.

In this chapter we shall detail some procedures for using various qualitative sources, alone and in combination, to generate theory effectively through comparative analysis.

Similarities between Field Work and Library Procedures

There are some striking similarities—sometimes obvious although often overlooked—between field work and library research. When someone stands in the library stacks, he is, metaphorically, surrounded by voices begging to be heard. Every book, every magazine article, represents at least one person who is equivalent to the anthropologist's informant or the sociologist's interviewee. In those publications, people converse, announce positions, argue with a range of eloquence, and describe events or scenes in ways entirely comparable to what is seen and heard during field work. The researcher needs only to discover the voices in the library to release them for his analytic use.

We say "discover" because, like field work, social research in the library must be directed with intelligence and ingenuity. Of course, in either the field or the library, the researcher may be lucky enough to stumble on conversations and scenes. These happy accidents are an invaluable addition to his data, especially if he knows what to do with them. But the effective researcher must direct his data collection, wherever he works; if he is good at field work he ought to embrace the library's resources with equal delight.

Various procedures, or tactics, available to the field worker for gathering data have their analogues in library research. One procedure in the field is to select a key locale, station oneself there and observe the passing scene. Where he goes is directed by what he expects or hopes to hear and see; the more advanced his research, the more directed his choice of locale. In the library, the researcher must go to those shelves where pertinent conversations and scenes can be discovered. At the outset of his study, he chooses those locales by guesswork and early crude hypotheses, while praying for lucky accidents. In beginning a research on American social mobility, for instance, one might start with shelves where materials on "success manuals" are stored, but then go to shelves bearing religious sermons or books about farming. One can use the same tactic with the topical indexes and reference guides to magazine articles.

As in all phases of field work except the initial ones, the researcher has to make daily decisions about where to station himself, which are directed by his emerging theory. For example: A hypothesis about how pictures or photographs taken from above the city are used to symbolize it was developed during a study of city images.[1] The researcher, after some thought, struck on the idea of looking at magazine articles about the Empire State Building, reasoning that these would include observations that would enable him to develop his hypothesis more fully.

Another persistent problem in field work is to figure out whom to talk with, listen to, query, or observe about a given issue important to the research. The library researcher has exactly the same problem, except that instead of traveling great distances to meet the informant, he finds his way to him in the library. One can interview an important psychiatrist about what he thinks about state mental hospitals; he can discover the same opinions in the psychiatric journals. If the field worker wishes

1. See Anselm Strauss, *Images of the American City* (New York: Free Press of Glencoe, 1961), pp. 8-9. Many examples referred to in this chapter derive from the research for this book.

to hear what antagonists or allies say about the same subject, he either makes certain that he is present when they are together; or he catches them when they are making comments (perhaps encouraging such comments) outside the others' presence. A skilled library researcher can do likewise. For instance, psychiatrists comment separately about state hospitals, but sometimes one can discover symposia proceedings that show antagonists and allies speaking in each other's presence.

The library shelves are amazingly rich in such resources. Here is an additional example: A researcher reasoned that during early years of the nursing profession, nurses would have commented about their profession, explicitly or implicitly signaling what "profession" meant to them. Of course, he discovered many such comments; but he also found, with no great trouble, conclaves of nurses discussing and arguing about their profession, including an early session at the Chicago World's Fair in 1893. Thus the field work tactic of going to "meetings" has its library analogue. Also, since discovering informants in field work includes finding congeries of information, one wishes to know what people in different social positions, or different places in a hierarchy, believe, say, and do about particular issues. When we take up the question of comparative groups, we shall discuss more fully how persons representative of different social positions, including "deviants," can be found in the library.

Another general procedure in field work is to check what different participants in, or observers of, an event say afterward. One may even wish to follow-up from time to time what is said later, when the event is long past. The library researcher often has no great trouble in using the same tactic. Thus, how different people saw, experienced and reacted to the Chicago fire is on record, including what men as far away as New York and London said and did, and why.[2] But reactions to much less dramatic or massive events are also recorded in the library (as the historians demonstrate constantly). The same object or event may be commented upon several times—during field work—either by the same person or by different persons. In library research, it is the researcher's job to locate such comments in suitable time series.

2. *Ibid.*, pp. 39 and 263-64.

For example, suppose one wishes to know what the same person said about his profession at different periods of his life. If he has been considerate enough of us to have written about it at intervals, we may be able to find what he has written. He may even have published all pertinent writings in a single volume. If we wish to know what different people have said about the same object or event, we have only to check sources for different years: for instance, what have different city historians said about their city—or about major events, such as the city's founding—during different periods of its history?[3] Or what have different generations of nurses said about physicians or nursng assistants over the years?

We shall briefly mention only three more parallel tactics in field and library research. First, it is, of course, quite possible to follow certain sequences of related events—for instance, changes occurring in an organization—through library materials (historians are perhaps best at this particular skill).

Second, a field worker often wishes to determine who is "involved" in an event and who is not, or who may know about it and who may not; the library researcher must also discover how different informants weigh such matters. These are only special instances of discovering what different informants, from different positions, say about the same or different objects.

Third, field workers frequently "track down" the meaning of a key word that they notice people are using constantly. For instance, the authors of *Boys in White* recount how the physicians' term *crock* eventually struck them as potentially revealing of important medical perspectives.[4] They then made careful analysis of each use of the term as they heard it. In library research, one may be similarly struck by key words. For instance, in reading popular literature about American cities, one may be struck eventually by how authors claim that their particular cities are peculiarly "American," and perhaps are the "most American." Careful analysis can then be made of each

3. Cf. R. Richard Wohl and A. Theodore Brown, "The Historiography of Kansas City: Sidelights on a Developing Urban History," presented at the annual meeting of the American Historical Society, 1956; see Strauss, *op. cit.*, p. 264.

4. Howard S. Becker *et al.*, *Boys in White* (Chicago: University of Chicago Press, 1961).

use of this adjective and any accompanying explanatory commentary by those who use it.[5]

Caches of Documents and Qualitative Interviews

The researcher looking for data in the library may discover caches of materials, such as are continually being discovered or stumbled upon by historians. For example, most of the historians who wrote chapters on phases of entrepreneurship in *Men of Business* [6] analyzed caches of data: correspondence between a French and an Egyptian banker, or the collected letters of an unsuccessful entrepreneur who emigrated from New England to Ohio. Such batches of data all in one place can be useful for sociological inquiry also, as Kai Erikson, for instance, has demonstrated in his study of deviancy in Puritan Massachusetts.[7] Caches of useful materials are everywhere in the library; the researcher needs only ingenuity, and as always a bit of luck, to discover them. For instance, in the annual reports of a welfare association, we found a marvelous collection of interviews and conversations with very poor New Yorkers, recorded during the late nineteenth century, and giving a vivid picture of poverty during this era.[8]

This last example of a cache suggests that it can be regarded much like a set of interviews, done with either a sample of people or representatives of different groups. In the above instance, these were actual interviews, albeit brief and informal. Most caches that would be useful for sociologists take other forms: collections of letters (published or unpublished), a collection of speeches or sermons, a set of proceedings, a symposium, or collection of articles on a single topic by one or several authors. Another instance of a cache is the remarkable series of articles published about American cities by the *Saturday Evening Post*, month by month between 1947 and 1950. Each article

5. Strauss, *op. cit.*, pp. 121-23.
6. William Miller (Ed.), *Men of Business* (Cambridge: Harvard University Press, 1954).
7. *Wayward Puritans* (New York: John Wiley and Sons, 1965).
8. Strauss, *op. cit.*

described one city, and together the series added up to a very useful "find" in the research for a book on city images.[9]

Whether one regards these caches as interviews or conversations, it is important to recognize that they are only one source of important qualitative data. They are probably not the most important source, either, for most studies directed at generating sociological theory. Since generation is most effective when it rests upon the search for comparative materials, caches can hardly be the chief source of data—any more than a bundle or two of interviews (no matter how extensive or on how numerous a population) can suffice for the field theorist.

Perhaps we should warn that the discovery of a cache can actually restrict the development of a researcher's theorizing. Some caches are so esthetically lovely in themselves, so interesting, that the researcher hates to leave the material. He feels he must explore every corner of it, even make it his very own by possessing it (much as some sociologists sentimentally "own" their carefully gathered qualitative interviews or field notes, or as anthropologists cherish their observations on particular tribes and villages). This kind of ownership can yield great depth of substantive knowledge but add little to social theory, as we noted in discussing theoretical saturation in Chapters III and V.

To be of optimal use for theory, caches need to be used in combination with data drawn from a *variety* of sources, all subjected to comparative analysis. A cache, no matter how interesting in itself, has no meaning for theory unless it is related to it. It must check out or correct or amplify the researcher's emerging hypotheses. If he is sufficiently shrewd, his theory will direct him to useful caches of data; or if he is lucky, he may stumble upon one and recognize its importance.

Theorizing, Rules of Procedure, and Comparative Method

In earlier chapters of this volume, we detailed various operations for generating theory. These included the discovery of important categories and their properties, their conditions and consequences; the development of such categories at different levels of conceptualization; the formulation of hypotheses of

9. Strauss, *op. cit.*, especially pp. 260-62.

varying scope and generality; and above all the integration of the total theoretical framework. We noted that the search for comparisons, involving the discovery of useful comparison groups, was essential to the generation of theory. What does theory-making necessitate when translated into procedures suitable in the library? Both our earlier discussions about theorizing or and our commentary on parallels with field tactic are relevant, but let us add a few rules and their associated procedures.

First, the researcher should, as usual, begin a systematic search for important categories relevant to his area of substantive concern. How should he proceed in the library? The answer is that he should use *any* materials bearing on his area that he can discover. For instance, explicit categories are offered in the writings of other men (whether sociologists or not) on the area. Suggestive data may occur in the form of quotations from informants if a social scientist has made a relevant study; for instance, by taxi-dancers in the book by Paul Cressey on *The Taxi-Dance Hall*.[10]

A very important early source of categories is an array of fiction (including "Pot Boilers") bearing on the relevant topic. For instance, in researching images of American social mobility, novels can be an incredibly fertile source of categories bearing on mobility. Often the researcher may know of some novels even before he begins his research, but he will easily find others as he scans the library's shelves, and a little ingenuity will unearth others through reference works and volumes in which American literature is reviewed. But comparative method should be brought to bear from the outset. Thus, one should think about regional novelists, about novelists of different ethnic groups, about novelists who wrote for different generations of Americans, about novelists who emigrated from America, and others who emigrated only to return, as well as about others who emigrated here from different parts of the world. One should think of novelists who portrayed rural life and those who pictured city life, those who focused on men and those who were most interested in women.

Reasoning about social mobility itself, one should attempt to maximize potentially relevant comparisons by self-consciously searching for novels about different periods of American his-

10. Chicago: University of Chicago Press, 1932.

tory. Since we are not concerned with the accuracy of a novelist's perceptions, but only with using his book to stimulate our generation of categories, we can throw aside an unstimulating book in favor of those that help us. Books that only repeat what others have told us need not be read carefully. They merely need to be noted as supporting our evolving belief that given categories are among the most relevant for our concern.

Of course, novels are not the only source of categories; any materials that force a range of comparisons will be useful: letters, diaries, newspaper accounts, or other miscellaneous nonfiction. For instance, many initial categories about urban images were derived from scanning a number of books and articles bearing directly on American cities—their number is legion. Understandably, these were among the first documents that attracted the attention of the researcher. Later he returned to them for stimulation in developing further categories, especially those bearing upon temporal images of cities.[11]

Another major procedure for discovering categories is to abandon the illusion that only materials bearing on "the principal topic" (the urban image), or its closely related synonyms (mobility, social classes, "success") are pertinent to the inquiry. Again, a self-conscious style of thinking comparatively is a great asset. Thus one goes to the library catalogs, or to the *Readers' Guide to Periodical Literature*, and thinks of numbers of terms that might relate to the principal topic. Labor unions—mobility through collective bargaining? Tramps and hobos—downward mobility? Agricultural migrants or Ozark mountaineers—permanently frozen low mobility? Industrial education—possibly related to strategies for rising? Chorus girls, show-biz girls, women of the theater—special mobility careers for women? Popular culture heroes—sudden propulsion upward? Police manuals—strategies for dealing with the poorer classes? Collections of sermons—images on the consequences of too much success, ideological counsel for the rich and consolation for those who fail to become rich? Even an ingenious peruser of library materials like C. Wright Mills (never mind how he handled his materials) used relatively straightforward, closely allied rubrics as he rummaged through the library for data on,

11. Strauss, *op. cit.*, especially Chapters 1 and 2.

say, his white-collar people. So the researcher needs to cultivate functional synonyms for his topic in order to explore relevant categories fully.

While developing categories, the researcher will also systematically explore their properties. Again he must stretch the limits of his thinking by discovering comparative materials. For instance, what properties are frequently assigned to sons of very successful men? (This "second-generation wealthy" is a persistent American cultural theme.) Among the answers are: they often are failures in some way—they turn out to be nonentities, become corrupt although remaining rich, see themselves as failures although seemingly not, even commit suicide; but they can also match their fathers' successes—they can increase the family fortune or name, perhaps even proportionately, they can turn their considerable talents into admirable nonaltruistic ventures, and so on. In pinning down answers to "What characteristics are assigned to sons of the successful?" we shall also be interested in the assigned causes and consequences of the son's attributes and actions. Inevitably these inquiries lead us to ask where in the library we can find a greater range of relevant answers.

At every step, appropriate hypotheses will develop and quickly integrate with each other. As hypotheses evolve, we are directed to new sources of comparative library materials. Is there some easily identified member of a group whose words can further development of our theory? For instance, what does William A. White say about social mobility in country towns, and what does he think are the dangers, concerning mobility, in big cities? Or what do rural-born migrants to Chicago—or Chicago compared with New York or Kansas City—say about "how to get ahead," in those cities?

Our theory also directs us to seek, and be alert for, possible caches of useful material. Is there some magazine whose files, taken together, represent a wonderful bunch of data bearing on certain hypotheses? For instance, what about engineering journals as they bear on social mobility? Journals for funeral directors? Florists? Songwriters?

Explicit, or even vaguely formulated, hypotheses can lead us directly to certain comparative materials, if only we calculate shrewdly where they are to be found. Suppose, for instance, that one begins to wonder about the relation of spatial mobility to vertical mobility. What about people's images of what "the frontier" meant for upward or downward mobility? And which frontier, spoken of in what terms? So we look for New Englanders (who may give us the safety valve theory of the midwest frontier) or others (who may give us the anti-civilization image of the frontier). We look for whether the frontiersman speaks of making "a success" by himself, or needs a wife, or needs something or someone else.

Or, thinking about the city as a locale for vertical mobility, we check what people have written about the city as a challenge, a den of iniquity which can cast man down, and so on. But who has said these things, why, and about what kinds of cities? Some cities are seen predominantly as terribly wicked (New York), and others are not nearly so bad but rather linked with the "innocent" hinterland (Indianapolis, Des Moines). Again, about intra-city movement, the novel *Marjorie Morningstar* tells us that a Jewish father moves his family from the Bronx to west Manhattan so that his daughter has better chances for marrying upward.

If we have developed well-grounded categories and their associated hypotheses, we shall be led inevitably to look for exceptionally revealing comparison groups (or persons representing them) who run somewhat counter ("deviant") to the mainline of our developing substantive theory. Turning again to mobility images, we might ask which particular groups would be genuinely distinterested in, but aware of, mobility? We look, for instance, at primary sources about religious sects (the Amish, the Jehovah's Witnesses, the Hutterites). These will indicate their views of mobility, both within the sect itself and toward the outside world. If we are lucky, or shrewd, we shall find how some sectarians have succumbed to the more usual American image of mobility and how the sect has had to counter this threat.

But disinterest in mobility is only one dimension of deviancy: what about direct action against mobility? Are there any martyrs who have given their lives in protest against mobility, or heroes extolled by other actionists? If we cannot find them, this itself is useful in our theory. If we can find them, theory will also be furthered. Another possible source of information about deviancy would be those groups who, cut off from the mainstream of American thought, never caught on to prevailing ideas about mobility. They were not so much disinterested as uninformed. Who would they be—recent immigrants? less recent immigrants? Kentucky mountaineers isolated for generations? Or will we need to examine earlier periods of American history to find these groups? In short, a calculated strategy of search and scrutiny for data on off-beat groups is a necessity and will be exceptionally rewarding.

"Pinpointing," a procedure that tends to be used relatively late in one's inquiry, pertains mainly to integrating theory through the checking of detailed points suggested by specific hypotheses.[12] It is an equally valuable tactic when used on library data. Here are two examples. During the study of urban images (which has provided us with several previous illustrations) the researcher wondered whether one useful source for pinpointing last points on rural and urban images might not be the utopian literature written by Americans. Like the field worker who often sees scenes before later recognizing their pinpointing potential, this library-researcher had earlier browsed hopefully but unimaginatively through such utopian literature. Now he returned to it with specific purpose.

Even later in his research, he pinpointed with still another source of data. It seemed sensible to see if all he had written would check out with the very "latest in urban imagery" being produced, hot off the presses. So he looked for the latest imagery, especially for the most recently coined terms ("Inter-urbia") and integrated this last analysis into his total theory.

In closing this section on procedures, we cannot refrain from reminding sociologists that the writings of sociologists, of any era, as well as the writings of other social scientists, are fair game for comparative researchers. Ordinarily, technical writings are scrutinized for the explicit hypotheses they contain. These stimulate the researcher in his theorizing or provoke him into empirical answer. But it takes only a minor adjustment of stance to use technical writing as a source of data *exactly* as one uses the writings of ministers, politicians, engineers, explorers, spies, or comedians. During the great era of social reform, Franklin

---

12. See Anselm Strauss *et al., Psychiatric Ideologies and Institutions* (New York: Free Press of Glencoe, 1964), p. 35.

Giddings and Edward A. Ross wrote reformistic pieces not very different from their contemporaries; they also wrote sociology that embodied reform orientations. And sociological writing on cities, no matter how technical, has never been very different than popular writing.

To bring the examples up to the minute: sociologists' publications about delinquency, or stratification, can be as useful for comparative analyses as anything in the popular prints. A close reading of textbooks on stratification, for example, combined with reading the publications of men like Martin Lipset, C. Wright Mills, W. Lloyd Warner and, to go further back, Thorstein Veblen, can yield a host of categories, properties, and hypotheses about American images of mobility. To press the point home, it is only fair to conclude that one's own past writings are grist for today's mill, someone else's or your own.

The Discovery of Accidents

Because the generation of theory directs so firmly the search for, and analysis of, library data, we must not suppose that fortunate circumstance plays a lesser role than it does in field research. As we have implied in preceding pages, the library researcher cannot help but stumble upon useful comparative data. He is checking through the *Readers' Guide* on one topic, when happily his eye lights on another relevant topic about which he never thought—or he wonders about an article with an intriguing title, and in checking it finds marvelously rich data. He ransacks books strung along several shelves, and not only finds useful books he could never find through the catalog but also finds books—perhaps even more useful—either as he walks toward those shelves or allows himself to browse through books on neighboring shelves. Or after reading a magazine article which he has tracked down, he allows himself sufficient time to riffle through the remainder of magazine.

We use the word "allow" because while some happy accidents are completely fortuitous, others are promoted by the researcher. Indeed, unless tactics for maximizing accidents are not worked out, the researcher must rely wholly on chance. While chance is a powerful goddess, it is wise not to rely solely upon her powers. So the library researcher ought to permit himself time to browse in unfamiliar journals, looking in the neighborhood of the journal he happens to be scrutinizing; he must visit unfamiliar parts of the library (what would cookbooks show, or books on athletics?); and he may wish to utilize the contemporary newspaper collection, as well as reading his daily newspaper with more than a casual eye for accidental data.

Again, an example may prove useful. In a study of the development of American industrial education, one sociologist—social historian gathered most of her data in the library.[13] At a late stage of the research, having worked out most of her theoretical framework, she selected one relevant comparison group that was contemporary enough to study mainly through interviews. So she visited one selected airplane company (first preparing herself by reading about the company, the airplane industry, and the geographical locale) and interviewed there just as one would when conducting an ordinary investigation in the field. In writing up this portion of the study, interview and library materials were used in close and effective conjunction.

Qualitative Data and Formal Theory

All of our examples in this chapter, so far, have been drawn from studies focused on the generation of grounded substantive theory. It should be readily apparent, however, that our discussion has been equally relevant to formal theory. Probably the intelligent, comparative use of diverse types of qualitative data is even *more* necessary for generating formal theory than for substantive theory. When developing formal theory, one is almost forced to consider data from many different substantive areas—at least, as we noted in Chapter IV, if he wishes to do this with maximum efficiency.

Although it is quite possible for one researcher to generate magnificent substantive theory in a relatively short time (using field or library data), it is virtually impossible for him to generate equally excellent formal theory through only his own field work. Usually he also needs either the primary field data

13. Berenice Fisher, *Industrial Education* (Madison: University of Wisconsin Press, in press).

gathered by other researchers or their published analyses and their illustrative quotes drawn from field notes. Of course, if he has engaged in many field studies of many substantive areas, then he is better equipped to formulate grounded formal theory. But consider how much more efficient in numbers of comparison groups—as well as in time, effort and money—it would be to use library materials. When the researcher has also engaged in some firsthand interview or field work studies, then those data should be combined, wherever useful, with his larger body of library materials.

Library Materials: Advantages and Limitations

Since most sociologists who work extensively with qualitative data rely on interviews and field notes, it may be useful to suggest a calculus whereby they may weigh those sources against library sources. This is not intended to imply competition between the sources. The important point is that when a researcher decides what sources of data to use in a given study, he makes decisions crucial to its outcome; so he ought to make those decisions with the utmost care. Our suggested calculus is entirely provisional and meant only to focus attention on some potential advantages or limitations of library and field work materials. For given studies, advantages and limitations need to be calculated and, to some extent, guessed at. Our discussion is necessarily very general.

The first item in our calculus pertains to *accessibility*. One of its aspects bears on informants now dead. Like interviews and field work, library sources can yield materials about the past, but with the immense advantage that they allow us to listen to and observe (if metaphorically) long-dead persons as if they were actualy still alive. So information from and about the dead is often rather accessible to the researcher. (It may seem flippant to remind ourselves that more men have lived than are now alive, but the point, perhaps, is worth pondering.)

A second aspect of accessibility bears on how much the researcher is separated from his data by spatial obstacles.[14] One

14. Its accuracy aside, the classic instance is Ruth Benedict's *The Chrysanthemum and the Sword* (Boston: Houghton Mifflin, 1946).

striking characteristic of library materials is that they bring distant actors to the researcher's neighborhood, without the necessity of his moving from it. The better his library facilities, the better his conquest of space. But even researchers who must draw their materials from rather poor local libraries do themselves injustice if they ignore its potentials. We have in mind not merely finding materials that bear on a geographically distant locale—anyone who has used library resources for finding the words of men scattered around the United States alone will understand the immense usefulness of a library for spanning space. Of course, a researcher can travel to a specific locale, or even visit informants all over the United States; but time, effort, or money may make such ventures impractical or impossible. Consequently, a bias against library materials will greatly restrict the data readily available to such a space-bound researcher.

A third aspect of accessibility to data pertains to informants' willingness to be observed or interviewed. Certain groups are unwilling to expose themselves to the sociologist's gaze, or require him to make a considerable effort to "get inside," yet they may have produced—or had produced—useful library materials about them and their institutions. Taken in conjunction with the use of materials on dead informants and disintegrated groups (from brigands or pirates to secretive religious sects or "society people") such library materials make accessible the otherwise relatively inaccessible. Used with great care, they can also minimize the possibility that your informants may lie to you, as living informants do when they cannot otherwise protect themselves against a researcher's inquiry.

A fourth aspect of accessibility to data is linked with late phases of a researcher's inquiry. Frequently in field research, and especially in interview studies, the researcher discovers, when well along in his analysis, that his data leave something to be desired. But he may already have left the field, and cannot fill the gaps in his data. (A field worker with an eye on theorizing, however, should not often have major gaps in his data.) By contrast, the library researcher can return again and again, unless of course he is using library facilities at some distance from his home. Usually he can easily return to the library to check a detail, pinpoint with more data, or even work on another comparison group, if necessary.

A fifth aspect of accessibility is a consequence of the scheduling of work in universities and colleges. Probably most sociologists and anthropologists confine the data-collecting phases of their field work to semesters when they are free from teaching—mainly during the summer vacation. Even interviewing, unless it can be done in the immediate locale, is either a free-time activity or done speedily around the fringes of teaching. With either interviewing or field work, the researcher sometimes faces the additional problem of fitting his activity to the daily routines of his subjects. Research with library materials is relatively free from such considerations. Often the researcher can work at home, with materials drawn from the library or collected by himself. He can work without concern for his subjects' fluid and sometimes unpredictable routines. Best of all, he can work intermittently, gather his data (and analyze it, too) whenever he has a few hours, or even minutes: the limits to effectiveness are set only by his flexibility.

Implied in our discussion of accessibility are considerations of *effort, cost,* and *speed* of data gathering. About effort: it should be evident that often library materials are unearthed with much less effort than the gathering of comparable materials through interviews or field work. Less travel and less work may be entailed, as well as less daily wear and tear in terms of social relations. Also, far less transcribing is entailed than with interviews and field notes where transcribing is a necessity. One's own newspaper and magazines can be clipped, and efficient systems of note-taking on the library's materials can be developed. If the researcher is a faculty member, usually he can keep the library's relevant books—with slips of papers marking important pages—until his study is completed; he will find that, unlike standard sociological works, most of his source materials have little attraction for other readers. As for cost: when library data comparable to data yielded by interviews can be gathered, then certainly they should be used. The expense for the library researcher is minimal, even when he needs to purchase certain materials himself (for instance, popular magazines which the local library facilities may not possess).

As for the speed with which library data can be discovered and scrutinized, this is especially worth underscoring. After all, interviewing and field work are relatively time-consuming activities. And though the search for, and reading of, library materials can also be time-consuming, skilled researchers can quickly improve both their searching and their scanning. From our own experience, library research is faster than either interviewing or field research, when these enterprises are personally conducted. (Of course, research teamwork also is possible with library materials.) And we have noticed that when certain types of library materials are discovered and analyzed, they need not be intensively re-analyzed to be extremely useful for entirely new inquiries; thus a group of novels used for generating theory about images of urbanization were equally useful for two later studies about images of mobility and of women.

Another means for assessing the potential usefulness of library materials pertains to their generating of theory. As we detailed earlier, theorizing begs for comparative analysis. The library offers a *fantastic range* of comparison groups, if only the researcher has the ingenuity to discover them. Of course, if his interest lies mainly with specific groups, and he wishes to explore them in great depth, he may not always find sufficient documentation bearing on them. But if he is interested in generating theory, the library can be immensely useful—especially, as we noted earlier, for generating formal theory. Regardless of which type of theory the theorist is especially interested in, if he browses intelligently through the library (even without much initial direction), he cannot help but have his theorizing impulses aroused by the happily bewildering, crazy-quilt pattern of social groups who speak to him. Ordinarily, the sociologist does not personally encounter in any depth this range of groups or their representatives. Even picking books randomly from the "books to be reshelved" section of his library tends to yield quick theoretical pay dirt. Even if he has decided upon a field or interview study, additional work in the library, by yielding comparison groups, may stimulate his theorizing about the substantive area under study. Whether he is interested in substantive or formal theory, the rule is: maximize those comparison groups! That rule may lead to the library.

Finally, we shall mention one further characteristic of library materials that adds to their potential usefulness. These materials often lend themselves to being *arrayed* chronologically, which enhances their usefulness when the social theorist is especially interested in temporality. The historians have made a virtual fetish of chronology and narrative; we need neither be so compulsive about nor so enraptured with the temporal features of library data. These data are useful even for the analysis of change and development. Many examples cited in this chapter ilustrate that point. In addition, it is worth considering that the historical depth of our materials is usually far greater than our interview and field data. For generating some sociological theory, that greater historical depth can be especially useful.

For instance, substantive theory about American images of anything (mobility, urbanization, women, science) cannot include much temporality unless library materials (other than studies by social scientists) are used. As for formal theory: it would be an obvious mistake to confine either it or its generation to contemporary materials. Max Weber knew this, although his use of library sources was fairly conventional, albeit of great scope and managed with great skill.

Now that we have listed the very substantial potential assets of library data for sociological theorizing, we need to look closely at some possible disadvantages. Again we underline that this calculus is highly generalized; in specific inquiries our sketching of limitations may not apply. The *first* stricture that must be made against library materials is that some groups or institutions evolve and disappear without leaving much, if any, documentary trace. If the sociologist is interested in a particular group, he may be quite defeated when he tries to gather data about it in the library. On the other hand, if he is interested principally in theory, and so can settle for comparable groups, he should not give up so easily in his search for documentation. With that proviso, it must still be admitted that even the most extensive libraries are richer in materials about certain given substantive areas and particular groups than about others. Even when the relevant materials exist they may be fragmentary or relatively useless for one's purpose.

A related question is whether such data exist in the dense detail (about important issues, relationships, roles, strategies, processes) that interviews, and especially field work, unearth. A skilled researcher can decide quite quickly whether adequate library materials are easily obtainable for generating theory— including their strengths and probably weaknesses—by using some of the procedures discussed in this chapter.

A *second* possible disadvantage of library materials, for some theorizing, is that information yielded by the writer (whether about himself or events described) can be purposely misleading. In fact, many sociologists and anthropologists tend to suspect almost all library materials on just such grounds, believing their own techniques either more accurate or better for unmasking real purposes and intentions. As every field worker knows, one cannot trust all statements made by the other person in an interview or conversation, not merely because of his personal reasons for misleading the researcher but because of social rules about what can and cannot be told. There is no question that library materials must be carefully scrutinized, but probably no more or less than interview or field materials.

A *third* potential disadvantage is that library sources may be deficient if events reported by observers are simply inaccurate renditions of those events. By contrast, the field worker has been trained to make careful observations, to note precisely which of his observations can be given more credence than others—and why, and to report his observations accurately in his field notes. But the men whose writings he reads may not be nearly so accurate; so that while they can be read for their own views, they cannot necessarily be relied on for accurate reporting of real events.

All one can conclude from these considerations is "maybe yes, maybe no," and so the researcher, as always, must use his materials with the best possible judgment and in accordance with the best available canons of research. A personal devotion to the accuracy of one's own eyesight in the field ought not to cause the researcher to overlook perfectly good documentary materials. Moreover, if his purpose is explicitly the generating of theory, the absolute accuracy of his library informants is, as we have said, not crucial. He can even be less concerned if he intends to use field materials for further verification.[15]

15. Apropos of this issue of historical informants' accuracy versus the researcher's, Kenneth Bock has correctly remarked that: "The belief that what men have observed and recorded about human social life is but a distorted, subjective reflection of what was really there is a debilitating assumption. This sort of skepticism jeopardizes the entire study of man, for not only does it deny us access to the great bulk of human experience, but it eventually casts doubt upon the reliability of all observation. For all recorded observations were at one time 'contemporary,' and there is little warrant for the current conceit that the intelligent and careful observer

A *fourth* potential disadvantage of library materials is that by comparison with careful field notes, they may not always afford a continuity of unfolding events in the kind of detail that the theorist requires. We say this despite our previous comment that library data can be excellent for theorizing about temporality. In some part, the adequacy of the library materials depends on the sheer bulk of material available concerning the topic under study, and also on who has produced it. This point can be underlined by noting that library data bearing on "interaction" (even face-to-face interaction) can be abundant enough to afford a theorist ample stimulation for generating effective theory. Nevertheless, in some substantive areas—such as the phases of interaction between terminal patients and hospital staffs—the library materials may not yield nearly so much stimulation (especially concerning developing events) as a few days spent on hospital wards.

Library research has a *fifth* disadvantage when compared with field, or even interview, research. Sometimes field researches are precipitated when the researcher realizes that he is already a participant in, or a privileged observer to, some interesting group's activity. He would be denying the richness of his own experience with the group if he chose not to study it in preference to doing library research. Of course, this is especially true if he is interested in generating theory, since he cashes in immediately upon his past observations as well as upon his own personal reactions as observer or participant. If in this instance he chooses a field or interview study, less effort is also required

---

is an exclusively modern phenomenon. The bright-eyed young sociologist armed with his scheduled interview might generously concede that the shrewd perceptions of a Hesiod, Machiavelli, or Voltaire deserve a place, alongside his own findings, in the broad fund of social knowledge. All records call for careful scrutiny, but the techniques devised by historians for establishing the reliability of their data are by no means inferior to those employed by the social sciences." See his *The Acceptance of Histories* (Berkeley and Los Angeles: University of California Press, 1956), p. 123. See also Tomatsu Shibutani and Kian Kwan, *Ethnic Stratification* (New York: Màcmillan, 1965), in which the authors make extensive use of materials published by demographers, economists, linguists, historians, psychiatrists, psychologists, and sociologists, as well as files of *The New York Times* and some historical records. As they say, "Although sociology originally developed out of the philosophy of history, thus far historical data have barely been tapped" (p. 14).

because he is already a visitor or participant and likely to continue as one. The cost of his study may even be minimal, either because little or no financial support is necessary, or because he is being paid for being a participant, as in an occupational group. (Graduate students, especially, have earned wages from the employers of men whom they have studied.)

These, then, are some of the respective advantages and disadvantages of library research versus field or interview research.[16] In weighing these, perhaps we have emphasized unduly the potential advantages of library research, in a conscious attempt to focus sociologists' attention upon the central issue— not which source is ideally most important, but on the need for assessing realistically which may be best used, alone or in combination, in a particular study. As always, our emphasis is upon use for generating theory, although implicitly we also have made claims relevant for the verifying theory.

16. Although we have focused on library research, documents useful for generating theory obviously are found elsewhere. Thus, documents in government archives and company files could be as useful for generating social theory as for revealing historical and political fact. When sociologists use such documentary materials, they tend to use them almost wholly for verification or description.

VIII

Theoretical Elaboration of
Quantitative Data

Quantitative data is so closely associated with the current emphasis on verification that its possibilities for generating theory have been left vastly underdeveloped. However, some of our best monographs based on quantitative data indicate that they can be a very rich medium for discovering theory. In these monographs, discovery cannot be stopped, but breaks through both verifications and preconceived conceptual schemes to provide us with very interesting and important theory.[1] Yet, since the authors are still so focused on testing provisionally what they have discovered, their work is mostly written in the hedging rhetoric of verification. The result is that their statements present tests as merely "plausible suggestions." The plausibly suggested test should not be construed with our goal of the purposeful generating and suggesting of theory. The generating capacities of these sociologists and the richness of their research are, therefore, not given the fullest impetus.

Typically, discovery made through quantitative data is treated only as a byproduct of the "main work"—making accurate descriptions and verifications. When discovery forces itself on an analyst, he then writes his induced hypotheses as if they had been thought up before the data were collected, so that they will seem to satisfy the logical requirements of verifi-

1. For examples see James Coleman, "Research Chronicle: The Adolescent Society," and Seymour Martin Lipset, "The Biography of a Research Project: Union Democracy," in Philip Hammond (Ed.), *Sociologists at Work* (New York: Basic Books, 1964).

cation.[2] Purposeful generation of grounded theory is found usually, if at all, in short papers where a single carefully worked-out explanation of a hypothesis is offered, after an analytic wrestle between the rhetoric of tentative qualification and alternative explanations and the carefully researched, accurate data—a slight beginning for an adequate theory.

When the sociologist consciously starts out to suggest a theory plausibly, rather than test it provisionally, then he can relax many rules for obtaining evidence and verifications that would otherwise limit, stultify or squelch the generation of theory. He must give himself this freedom in the flexible use of quantitative data or he will not be able to generate theory that is adequate (as we have discussed it) in terms of sampling, saturation, integration, density of property development, and so forth. In taking this freedom he must be clear about the rules he is relaxing (which could not be relaxed for purposes of accuracy and verifications) and he should explain his position to readers. *The freedom and flexibility that we claim for generating theory from quantitative data will lead to new strategies and styles of quantitative analysis, with their own rules yet to be discovered.* And these new styles of analyses will bring out the richness of quantitative data that is seen only implicitly while the focus remains on verification. For example, in verification studies cross-tabulations of quantitative variables continually and inadvertently lead to discoveries of new social patterns and new hypotheses, but are often ignored as *not* being the purpose of the research.

In this chapter we shall present *one* new strategy of quantitative analysis that facilitates the generation of theory from quantitative data. It is a variation of Lazarsfeld's elaboration analysis of survey data.[3] In our presentation we shall indicate how, at strategic points, the rigorous rules for accuracy of evidence and verification can be relaxed in order to further the

---

2. This way of presenting one's work in a publication on research is not chicanery, but an established form in many circles of science. See Bernard Barber and Renee C. Fox, "The Case of the Floppy-eared Rabbits: An Instance of Serendipity Gained and Serendipity Lost," *American Journal of Sociology*, 64 (1958), pp. 128-29.

3. Paul F. Lazarsfeld, "Interpretation of Statistical Relations as a Research Operation," in Lazarsfeld and Rosenberg (Eds.), *The Language of Social Research* (Glencoe, Ill.: Free Press, 1955).

generation of theory. To be sure, there are many styles of quantitative analysis with their own rules. Our focus here is an illustration of how these numerous other styles can also be flexibly adapted to generating theory. However, we do touch on some existing general rules of quantitative analysis (*e.g.*, indexing and tests of significance); the way they are relaxed for purposes of generating theory could apply to many styles of analysis. And we shall also develop some general rules governing how to relax the usual rigor of quantitative analysis so as to facilitate the generation of theory.

The organization of this chapter is based on the successive stages of building up to theory from quantitative data. We discuss in turn the most frequent source of data used for generating theory, how one indicates his categories and properties with the data, how one discovers hypotheses with his conceptual indices, and how the hypotheses are then theoretically elaborated. In an appendix to this chapter we provide examples of theoretical elaboration. For some longer examples of certain specific points, we have referred the reader to other literature.

Secondary Analysis of Quantitative Data

The sociologist whose purpose is to generate theory may, of course, collect his own survey data, but, for several reasons, he is more likely to analyze previously collected data—called secondary analysis. Surveys are usually financed for providing large-scale descriptions of current populations; and the sociologist whose interest is in theory may not wish to be involved in this part of a study, for it takes considerable time and concentration that might otherwise be used for theoretical analysis. It is easier to analyze previously collected data, for then his only responsibility is to generate theory. Sometimes, of course, after the large-scale descriptions have been accomplished, the director of the study returns to his data to engage in secondary analysis for generating a theory on an idea initially stimulated by the earlier descriptive phase.

Generating theory is a more limited, narrowly focused effort (even though the theoretical concept may be very general) than presenting the broad description of a population given by the total survey. The description may involve thousands of questionnaire items, while the theoretical analysis only requires consideration of a few hundred.[4] Therefore, the tasks of description and analysis can conflict unless the sociologist has adequate money and time (a likelihood only for the study director and a few assistants). Theoretical analysis of quantitative data is, of course, an opportunity to be taken by many sociologists other than study directors or their assistants,[5] and so most generation of theory from quantitative data will be based on secondary analysis.

Comparative analysis requires secondary analysis when populations from several different studies are compared, such as different nations or factories. Comparative analysis of groups internal to one study does not require secondary analysis, but again it often is.

Trivial data, such as found in market surveys on consumption of products, can also have very important theoretical relevance. For example, from a study of meat consumption one can gain knowledge about the life styles of social classes. Secondary analysis is a necessity in such cases because sociologists with a theoretical bent do not usually collect such data.

When using secondary analysis of quantitative data for generating theory, one point must be kept clear. Because of the heavy emphasis on accurate evidence and verification of hypotheses, the analyst usually wishes to start out with the facts as facts. One limitation of secondary analysis is the difficulty of pinning down the accuracy of findings in what is necessarily a secondhand view—often without much knowledge of collection procedures and meanings of data. Also, since populations are in constant change, we have no way of knowing whether a survey accomplished some years ago for other purposes still applies meaningfully to the specific population. This problem

4. For example, compare the theoretical analysis in Barney G. Glaser, *Organizational Scientists: Their Professional Careers* (Indianapolis: Bobbs-Merrill, 1964) to the description from the same study using over 100 different IBM card decks and comprising four volumes. *Human Relations in a Research Organization*, Volumes I and II (1953) and *Interpersonal Factors in Research*, Parts I and II (1957) (Ann Arbor, Mich.: Institute for Social Research). For another example see Hanan C. Selvin, *The Effects of Leadership* (New York: Free Press of Glencoe, 1960).
5. See Barney G. Glaser, "The Use of Secondary Analysis by the Independent Researcher," *The American Behavioral Scientist* (1963), pp. 11-14.

of accuracy is not as important for generating theory about a type of social unit as it is for describing a particular social unit or verifying a hypothesis. What are relevant for theory are the general categories and properties and the general relations between them that emerge from the data. These can be applied to many current situations and locations as very relevant con‑ cepts and as hypotheses of interest to sociologists and laymen, regardless of whether the specific descriptions yielded by the data are currently accurate for the research population. Sec‑ ondary analysis, then, is uniquely well suited for the generation of theory but is often severely limited for description and veri‑ fication—for which it is still mostly used, with a typical pre‑ amble about "limitations."

Another limitation of secondary analysis that makes its use in description and verification questionable, but does not affect the generation of theory, is the representativeness of the popu‑ lation studied. Accuracy is, of course, crucial in description and verification, and the sample must therefore be carefully chosen by some form of random sampling. Secondary analysis of a random sample chosen for other reasons may introduce system‑ atic and random biases into the secondary study, making claims to accuracy questionable. Indeed, it is often difficult to ascertain from previously collected data what kind of sample was taken for what purpose, since records may have been destroyed, lost, misplaced or made unavailable. Many important questions con‑ cerning the sampling become unanswerable, such as how many people did not respond, how many cards were lost, and how many questionnaires were not usable. But when theory is the purpose (as stated in Chapter II), there are two reasons why the representativeness of the sample is not an issue. First, the direction of a relationship used to suggest a hypothesis is assumed to exist until disproved, in both biased and unbiased populations; and, second, theoretical (not statistical) sampling guides the choosing and handling of the data.

What is more important for generating theory is the *scope* of the population, which can be increased when the analyst is less concerned about representativeness. Representativeness usually requires some purification of the original sample to obtain a clear-cut population for a smaller study; the sociologist takes for his analysis carefully stratified samples from a larger survey sample. This tactic cuts down on scope by weeding out the possible (but never proven) "contaminating" influences of some respondents. For example, one may wish to take all scientists out of a national survey for study, but then, if he purifies the group by weeding out all but the PhD's, he loses the population scope that could have been afforded by keeping the scientists with the MD's, MS's, and BS's.

Concepts and Indices

In the last decade, the flexible use of concepts and their empirical indices in quantitative analysis has been advanced greatly by Lazarsfeld. A number of publications [6] have carried his work on the "process by which concepts are translated into empirical indices." We wish to mention here only a few general points and urge the reader to study the footnoted references for the general argument and the examples.

When the discovery and generation of theory is the goal of a survey analysis, "crude" or "general duty" indices (as described in detail by Lazarsfeld) suffice to indicate the concepts of the theory and to establish general relationships between them, which in turn become the basis for suggesting hypotheses for the emerging theory. Similar crude indices, usually a single questionnaire item or a simple summation index of two to six items, are often interchangeable when based on similar, but different indicators. "Interchangeability of indices," as Lazarsfeld demonstrates, means that we obtain the same findings in cross-tabulations with other variables when two indices of the same category are based on reasonably similar but different sets of indicators. Therefore, the analyst does not have to be certain that he has the most accurate index, judged on the basis of either precision or the best set of indicators.

Crude indices, when correlated with other variables, also yield the same relationships in direction as the more precise

6. Paul F. Lazarsfeld, "Problems in Methodology," in R. Merton, L. Broom and L. Cottrell (Eds.), *Sociology Today* (New York: Basic Books, 1959), pp. 47-67; "Evidence and Inference in Social Research," *Daedalus*, LXXXXVII (1958), pp. 100-109; and, with Wagner Thielens, *The Academic Mind* (Glencoe, Ill.: Free Press, 1958), pp. 402-407.

indices yielded by factor analysis, latent structure analysis, a Guttman scale, or elaborate scales involving dozens of items. Since for generating theory we are only looking for general relationships of direction—a positive or negative relation between concepts, and not either precise measurement of each person in the study or exact magnitudes of relationship—it is easier, faster, and considerably more economical to use the crude index. Even when crude indices result in obvious misclassification of some cases, they still yield the information necessary for generating a grounded theory.[7]

Crude indices of categories or properties can also be based on either a single questionnaire item or a series of items summed into an index. However, for indices of the core categories, it is perhaps preferable to use two to six item summation indices, since the category will usually be based on at least two dimensions and each should be indicated by at least one item. Further, crude indices need only be dichotomized to obtain comparative groups, not cut into several groups. Whether an index is cut in two, three, or four groups, the same general relation will appear when it is cross-tabulated with another variable, provided that the cutting point is statistically established with criterion variables as a meaningful break in the data.[8] Dichotomizing an index is financially economical and saves cases for cross-tabulation when the number of cases is small and when the analyst engages in the multivariate analysis of three or more variables. Indeed, even if a trichotomous index is used, the analyst, except in cases of exceptional patterns, still ends up talking about the general positive or negative relation between two variables.

When generating theory, validation of a core index—demon-

7. It is at this point, Lazarsfeld suggests, that technicians, who perhaps have no generative powers, take flight into precision by blaming their crude methods and trying to refine their indices instead of thinking about what they have found.

8. In constructing a summation index, the analyst first obtains one more group than the number of indicators he is using: four indicators lead to five groups. Before combining these groups he should cross-tabulate the five groups with a criterion variable—he knows the relationship exists —to find out between which groups the direction of the relationship changes. He then combines all those groups positively related to the criterion variable and all those negatively. He cannot just dichotomize the index where he pleases, because he may reduce its discriminating power by combining positive and negative degrees.

strating that the index measures the concept to a sufficient probable degree—need not be a special operation in which a theoretically relevant relation between two variables is sacrificed from the substance of the analysis itself to prove the validity of the argument, as is typically necessary in verifications.[9] If the index "works"—that is, if it is consistently related to a whole series of variables that, when put together, yield an integrated theory—this is validation enough of a core index. Integration of the theory is, in fact, a more trustworthy validation of an index than the standard method of merely showing that an obvious relationship exists between the index and another questionnaire item, and that therefore the index must measure what it is supposed to measure.[10]

For example, the core index of "professional recognition" in *Organizational Scientists* (by one of this book's co-authors) could easily have been validated by showing that professional recognition is positively related to receiving promotions; but instead the whole book shows the validity of the index by the way the substantive theory on scientists' organizational careers is integrated.[11] In fact, the theory becomes integrated around the core index of recognition because of the multiple relationships with that index, indicating that the theory works—it provides relevant explanations and consequences of organizational careers. Lazarsfeld's methods for specifying concepts and for selecting sub-sets of items to construct indices of the concepts are excellent for ensuring that categories will fit the data and will work or be relevant. This fulfillment of the two major requirements of grounded theory explains why the index becomes validated by the whole theory.

We make these statements in the service of generating theory. If the analyst wishes to describe or verify, these issues must be argued on different grounds, because his problems of precision, dichotomization, and validation of indices are different. The analyst must therefore be clear about his purpose. However, most survey analysts are *not* clear, because Lazarsfeld

9. For an example see Lazarsfeld and Theilens, *op. cit.*, pp. 89-90.
10. This is a specific case of Zetterberg's rule that the total integration of a theory tends to make any one of its parts "highly plausible." See Hans L. Zetterberg, *On Theory and Verification in Sociology* (Totowa, N.J.: Bedminster Press, 1963), Chapter 6.
11. Glaser, *op. cit.*

never has made the distinction between the purpose of generation and those of verification and/or description with accurate
findings. He writes not of theory but of "empirical propositions"
and "statistical relations." We see clearly how his work on concepts and indices is valuable for generating theory through
conceptual indices and general relations between them. But
others who wish to discover "facts" and verify hypotheses, especially by secondary analysis, must argue for Lazarsfeld's
methods on their own. Indeed, there are many sociologists who
use his methods and stay on the empirical level of description
or harp on their findings in the verification rhetoric, even when
attempting to suggest theoretical hypotheses.

The survey analyst chooses his categories in the same manner as the researcher doing qualitative analysis. An initial scheme
of concepts and hypotheses, usually applied to quantitative data
in attempting verifications, is not needed. Concepts whose fit
will be emergent are found in previous descriptive analyses
with the quantitative data, or in other quantitative or qualitative data on the same subject. Also, categories and properties
emerge during the collecting and analyzing of quantitative data
as readily as they do with qualitative. It must be remembered
that qualitative data suggesting a category may also be used as
another slice of data for the quantitative analysis.

The theoretical relevance of the concept is soon demonstrated by whether or not its index actually works in a multitude of cross-tabulations. If the index does not work, then the
analyst should question the theoretical relevance of his concept before he questions the method of index formation. In quantitative analyses it is typical to observe a non-emergent category
derived from a logico-deductive theory (say, on self-image, role
conflict, or status congruency), forcibly indexed—and then
found to be related to nothing of theoretical relevance. The
analyst then finds fault with the precision of the method of
index formation, rather than with the relevance of a category
derived from an ungrounded theory, since he seldom questions
his faith in the logico-deductive theorist when the latter is a
charismatic figure in the profession. Much survey analysis fails
for this reason, but we hear of failures only through our friends;
tact prevents citing examples.

It is possible to index any category, but while, with emergent categories, the analyst is almost sure to discover many relations between indices, "ought" categories from ungrounded theories are a risk. To stay on the empirical level, using no theoretical categories, is one alternative to taking the chance of directing theoretical research through logically deduced categories such as "anomie" or "authority relations." Yet people who do not trust logico-deductive theory, but who wish to do theoretical work, could very safely attempt discovery of grounded theory as another alternative.

Discovering Hypotheses

In generating theory, preconceived hypotheses are not necessary for correlating or cross-tabulating two variables (called runs) with indices of core categories and properties. Indeed, the rule for generation of theory is *not* to have any pre-set or valued hypotheses, but to maintain a sensitivity to all possible theoretical relevances among the hundreds of possible runs afforded by large surveys. In contrast, necessarily preconceived hypotheses direct exactly what two variable correlations to use as tests in verificational studies. Indeed, verificational rules state that data should be collected for tests *after* the hypothesis has been formulated—though they seldom are. For generating theory the data can be collected at *any time*. As we have said, it is usually collected beforehand because most discovery and generation is a secondary analysis of data collected for other purposes, and because the hypotheses come after the analysis— they are suggested from findings, not tested with them.

In order to saturate all possible findings for suggesting hypotheses, the analyst may take his core concepts and run them with literally *every* other questionnaire item in the survey that seems remotely relevant to his area of interest.[12] At this point the theory of the core indices starts to emerge. Clusters

12. If the analyst has enough time and money, he can run the index open (use all groups) and then dichotomize them at the breaking point for each item. This will yield more diverse information on each relationship and make the index more sensitive. This strategy is an alternative to dichotomizing on a criterion variable, but is cumbersome; and once the analyst is sure his break in the index is the most sensitive one, it may seem a waste of time for the yield of information.

TABLE I

COSMOPOLITAN ORIENTATION

	Motivation to Advance		Knowledge
	High	Low	Difference
Personal contacts outside organization are very important as sources of scientific information	56%	35%	+21%
If had to, would prefer to move to a university	72%	43%	+21%
Belonging to an organization with prestige in the scientific world is of the utmost importance	40%	21%	+19%
Very strong involvement with close professional work associates	40%	26%	+14%
Very strong sense of belonging to section (principal research work group)	44%	27%	+17%
Basic research, as a result of clinical program, is likely to			
—benefit	42%	56%	—14%
—suffer	40%	29%	+11%
Those who would worry about a substantial emphasis on applied as well as basic research	38%	19%	+19%
Base for each per cent	(186)	(146)	

LOCAL ORIENTATION

	Motivation to Advance		Knowledge
	High	Low	Difference
Having an important job in the organization is of the utmost importance	30%	12%	+18%
Association with high-level persons having important responsibilities is of the utmost or considerable importance	55%	42%	+13%
Having a very strong sense of belonging to the organization	31%	19%	+12%
Interested in a higher level job in the organization which entails stimulating or advising subordinate professionals about their work	77%	67%	+10%
Interested in a higher level job entailing administrative planning or coordination	68%	56%	+12%
Base for each per cent	(186)	(146)	

of items are discovered as associated with the index. Indeed, this strategy (an unbelievable "sin" in verificational studies) virtually discovers theory for the analyst by providing associations to be conceptualized and analyzed. He induces a theory simply from the general relationships he has found. He need not concern himself with theoretical explanations of what he has found in comparison with what he was supposed to find, as is done in verificational studies.

One comparative strategy for generating theory from findings is to compare clusters of relationships within the context of the emerging theory. For example, in Table I we see that "motivation to advance knowledge" (a crude index) is consistently related to two clusters of items, those indicating a *cosmopolitan* orientation—toward the profession—and those indicating a *local* orientation—toward their research organization. Thus we discover and suggest theoretically that highly motivated scientists within research organizations devoted to basic research (a structural condition) possess the property of being local-cosmopolitans.[13] Table II bears out the suggested hypoth-

TABLE II

Consecutive addition of hours per week spent on various work activities	Motivation to Advance Knowledge High	Low	Difference
21 or more hours: own research	76%	61%	+15%
36 or more hours: plus other professional productive work	63%	49%	+14%
41 or more hours: plus nonproductive professional work	69%	48%	+21%
51 or more hours: plus other organization activities for total work week	55%	48%	+17%
Base for each per cent	(186)	(146)	

esis, by showing that in their work activities highly motivated scientists are both local and cosmopolitan oriented: as more working hours and activities are added to the work week, the

13. For the theoretical discussion of Tables I and II, see Glaser, *Organizational Scientists: Their Professional Careers, op. cit.*, Chapter 2.

highly motivated scientists spend more time on both professional
and organizational activities.

Consistency Indices

These two variable runs showing clusters of associations are
analyzed comparatively in two ways: *within* and *between* consistency indices. A consistency index is a list of single questionnaire items which all indicate the same category, such as cosmopolitan, and all relate separately to the core index in the

TABLE III. PERCENTAGE OF RESEARCHERS WITH HIGH MOTIVATION AS
RELATED TO THEIR PREVIOUS EXPERIENCE

Background Experience	Previous Experience %	No Previous Experience %	Difference %
Emphasis on advance of knowledge:			
University employment	65 (180) *	45 (152)	+20
Research and teaching	61 (247)	42 (85)	+19
Ph.D. Education	62 (164)	40 (58) † 55 (110) #	+22
Emphasis on application of knowledge:			
Medical or clinical practice	58 (244)	55 (88)	+3
Hospitals	57 (111)	55 (121)	+2
Industry	58 (78)	56 (254)	+2
Private practice or business	58 (36)	56 (296)	+2
Government agencies	48 (117)	61 (215)	−13
U.S. Public Health Service	47 (68)	58 (264)	−11

* Figures in parenthesis indicate number of cases.
† Education less than doctorate.
# M.D.

same consistent direction. The indicators are not added together
first and then related to the core index, as in summation indices.
Summation indices are best for the core categories, but consistency indices are best for the categories to which a core index
is to be related. This strategy allows the analyst to see how the
core concept relates to each individual indicator of another
category. If inconsistencies in associations between the consistency index and the core index occur for what appeared to be
substantively consistent indicators, they are quickly caught and
compared for the underlying meaning of the differences within
the set of indicators and the emerging theory.

For example, in Table III we see that *within* the consistency
index of applied experience, high motivation to advance knowledge (not to apply it) is not related to previous experiences
in private or group practice, hospitals or industry.[14] These
particular applied experiences, then, we theoretically suggest,
neither engender nor inhibit motivation to advance knowledge.
But the problem remains: why is motivation negatively related
to applied experience in government agencies and the U.S.
Public Health Service, or (theoretically) why do these experiences inhibit or reduce motivation to advance knowledge? We
suggest that it is because these two experiences, in contrast to
the first four, imply routine service in the application of
knowledge.

If all the items on "experience in application of knowledge
experiences" had been combined first in a summation index,
and then related to motivation, these inconsistent comparisons
of groups within the consistency index (from which we discovered strategic structural conditions varying the core category)
would have been missed; hence, so would an important hypothesis of the theory: the effect of "routine" applications on the
scientists' motivation to advance knowledge. The property of
"routine application" would have been missed had the analyst
simply constructed a summation index, since all the items on
applied experience would have seemed internally consistent
when tested—all items positively related to each other. Therefore there would have been no suspicion that correlating an

14. For the theoretical discussion of Tables III and IV, see Barney
G. Glaser, "Differential Association and the Institutional Motivation of
Scientists," *Administrative Science Quarterly,* 10 (1965), pp. 81-97.

applied experience index with another index was actually sum- ✓
ming inconsistencies.

Comparisons *between* different consistency indices are also
used as a strategy of comparative analysis. We saw in Table I
that, since high motivation is positively associated with both a
local and cosmopolitan orientation, the analyst can suggest, on
the basis of this comparison between consistency indices that
scientists highly motivated in research are local-cosmopolitans in
a basic research organization.

These two comparative strategies—comparing within and
between consistency indices associated with a summation index
—occur in three or more variable associations also; but then
the analyst is using additional analytic strategies, which we
discuss in the next section. Also, once a detailed analysis of an
association with a consistency index is accomplished, then the
consistency index can be summed and dichotomized for further
analyses with three or more variables. These analyses are more

TABLE IV. RELATION OF RECOGNITION TO SCIENCE EXPERIENCE FOR
RESEARCH WORKERS WITH HIGH MOTIVATION

Science Experience	High Recognition %	Low Recognition %	Difference %
Full	76	69	+7
	(46) *	(52)	
Some	68	42	+26
	(75)	(99)	
None	44	35	+9
	(23)	(37)	

* Figures in parenthesis indicate the number of cases.

complicated, requiring reduction of details and the saving of
cases for cross-tabulation. For example, the first part of Table
III shows motivation to advance knowledge related to a consistency index on one kind of previous experience in science—
experience emphasizing advancement of knowledge. Table IV
shows the summation index of previous experience in science
related to two other summation indices—motivation to advance
knowledge and professional recognition—for the theoretical
purpose of suggesting hypotheses bearing on the interaction
between the three indices.

Tests of Significance

Statistical tests of significance of an association between variables are not necessary when the discovered associations between indices are used for suggesting hypotheses. Selvin [15] has argued that this rule should be relaxed for *all* survey analysis, but he can take this stand only because he has not made the distinction between the generating and the verifying or describing purposes of research. He questions whether these tests are appropriate with survey data, since the statistical assumptions necessary to use them cannot be met with such data and also are ineptly applied according to general sociological theory. His critics, however, seem to be more concerned with keeping the tests of significance to ascertain accuracy of evidence used for verification and description.[16] We wish to stay clear of this controversy because we are making an argument concerned only with these tests in relation to the generation of theory.

Testing the statistical significance of an association between indices presents a strong barrier to the generation of theory while doing nothing to help it, since the resulting accuracy (if one can actually trust the test) is not crucial. These tests direct attention away from theoretically interesting relationships that are not of sufficient magnitude to be statistically significant. The analyst usually does not think of the associations as a grounded foundation for an hypothesis, although weak associations may be highly theoretically relevant. Also, the test, not the relationship, may be weak.

Believing that he has no findings relevant for generating theory, the analyst also usually neglects to ask what the partial relationships look like under several conditions. It is easy to

15. Hanan Selvin, "A Critique of Tests of Significance in Survey Research," *American Sociological Review*, 22 (1957), pp. 519-27; "Statistical Significance and Sociological Theory" (July, 1960) (mimeographed, University of California, Berkeley).

16. Robert McGinnis, "Randomization and Inference in Sociological Research," *American Sociological Review*, 23 (1958), pp. 408-14; Leslie Kish, "Some Statistical Problems in Research Design," *American Sociological Review*, 24 (1959), pp. 328-38; and critical comments by David Gold and James Beshers in *American Sociological Review*, 23 (1958), pp. 85 and 199.

forget that partials may be statistically significant even if the general relationship is not, because the partials can cancel themselves out. "Canceling out" means that the relationship may be positive under one condition and negative under another; so that when combined the partial relationships cancel themselves out to result in a weak general association. However, it is theoretically very relevant and interesting to be able to say how conditions minimize, maximize, or cancel out a relationship. Also, even if partials are weak, the theoretical relevance of a weak relationship between two indices may be the *weakness* itself.

Believing in tests of significance can also dissuade one from trusting consistent but weak relationships within and between consistency indices. Yet consistency validates the merit of relationships when it comes to the plausible reasoning required in a credible theoretical analysis.[17] And, as just noted, whether the level of the relationship is zero, weak, or strong, it may, if relevant, be grist for the theory.

A belief in tests of significance can also, in the process, direct one's attention away from theoretical relevance of content toward confusing statistical significance with theoretical signficance, and a statistical method labeled "analysis" with theoretical analysis. Merely being statistically significant does not mean that a relationship is or should be of theoretical relevance. Such relevance depends on the meaning of the association as it relates to the theory. Also, the statistical analysis methods (for example, "factor analysis," or "analysis of variance") are not theoretical analyses. They are merely techniques for arriving at a type of fact. It is still up to the analyst to discover and analyze the theoretical relevances of these facts. In sum, the basic criterion for generating theory is theoretical relevance, and the analyst should sample his quantitative findings on this basis.

In place of making tests of significance, the sociologist can establish working rules to fit his particular situation. For example, two rules for establishing an acceptable percentage-difference level are not to consider any relationship of, say, less than

17. That consistency validates is a basic pattern of plausible inference. See G. Polya, *Patterns of Plausible Inference* (Princeton, N.J.: Princeton University Press, 1954), Vol. II, Chapter XII.

10 per cent difference; or any relationship in which three people's changing their minds or being misclassified would change the percentage to below an establshed level. These levels change with the number of cases used, smaller numbers of cases requiring a higher percentage-difference level. Selvin has also developed an internal replication procedure for establishing the possibility that a relationship exists.[18]

Standing by the rules that he may have initially established for his research is pertinent only to the beginning phases of generating theory. When the analyst has achieved theoretical relevance with his data, consistency arises in percentage-difference levels as well as in content, and he will readily learn to understand when and why a lower difference is relevant as well as a higher one. The absence of a relationship becomes just as important as an increase above the consistent percentage level, for any degree of association (or lack of it) may be part of the theory. For example, in Table III the relationship of motivation to previous experience varies at consistent percentage-difference levels—positive (20 per cent) to zero (2 per cent) to negative (−12 per cent)—thus theoretically indicating that these levels are engendered by experiences emphasizing basic research, unaffected by those experiences emphasizing applied research, and inhibited by experiences involving routine service in applied research. In Table V, a consistent percentage-difference

TABLE V. EFFECT OF RECOGNITION ON SCIENTISTS' SATISFACTION
WITH DIVERSE ORGANIZATIONAL PERSONNEL *

| | Organizational Position of Scientists | | |
	Junior	Senior	Supervisor
Assisting personnel			
Very and fairly satisfied	+10%	+5%	+11%
Scientific personnel			
Very satisfied	+16%	+5%	+22%
Leadership			
Very satisfied	+28%	+26%	+12%
Fairly satisfied	−11	+11	+16
Institute director			
Very competent	+10%	+7%	+28%
Fairly competent	+7	+2	......

* This is a table of differences accounted for by high compared to low recognition.

18. Selvin, *op. cit.*

level of 10 to 16 per cent shows in comparative relief the theoretical relevance of the stronger and weaker relationships as conditions varying the effect of recognition on satisfaction with organizational personnel.[19]

Liberties in Presentation of Data

When quantitative data are reported in verificational and descriptive studies, typically each association is given in table form with a technically exact discussion of it; and then the finding is qualified by tentative statements and alternative explanations or interpretations. This style of presentation need not be used in generating theory, nor, in fact, could it be used. The multitude of relationships on which grounded theory is based is so large that this style applied to each relationship would make the report of the theory unreadable—too long, cumbersome, and slow-moving—to colleagues and quite inaccessible to laymen. It is particularly important that both colleagues and laymen readily understand the theory,[20] since quantitative data are usually not as interesting to read as qualitative, and do not carry the reader along as easily. Therefore, the analyst must take some liberties both in presenting tables and in making statements about them. Needless to say, the liberties in presentation should not in any way change the data upon which the theory is based; it is just that for generating theory not all data must be presented and stated in exact detail. Since the possibilities are great, each analyst must decide on various liberties according to his particular directions of effort.

Let us consider here a few general liberties of presentation. Unlike Tables I through IV, Table V is a table of percentage difference. The proportions that were compared to arrive at the differences are left out, since they were not necessary for the theoretical analysis. If it is necessary to know about a particular set of proportions, they should be mentioned in text. However, the focus of the analysis in this table was on comparing percentage differences for indicating direction and magnitude of many relationships: that is, differences in satisfaction with organ-

19. For theoretical discussion of Table V see Glaser, *Organizational Scientists: Their Professional Careers, op. cit.*, Chapter 6.
20. In contrast, verifications usually only require the understanding of a small group of colleagues working in the area.

izational personnel accounted for by the high and low recognition achieved by scientists at different stages of their organizational careers. Both the direction and magnitude of these relationships were important for the analysis; if only direction of relationship had been important, the table could have been further simplified by leaving out numbers and using only plus and minus signs. These flexible renditions of quantitative evidence are in the service of generating theory. No information is lost, distorted, or purposively concealed. It is just that only enough information is presented to show, in the simplest possible manner, the grounded basis of the emerging theory. Verification requires a more detailed rendition of the data—showing all N's, sub-N's and compared high and low percentages—so that the reader can verify the verification for himself.

Because of the overabundance of separate associations necessary in generating theory (literally hundreds, in contrast to the few necessary in verificational studies), another general liberty may be taken in presenting tables, particularly two variable tables. Unless a whole configuration of consistency indices are shown together in a table for visual comparisons, it is enough to state in the written text two variable associations in their direction and (if necessary) magnitude; presenting a table would be repetitious. When theoretically necessary, proportions and N's can be provided in a footnote.

While verificational studies require exactitude, statements about associations can be more flexibly written when theory is the goal. For example, "more successful investigators have satisfactory research facilities provided to them as a reward by the organization" is a statement that assumes the reader understands that three liberties have been taken with this reporting of a two-variable table. First, the "successful" investigators have been *compared* with less successful investigators—the statement is comparative. Second, "more" means *proportionately* more—the comparison is relative, not absolute. And third, that the organization provides these research facilities as rewards to the successful investigators is a theoretical *inference* from the finding that they simply have more satisfactory research facilities than the less successful investigators. Such a hypothesis is more readable than the precise, literal statement: "A higher proportion of those scientists with high professional recognition than those scientists with low professional recognition have satisfactory research facilities. We tentatively suggest that these facilities are provided as rewards to the more successful scientists by the organization."

These three liberties in writing can also sometimes be taken when rendering three-variable tables, and the table need not be put in text. But more often, as noted in the next section, three-variable tables have complex purposes—for example, an interaction table showing the joint effects of two variables on a third (example 4 below). A table and some explicit reporting of it are required for the theoretical inference to be easily understood as being based on evidence.

Theoretical Elaboration

The previous section presented the first step in our style of theoretical analysis of quantitative data: saturating core indices with all possible two-variable runs; discovering relationships among the runs with theoretically relevant consistency indices, summation indices and single questionnaire tems; then analyzing the findings with theoretical inferences. The next step, which cannot be neglected, is *elaboration analysis*—to make three or more variable analyses in order to saturate categories further by developing their properties and thereby achieving a denser theory. Thus, the discovery of relationships among indices provides the analyst with beginning suggestions for a theory, plus a theoretical direction and focus for its elaboration.

By "elaboration" we mean that the two-variable associations, which are the basis of theoretical hypotheses, must have their structural conditions specified; their causes and consequences sought, with possible spurious factors checked for; and their intervening variables (delineating processes between the variables) discovered. Although this, of course, is Lazarsfeld's elaboration analysis,[21] we shall contribute something new to his method for our own purpose of generating theory. The next several paragraphs assume an understanding of elaboration analysis (which can easily be gained by a study of Hyman's

21. See references in Footnotes 3 and 6.

rendition of it [22]). The notions on consistency analysis discussed in the previous section are subsumed in elaboration analysis.

Lazarsfeld has provided three ways of ordering the variables in an elaboration analysis: (1) temporal, (2) structural level of complexity, and (3) conceptual generality. Temporal ordering is simply the time sequence of the variables involved. Structural complexity is an ordering in terms of the encompassing structural levels that characterize the unit of analysis under study. For example, a nurse can be characterized by the ward she works on, the hospital she works in, the city in which the hospital is located, and the nation where the city is. Conceptual generality is an ordering by degree of abstractness of the variables. For example, a nurse says that all patients should be bathed every day, which is specific opinion derived from a broader attitude of obeying all hospital rules, which attitude in turn derives from a basic value in medicine that nurses should obey hospital rules.

Lazarsfeld's elaboration analysis is seldom used in research, except for the simple task of specifying the conditions of a finding; for this task, one need not understand or expressly use his formula. The reason for this lack of use is simple: the only type of ordering of variables that Lazarsfeld has actually worked out is temporal ordering—the other two types have only been suggested.[23] Since survey data is typically cross-sectional in time, analysts are hard put to establish clear-cut, *factual* time orders in which colleagues will have confidence, because of the emphasis on accurate facts in verification and description.[24] Usually there is too much temporal interrelation among cross-sectional survey variables—over time, either one could, and probably does, result in the other. Thus, elaboration analysis is often stopped in its tracks before it has a chance to prove its usefulness. And the analyst who does not give it a chance stifles, rather than stimulates, his theoretical imagination. He has been

22. Herbert H. Hyman, *Survey Design and Analysis* (Glencoe, Ill.: Free Press, 1955), Chapter VII.

23. See Lazarsfeld's introduction to Hyman, *ibid.*

24. The evaluator of an article for one journal remarked on an elaboration table, "More generally the whole argument about establishment vs. persistence (or stability) of the relationships suffers because the author really has no time trend data—and that is necessarily implied in statements about persistence or stability." The paper was rejected because temporal order was not an incontrovertible fact.

taught not to let his imagination range on data that he cannot himself believe completely accurate, much less argue for their credibility with his colleagues. He has been taught to be skeptical of such strategies for survey data to the point of keeping an empty head about data felt unreliable.

Elaboration analysis is stimulating because the findings it produces *fit* the thought patterns of sociological theory. With it, the analyst can show interpretations, processes, conditions, causes, spurious factors, and consequences with actual data— not an interpretation of the data. The analyst can literally speak through elaboration tables. He need only infer from his indices the conceptual level of his talk since the tables provide the theoretical arrangement of the variables. But if temporal ordering is believed impossible in most cases, how can we allow theory to emerge from elaboration tables?

Theoretical Ordering

The theory ran emerge from these tables if, first, the analyst decides that his purpose is to generate theory, for then the accuracy of temporal ordering that would be required for verification and description is no longer crucial. He must then proceed to order his variables *theoretically*: a new principle of ordering. Lazarsfeld comes close to suggesting this principle with his "substantive" orderings by structural complexity and conceptual generality, for these are two specific examples of the general principle of theoretical ordering. But Lazarsfeld misses developing a general theoretical ordering principle because he does not consider their underlying similarity, nor how and why they can be used for the generation of theory. He misses this consideration because he is involved exclusively in establishing facts for description and verification. He never comes close to understanding that temporal sequence can be handled theoretically as well as factually.

Theoretical ordering of variables occurs by two strategies: (1) running all possible three-variable associations with each theoretically relevant two-variable association; and (2) running particular tables to fill in gaps or to answer questions, which emerge as the theory develops, by arranging elaboration tables according to the dictates of the theory. From the findings in both strategies there emerge theoretical orderings of variables already integrated with core categories and hypotheses. The analyst then infers or suggests them as his theory.

Theoretical ordering of variables by all possible three-variable associations on core two-variable relationships is done by comparing the partial association percentage differences to the percentage difference of the original relationship. When the partials vary above and below the original relationship, then the analyst discovers conditions that minimize and maximize his core relationship. From these findings he generates theory stating "under what conditions" a phenimenon exists. Some of these conditions are antecedent to the original association and may be suggested as partial causes; others, which occur at the same time, may be called contingencies. When the partials are equal to the original relationship, then a particular condition does not vary the relationship. The analyst either regards it as theoretically relevant or ignores the finding.

When both partials are less than the original relationship (they never completely disappear), then the analyst must theoretically suggest whether the third variable is (1) an intervening variable, thus suggesting a theoretical process between two core variables, or (2) an antecedent variable. An antecedent variable that reduces partials may have several theoretical meanings. The original relationship may be spurious; that is, both original variables are the consequences of the third variable. This finding may be theoretically very relevant. For instance, "the more fire engines that come to a fire, the greater the damage" is a spurious relationship, with both factors accounted for by size of the fire. The antecedent variable may also suggest a process in which the third variable leads to one of the original variables, which in turn leads to the other. This inference can be tested with the second strategy of theoretical ordering, which is to answer the question "Is this a process?" by rearranging the table to fit, thus testing for the theoretically assumed ordering of an intervening variable. If the inference proves correct, the analyst has found a value-added process— without the first variable the other two variables do not occur in process.[25] Thus the analyst can actively check on his theory as

25. See for a discussion of this type of process Neil Smelser, *Theory of Collective Behavior* (New York: Free Press of Glencoe, 1963), Chapter I.

it emerges, by testing assumed theoretical orders. (This will be illustrated shortly.) Third, the antecedent variable may be a cause of a cluster of two variables. These two variables always occur together and therefore are truly, not spuriously, associated, but they do not occur without the discovered cause, which the analyst might wish to call a necessary condition. Thus fire engines and fires are truly associated, but are not found together unless someone has put in the alarm.

The first strategy of theoretical ordering is based on emergence: the data provides possible orders for the analyst. He need only induce theory about what he has found. This can be difficult when he has to overcome current training in quantitative analysis. He must remember that he is only looking for plausible orders among variables to suggest a theory. He is not looking for the "facts" of a description or verification. *He must think developmentally by remembering that only the data is static or cross-sectional—not his mind!* Although the data may admit of no temporal sequence, his creative imagination can consider any ordering principle for the related variables, and this principle becomes his ingenious suggestion. With imagination and ingenuity he can theoretically order his variables by time, structural complexity, conceptual generality, or in any other theoretical manner. His job is to suggest a theory based both on the *theoretically relevant order* of elaborated relationships and on the *content* of the variables he employs. He cannot think methodologically or statistically with symbols such as *t* factors or *x* leads to *y;* he must think *theoretically* about the content of his indicated categories and infer why the order of their possible relationships may be as he found them. In short, he must free himself from the exact rules of elaboration ordering as applied to descriptive and verificational studies, so he can be flexible in an imaginative, post hoc theoretical analysis of what he has discovered from the four elaboration possibilities: antecedent or current conditions (PA and PI), antecedent or intervening variables (MA and MI).

In generating theory as it emerges, the analyst first discovers two-variable relationships; second, he discovers their elaboration. Then he moves into a third stage, in which he starts generating possible further elaborations of two-variable relationships within the previous elaboration, using the second strategy of arranging variables to test theoretical orderings. He looks through his data to find indicators for the concepts he thinks are related in theoretical ways to his emerging theory. Then he arranges his elaboration tables to test if they bear out his hypotheses (for suggestion, not verification), or to discover what actually happens. At this stage of the analysis, he is theoretically sampling his data as directed by his emerging theory and he is actively directing his further runs accordingly; much as the field researcher directs his final work toward theoretically sampling data on hypotheses for filling gaps and answering the remaining questions in order to saturate categories. And much as the field worker at this stage moves quickly between situations, achieving greater relevance with smaller amounts of data, the quantitative analyst may literally camp in the IBM machine room, having successive tables run to continually check his hypotheses as he thinks them through and theoretically samples his data for them.[26] At this stage an active dialogue of discovery and generation develops between himself and his data. He knows what his data should look like in various runs, and the runs set him straight. By this time the analyst has looked at hundreds of tables, trying to discover what he anticipates finding because of directions provided by the first two stages of his research. Consistency and elaboration analyses join together to provide him a grounded basis for his theory. (The appendix to this chapter gives examples.)

Conclusions

The point of this chapter has been to illustrate the careful relaxation of rules surrounding quantitative analysis, a relaxation for generating theory. The styles of quantitative analysis are multitudinous, so our discussions here include but few illustrations pertaining to the rich veins in quantitative data that can be mined when analysts relax their rigór.

One topic that we have not yet dealt with in this chapter bears mention: comparative analysis within and between surveys. To be sure, the discovery of relationships and their elabo-

---

26. This is a frequent activity among some survey analysts; see Coleman's discussion of continually having tables run as he thinks them through, *op. cit.*, pp. 203-04.

ration are all based on comparative analysis of subgroups that are readily found in the same body of data. However, sociologists have yet to explore the many possibilities for generating theory by the active creation of diverse comparison subgroups within a survey (beside core index and typologies), and by the active search for comparison subgroups in other surveys. The various survey-data libraries scattered around the nation now facilitate comparisons between surveys.

We can suggest a few general rules for beginning this kind of exploration. The analyst can use *similar* groups for comparisons between surveys; they do not have to be identical. For example, "working class" may be indicated by residential area in one study, income in another, and low degree of organizational affiliation in another (remembering that crude indications are sufficient and interchangeable).[27] Further, the analyst should search for ways of comparing quickly and easily the multiple comparison groups within many different, particularly large, surveys, since one or two surveys can easily run thin on data, and what is needed for a dense, adequate theory is a great amount of data. Also, multiple comparisons should be sought and flexibly done with qualitative data on other relevant groups.

In making these multiple comparisons, the analyst should constantly focus on generating and generalizing a theory, not on the comparison of differences to verify or account for a fact. Generating from differences is not easy to manage with quantitative data, since sociologists are trained to verify, and verification from differences comes very easily with quantitative data. Verifying and accounting for facts by differences are subsumed in the process of generating theory; they are not the product of quantitative research for this purpose.

Appendix to Chapter VIII: Examples of Theoretical Elaboration

Following are several examples of theoretical ordering of elaboration tables, which tell the analyst if it is possible to suggest a theoretical statement. We focus particularly on the

27. See Herbert H. Hyman, *Political Socialization* (Glencoe, Ill.: Free Press, 1959), for examples of combining similar categories for comparative analysis.

second strategy of theoretically arranging tables to discover possible orderings for hypotheses.

1. *The discovery and generation of a performance-reward process.* In a study of organizational scientists, the analyst discovered that scientists' motivation to advance knowledge was positively associated with professional recognition for doing so. This finding suggested the theoretical inference that recognition from others maintains motivation.[28] The analyst then elaborated this relationship by suggesting the following theoretical ordering: if recognition (which indicates previous performance) maintains motivation, then motivation should result in high quality performance in research and this, in turn, should result in more professional recognition. This ordering could then be suggested as a circular, snowballing, reward process for performance within science. The problem then became to order the elaboration tables to test if theoretically (not factually) this process was grounded.

In Table VI, the magnitude of association between recognition and performance is *diminished* when the intervening effect of motivation is removed. Therefore, high motivation tends to be a link between receiving recognition and accomplishing further high quality research performance, tentatively demonstrating the performance-reward process as a grounded basis for a theory of this process. As a social pattern, this circular process will continue if the performance measured here results in new recognition.[29]

TABLE VI

| | Recognition | | |
	Average	Less	Difference
High performance	56%	44%	+12%
	(144)	(188)	
Proportion with high performance and:			
High motivation	60%	53%	+7%
	(96)	(90)	
Low motivation	46%	37%	+9%
	(48)	(98)	

28. Glaser, *Organizational Scientists: Their Professional Careers, op. cit.,* Chapter III.

29. See *ibid.,* p. 32.

At this point the analyst suggested that, besides research performance, it was also possible to predict behavior associated with research on the basis of intensity of motivation. This assertion was borne out by one indicator of research behavior: the amount of time in a typical work week that the scientist puts into his own research activities. Fifteen per cent more of the highly motivated investigators worked 21 hours a week or longer on personal research. Furthermore, 11 per cent more of those who worked 21 or more hours a week on their own research had a high quality performance score. (Note the discovery of two additional associations.)

TABLE VII

| | Motivation | | |
	High	Low	Difference
High performance	57%	38%	+19%
	(186)	(146)	
Proportion with high performance who put:			
21 or more hours per week into own research	60%	43%	+17%
	(142)	(89)	
Less than 21 hours per week into own research	48%	35%	+13%
	(44)	(57)	

Next, in theoretically ordering motivation, personal research time, and performance (Table VII), it can be suggested that the highly motivated investigators will tend to put more time into their own research work, and that this time in turn will tend to result in higher quality performance. The magnitude of association between motivation and performance is *diminished* when the intervenng effect of personal research time is removed. This finding then adds a subsidiary link to the circular performance-reward process (diagramed below).

PERFORMANCE-REWARD PROCESS IN SCIENCE

Recognition → Motivation → Time in Own Research → Performance

This theory is based on one possible one-time sequence. The reverse time is also possible: some investigators may have developed a high degree of motivation because they put in more than 21 hours per week. Hard work could generate interest. Therefore, we may have another time sequence in the performance process—longer hours in research leading to high motivation, resulting in high performance. However, this cannot be suggested because the data leave it ungrounded. In comparing proportions downward in Table VII, among those with high motivation 12 per cent more of those who worked 21 or more hours a week on their own research had a high performance score. Among those with low motivation, 8 per cent more who worked 21 hours or more a week on personal research had a high performance score. The original relation between time in own research and performance is 11 per cent. So high motivation, instead of being an intervening variable between time and performance, is a condition that creates a slightly stronger relation between the two. This is, of course, the time sequence originally assumed, which shows it to be the only theoretically grounded sequence.

This example indicates the discovery of two-variable relationships and their theoretical elaboration in order to generate a processual theory. The theory is suggested, not tested, because obviously the temporal ordering is theoretical, not factual; the data were collected on one day, except for the performance index, for which data were collected three months after the survey. However, *even theoretical ordering provides checks on itself;* even when the two elaboration tables were rearranged, the order of the process did not change.

2. *Structural complexity process.* In the same study of organizational scientists, the following consequences of two different promotion systems in the organization were discovered.[30] The "recommend" system (in which initial consideration for a scientist's promotion was based on a supervisor's recommendation) resulted in more discrepancies between rank and actual responsibilities and in more unsatisfactory evaluations of the system than did the "routine" system (in which initial consideration for promotion was based on periodic reviews). Theoretically, it seemed that a process was involved, whereby the relative frequency of perceived discrepancies resulting from each promotion system was a reason for the relative number of unsatisfactory evaluations of each system. The analyst then arranged

30. *Ibid.,* Chapter III.

an elaboration table to test for this theoretical order (Table VIII), and the findings supported it—the partial associations (22 and 25 per cent) were less than the original association (29 per cent), showing that discrepancies were an intervening variable between systems and evaluations. This theoretical process was supported by another consistency finding that among scientists in the "recommend" system there was considerably less satisfaction (29 per cent) with chances for a promotion.

TABLE VIII

| | Promotion System | | |
	Recommend	Routine	Difference
Evaluate promotion process as unsatisfactory	58% (184)	29% (145)	+29%
Proportion who evaluate promotion process as unsatisfactory and who observed discrepancies			
Frequently	83% (59)	61% (28)	+22%
Occasionally	45% (125)	21% (117)	+25%

Here the theoretical ordering of variables is based on structural contexts at different levels, and assumes that the more encompassing level has a greater effect on the lesser level rather than vice versa. Thus "promotion systems" is a contextual unit that causes discrepancies in rank and responsibilities among personnel; while "discrepancies" is a property of the system that provides a structural condition affecting the way scientists evaluate their systems' promotion procedures. Thus, mixed into this structural level process are contextual properties of individuals or structural conditions under which they have a career (promotion procedures and characteristic discrepancies in rank and responsibility); consequences for individuals (discrepancies) and for a system (evaluations); properties of a system (procedures, discrepancies, and dissatisfied individuals); properties of individuals (evaluations), and so forth—depending on how the analyst wishes to render and focus his theory. In short, even within this simple structural process, as found in one elaboration table, the analyst can find much grist for sociological theory.

3. *Theoretically rearranging a table to test for alternative career processes.* The question arose about how those scientists who planned to move to relieve the pressure of a currently unsuccessful career have made this decision.[31] They may (1) decide to leave the organization, and then choose the goal they plan to work for—perhaps still basic research (by going to a university) or perhaps a change to practice or applied research (by going to either a private, industrial or governmental research organization); or (2) decide to change the goal of their work from basic research to another goal, such as applied research or "practice," and this change would necessitate leaving their organization as soon as possible.

Table IX is arranged to test for the sequence of factors in the first process: "plans to move" is tested as an intervening variable, coming between degree of recognition and preference for a preferred affiliation in a university, if the move is made. Since the original relation is nil, we discover that this theoretical elaboration test for an intervening variable is a test if the non-existent original relationship was actually a canceling-out of a strong positive relationship (between recognition and preference under the condition of planning to move soon) and a strong negative relationship (between recognition and preference when planning to stay on in the organization). Thus this table corrects our theoretical ordering by yielding a finding that suggests that unsuccessful scientists who plan to move (11 per cent in Table X) have not as yet planned to go on with either basic research or applied research or practice. They are still just planning to move because of a poor career, and they have not decided where or for what purpose.

TABLE IX

| | Recognition | | |
	High	Low	Difference
Prefer move to university	62%	63%	−1%
	(144)	(188)	
Proportion who prefer move to university and who plan to:			
Move soon	66%	69%	−3%
	(12)	(36)	
Stay for time being or permanently	58%	57%	+1%
	(130)	(152)	

31. *Ibid.,* Chapter VIII.

Table X is arranged to test the second-mentioned process in making plans to move. Preference for the university or for other organizations is tested as intervening in the decision to move as soon as possible made by those who lack recognition. Again, planning to move because of low recognition is not a result of planning to change work goals—both partials are *not* less than the original relationship of 11 per cent. What this table tells us is that the scientists' plans to move as soon as possible material- ize (15 per cent) under this condition of a certain preference for moving to a university where their research goals would be the same. On the other hand, plans to move soon hardly mate- rialize (7 per cent), if at all, when the scientists prefer an or- ganization offering them another work goal.

TABLE X

| | Recognition | | |
	High	Low	Difference
Plan to move as soon as possible	8%	19%	—11%
	(144)	(188)	
Proportion who plan to move as soon as possible and who prefer to move to:			
University	10%	25%	—15%
	(84)	(111)	
Other organizations	7%	14%	—7%
	(60)	(77)	

Thus, theoretical arrangements of elaboration tables, while not necessarily bearing out our theoretical guesses, discover for us *what is going on* (in, say, the decision to leave an organiza- tion because of a failing career). They fill gaps in the total theory of organizational careers and answer our specific questions.

4. *Specifying joint effects of conditions.* Seldom are both par- tial associations less than the original association; the most fre- quent findng specifies antecedent or contingent conditions that minimize and maximize relationships. These findings yield per- haps the most frequent of theoretical statements: the varying conditions under which a phenomenon exists. As we have said, the specification of conditions may apply to a single index, but as an elaboration procedure it applies to two or more variable relationships. Antecedent conditions (such as previous research

experience, Table III) may, if the theory warrants, be suggested as partial causes. Conditions occurring at roughly the same time are called contingencies, denoting whether a relationship is contingent on a condition that makes it more or less pronounced. Further, for his theory the sociologist may choose to reverse the temporal order of his specifications of conditions to obtain statements on the varying consequences of diverse aspects of a condition (types, dimensions, or degrees of the condition). Thus, this type of elaboration table yields findings that suggest several ways to generate a theory.

TABLE XI. PERCENTAGE WHO ARE VERY SATISFIED WITH JOB SECURITY

Organizational Position	Felt Recognition High	Low	Difference
Junior Investigator	67%	43%	+24%
	(57)	(84)	
Senior Investigator	70%	58%	+12%
	(40)	(60)	
Supervisor	73%	73%	......
	(47)	(44)	

Joint effects is another theoretically interesting way of talking about the specification of conditions. In Table XI we see the joint effects of scientists' organizational position and degree of professional recognition on their satisfaction with the security of their job in the organization. A standard means for rendering this table is to say that when we hold organizational position constant, professional recognition only makes for job security in the investigator position. But "holding constant" is a notion used in verification of theory, when the analyst is trying to reduce the contaminating effects of any strategic variable not in focus with his variable of interest.

To view the table in terms of joint effects of two conditions on a third lends itself better to generating theory, since no variable is assumed a constant; all are actively analyzed as part of what is going on. For example, in Table XI we see that as a scientist's organizational position advances (or for the theory, as his career advances), professional recognition becomes less important for job security (the percentage differences decrease). Another joint effect for theoretical inference is that, as the scientist's career advances, he becomes more secure in the organization through seniority, and less dependent upon his degree of professional recognition for this security (under "low recognition" security percentages increase with position). Or the analyst might say that a scientist with professional recognition to his credit tends to have a secure job no matter what his organizational position. (See percentages under "high recognition.") Thus, statements of joint effects tell us how conditions interact together to affect a third variable—and this is theoretically rich and relevant information.

TABLE XII. PROPORTION OF JUNIOR INVESTIGATORS WHO ARE VERY SATISFIED WITH SECURITY OF JOB

Promotion System	Recognition		
	High	Low	Difference
Recommend	63%	37%	+26%
	(30)	(51)	
Routine	69%	50%	+19%
	(26)	(32)	

Two other ways of making inferences about this table are in terms of "differential impact" and "differential sensitivity." [32] For Table XI the analyst can say that position has a *differential impact* on the relationship between recognition and security. In Table XII, we see the differential impact of promotion systems on junior scientists' satisfaction with job security under different conditions of professional recognition. These, again, are forms of contextual and conditional comparative analyses. Referring again to Table XI, the analyst can say that the security of the scientists with low recognition is very sensitive to organizational position, while the security of scientists with high recognition is insensitive to organizational position—thus indicating the *differential sensitivity* of the successful and unsuccessful in their job security.

Finally, the analyst can generate minimal and maximal *configurating* conditions (a useful theoretical model) for his theory from a joint-effects table like Table XI. To be at the beginning stages of a career without recognition is to feel comparatively little satisfaction with job security. Maximum security comes at

32. *Ibid.*, Chapter IV.

the peak of one's career in the organization, because of tenure. Though it took professional recognition to achieve this position, recognition is no longer a condition for job security.

We could suggest more ways to generate theoretical statements from joint-effects tables, as well as from the first three illustrations of elaboration tables. However, we wish only to conclude from these brief illustrations that *if quantitative data is handled systematically by theoretical ordering of variables in elaboration tables, the analyst will indeed find rich terrain for discovering and generating theory.* We hope by our slight but purposeful loosening of the rules, via our principle of theoretical ordering, that elaboration analysis will be used more than heretofore. Its richness for research has not yet been tapped because of difficulties in using it on cross-sectional survey data to produce accurate facts for description and verification.

PART III:

IMPLICATIONS OF GROUNDED THEORY

IX

The Credibility of
Grounded Theory *

The change of emphasis in sociology toward verification of theory, which has been linked with the growth of rigorous quantitative research, has had the unfortunate consequence of discrediting the generation of theory through flexible qualitative and quantitative research. The qualitative research is generally labelled "unsystematic," "impressionistic," or "exploratory," and the flexible quantitative research "sloppy" or "unsophisticated." These critics, in their zeal for careful verification and for a degree of accuracy they never achieve, have forgotten both the generation of theory and the need for carefully appraising the different degrees of plausibility necessary for sociology's diverse tasks.

In each chapter of this book, we have for a proposed phase of research detailed its level of credibility, plausibility, and trustworthiness; what accounts for this level; and the purposes for which its techniques are used. For instance, we have discussed the level of accuracy of data needed for generating theory. We have focused on how comparative analysis and different slices of data correct the inaccuracies of data. We have shown how integration of a theory tends to correct inaccuracies of hypothetical inference and data.[1] We have discussed at length

* We wish to thank the *American Behavioral Scientist* for permission to include in this chapter large sections of our article "Discovery of Substantive Theory," 8 (February, 1965), pp. 5-12.

1. This theme of integration into a theory as a way of confirming a fact or a proposition is extensively developed in Hans L. Zetterberg, *On Theory and Verification in Sociology* (Totowa, N.J.: Bedminster Press, 1963).

the proper way to generate a substantive or formal grounded theory that is "accurate" in fit and relevance to the area it purports to explain.

These many references to credibility enable us to controvert the frequent discrediting of the generating of grounded theory, with its associated flexible techniques and strategies of quantitative and qualitative research. This criticism stems from sociologists' taking as their guide to credibility the canons of rigorous quantitative verification on such issues as sampling, coding, reliability, validity, indicators, frequency distributions, conceptual formulation, hypothesis construction, and presentation of evidence. But in this book we have raised doubts about the applicability of these canons of rigor as proper criteria for judging the credibility of theory based on flexible research. We have suggested that criteria of judgment be based instead on the detailed elements of the actual strategies used for collecting, coding, analyzing, and presenting data when generating theory, and on the way in which people read the theory. And we have set forth some details to be used in both discovering grounded theory and judging its credibility.

In this chapter we detail more explicitly the implications of grounded theory for the issue of credibility. First, we shall give our position on the credibility of grounded theory from the point of view of the analyst who feels he has completed the generation of his theory, and now trusts it enough to convey it to others in publications. We discuss then how readers may judge his theory and how the discovery of theory is related to its further rigorous verification. Though our references are mainly to field work, many details pertain to all kinds of data used for generating theory.

Bringing the Research to a Close

The continual intermeshing of data collection and analysis has direct bearing on how the research is brought to a close. When the researcher is convinced that his conceptual framework forms a systematic theory, that it is a reasonably accurate statement of the matters studied, that it is couched in a form possible for others to use in studying a similar area, and that he can publish his results with confidence, then he is near the end of his research. He believes in his own knowledgeability and sees no reason to change that belief. He believes not because of an arbitrary judgment but because he has taken very special pains to discover what he thinks he may know, every step of the way from the beginning of his investigation until its publishable conclusion. The researcher can always try to mine his data further, but little of value is learned when core categories are already saturated (as we have pointed out in Chapter VI). The analyst also realizes that his theory as process can still be developed further, but that it is now sufficiently formulated for his current work to be closed and be published.

The theory that emerges from the researcher's collection and analysis of qualitative data is in one sense equivalent to what he *knows systematically* about his own data. Why does the researcher trust what he knows? If there is only one sociologist involved, he himself knows what he knows about what he has studied and lived through. They are his perceptions, his personal experiences, and his own hard-won analyses. A field worker knows that he knows, not only because he has been in the field and because he has carefully discovered and generated hypotheses, but also because "in his bones" he feels the worth of his final analysis. He has been living with partial analyses for many months, testing them each step of the way, until he has built his theory. What is more, if he has participated in the social life of his subject, then he has been living by his analyses, testing them not only by observation and interview but also by daily living.

By the close of his investigation, the researcher's conviction about his own theory will be hard to shake, as most field workers would attest. This conviction does not mean that his analysis is the only plausible one that could be based on his data, but only that he has high confidence in its credibility. What he has confidence in is not a scattered series of analyses, but a systematic ordering of them into an integrated theory.[2] He has, in

2. *Ibid.* It is important that one distinguish between the researcher's conviction about the credibility of his theoretical analysis and his conviction that he understands much about the perspectives and meanings of his subjects. Researchers will readily agree that their own theoretical formulations represent credible interpretations of their data, which could, however, be interpreted differently by others; but it would be hard to shake their conviction that they have correctly understood much about the perspectives and meanings of the people whom they have studied.

fact, discovered, through principally inductive effort, a substantive theory about delimited arrays of data, which he is ready to publish.

If a research team is involved, then of course their shared knowledge constitutes the final substantive theory offered to colleagues. Each member not only knows his own data and analyses intimately, but has shared his colleagues' observations and experiences during numerous discussions, "talking out," and memo-writing sessions. The inevitable debates among team members have also contributed to the development of a shared conceptual analysis.

The "real life" character of field work knowledge deserves special emphasis, because many critics think of this and other qualitatively oriented methods as being merely preliminary to "real" (scientific) knowing. But a firsthand immersion in a sphere of life and action—a social world—different from one's own yields important dividends. The field worker who has observed closely in this social world has had, in a profound sense, to live there. He has been sufficiently immersed in this world to know it, and at the same time has retained enough detachment to think theoretically about what he has seen and lived through. His informed detachment has allowed him to benefit both as a sociologist and as a human being who must "make out" in that world. This is true despite the fact that the people there generally do not expect perfect adherence to their ways from the outsider. His detachment has served also to protect him against "going native" while still passing as a native to a large extent, when the people whom he is studying either have temporarily forgotten his outsider status or have never recognized it. Meanwhile his display of understanding and sympathy for their mode of life permits sufficient trust in him so that he is not cut off from seeing important events, hearing important conversations, and perhaps seeing important documents. If that trust does not develop, his analysis suffers.[3]

The evolving systematic analysis permits a field worker quite literally to write prescriptions so that other outsiders

3. For a field work account of how tightly closed doors were finally opened after trust was established, see R. Wax, "Twelve Years Later: An Analysis of Field Experience," *American Journal of Sociology,* 63 (1957), pp. 133-42.

could get along in the observed sphere of life and action. That is one benefit of a substantive theory. If he has "made out" within the particular social world by following these prescriptions, then presumably they accurately represent the world's prominent features; they are workable guides to action and therefore their credibility can, on this account too, be accorded our confidence.[4]

In effect, this is how shrewd or thoughtful visitors to any social world feel about their knowledge of these worlds. Not infrequently people successfully stake their money, reputations, and even lives, as well as the fate of others, upon their interpretations of alien societies. What the field worker does is to make this *normal strategy* of reflective persons into a successful *research strategy*. In doing so, of course, a trained, competent researcher is much more systematic in generating his ideas than is the ordinary visitor; if he is a superior researcher, his knowledge is likely to be generalized and systematically integrated into a theory. Such bias as he brings to the field is more likely to be checked upon, while his hypotheses are more likely to arise within the field of observation than to be imported from the outside. In the latter regard, he also differs from researchers who bring such a working baggage of preconceived formal theory into the field that they end not by discovering much substantive theory but by merely writing footnotes to the imported theory. They are not likely, either, to do very well in the pragmatic test of living by their theory while in the field.

Finally, it is worth special mention that those field workers who do not really believe in their own hard-won substantive theory are tempted toward a compulsive scientism. Because they do not trust themselves—their own ability to know or reason—they rely in addition upon questionnaires or other "objective" methods of collecting and analyzing quantified data. When used for this purpose, these methods do not necessarily lead to greater credibility, but they do permit the insecure researcher to feel greater security in his "results" without really considering what specific queries do or do not need this addi-

4. The most vigorous of quantitative researchers may write a methodological article "from the heart" with no data collection or coding, because he simply knows what he knows. He has lived it and he was successful. People will believe him because they know he has been through it. In writing this article, he is merely doing field work on himself.

tional "hard" data. This insecure field worker may know that he is running away from his own ideas, because of a lack of confidence in his ability to render his knowledge credible, but he probably cannot stop running!

Conveying Credibility

When the researcher decides to write for publication, he faces the problem of conveying to colleagues and laymen the credibility of his discovered theory so that they can make some sensible judgment about it. The problem of conveying credibility is dividable into two sub-problems, each of which deserves discussion.

The first sub-problem is that of getting readers to understand the theoretical framework. This is generally done by giving an extensive abstract presentation of the overall framework and its principal associated theoretical statements, usually at the beginning and/or end of the publication and also in segments throughout it. This presentation is not particularly difficult since there exists an abstract social science terminology that is quite as applicable to qualitative as to quantitative data, as well as a common sociological perspective that furthers the communication. The presentation can also be aided by the use of emergent concepts (of the type discussed in Chapter II) that are both analytic and sensitizing.

The related second sub-problem is how to describe the data of the social world studied so vividly that the reader, like the researchers, can almost literally see and hear its people—but always in relation to the theory. The standard approach to this problem is to present data as evidence for conclusions, thus indicating how the analyst obtained the theory from his data. Since qualitative data do not lend themselves to ready summary, however, the analyst usually presents characteristic illustrations and, if also attempting provisional proofs, various accompanying crude tables. If the theory encompasses a multitude of ideas, illustrating each one is too cumbersome and too disrupting to the flow of general ideas.[5] Thus the qualitative analyst will

5. See detailed discussion on this point in Anselm L. Strauss, Leonard Schatzman, Rue Bucher, Danuta Ehrlich, and Melvin Sabshin, *Psychiatric Ideologies and Institutions* (New York: Free Press of Glencoe, 1965), Chapter 2, "Logic Technique and Strategies of Team Fieldwork," pp. 18-37.

usually present only enough material to facilitate comprehension, which is usually not enough data to use in evaluating all suggestions. So the researcher also ordinarily utilizes several of a considerable armamentarium of standard devices. He can quote directly from interviews or conversations that he has overheard. He can include dramatic segments of his on-the-spot field notes. He can quote telling phrases dropped by informants. He can summarize events or persons by constructing readable case studies. He can try his hand at describing events and acts; and often he will give at least background descriptions of places and spaces. Sometimes he will even offer accounts of personal experience to show how events impinged upon himself. Sometimes he will unroll a narrative. Chapter headings can also help to convey sights and sounds.[6]

Another way to convey credibility of the theory is to use a codified procedure for analyzing data (such as presented in Chapter V), which allows readers to understand how the analyst obtained his theory from the data. When no codified procedure is used in qualitative analyses, the transition from data to theory is difficult, if not impossible, to grasp.[7] Without this linking process in mind, the reader is likely to feel that the theory is somewhat impressionistic, even if the analyst strongly asserts he has based it on hard study of data gathered during months or years of field or library research.

Even such codified procedures, however, as a search for

6. The researcher's task of conveying credibility is actually much like that of the realistic novelist, though the latter's analytic framework—his interpretation—is generally much more implicit. Often the novelist's tactics for getting the reader to imagine social reality are more subtle, both because he may be a more skilled writer and because he may feel that he can use more license in his presentation. Sometimes, too, his descriptive task is simpler because his analytic framework is much simpler. Nonetheless, the great novelists have conveyed views of society that readers have long felt to be both complex and real (*i.e.*, credible). We say this not to pit researchers against novelists, but to point out where their respective tasks may be similar and where different.

7. Following Merton's suggestion (see Chapter V, Footnote 3) about the need for codifying actual qualitative methods, we require more descriptions of methods of transition from qualitative data to analysis. Barton and Lazarsfeld, in their delimiting of the various functions of qualitative analysis, have indicated a full range of purposes for which other methods of transition can be developed. In focusing discussion on these purposes, they hit upon what might be considered elements of possible methods. To analyze a purpose and the analytic operations involved in its final achievement is not, however, to be construed as a method of transition that guides one the full route from raw data to accomplished purpose.

negative cases or a consideration of alternative hypotheses [8] will leave a reader at a loss, since these analytic procedures are not linked specifically with the procedures for using qualitative data. Consequently, there are no guidelines specifying how and how long to search for negative cases or how to find alternative hypotheses given a specified body of qualitative data. Thus the analyst's attempt to convey his theory's credibility may still be unsuccessful because of possible bias in his search for negative cases or for reasonable alternative hypotheses. The constant comparative method, however, joins standard analytic procedures with directives for using the data systematically.

In addition, the constant comparative method's requirement of keeping track of one's ideas increases the probability that the theory will be well integrated and clear, since the analyst is forced to make theoretical sense of each comparison. Making sure the categories of the theory and their properties are meaningfully interrelated is difficult enough; keeping all the interrelations clearly delineated is an added difficulty. The integration and clarity of the theory will, however, increase the probability that colleagues will accept its credibility.

Judging Credibility

Several aspects of the presentation enter into how the reader judges the credibility of the theory. First of all, if a reader becomes sufficiently caught up in the description so that he feels vicariously that he was also in the field, then he is more likely to be kindly disposed toward the researcher's theory than if the description seems flat or unconvincing.

Second, the reader's judgment of credibility will also rest upon his assessments of how the researcher came to his conclusions. He will note, for instance, what range of events the researcher saw, whom he interviewed, who talked to him, what diverse groups he compared, what kinds of experiences he had, and how he might have appeared to various people whom he studied. That is, the reader will assess the types of data utilized

8. See Howard S. Becker and Blanche Geer, "The Analysis of Qualitative Field Data," in Richard N. Adams and Jack J. Preiss (Eds.), *Human Organization Research* (Homewood, Ill.: Dorsey Press, 1960), p. 290.

from what is explicitly stated as well as from what he can read between the lines. It is absolutely incumbent upon the reader to make such judgments, partly because the entire publication may be a complete fabrication,[9] but primarily because any analysis may require some qualification.

Multiple comparison groups make the credibility of the theory considerably greater. By precisely detailing the many similarities and differences of the various comparison groups, the analyst knows, better than if he had studied only one or a few social systems, under what sets of structural conditions his hypotheses are minimized and maximized, and hence to what kinds of social structures his theory is applicable. In increasing the scope and delimiting the generality of his theory, he saves his colleagues work. Ordinarily, readers of field work must figure out the limitations of a published study by making comparisons with their own experience and knowledge of similar groups. They can then figure that the reported material jibes just so far and no further—for given structural reasons. When multiple comparison groups are used much of this burden of delimiting relevant boundaries for the theory is taken away from the reader.[10]

Such reader qualification of the theory we may term "the discounting process." Readers surely discount aspects of many, if not most, published analyses (whether they rest upon qualitative or quantitative data).[11] This discounting takes several forms: the theory is *corrected* because of one-sided research designs,[12] *adjusted* to fit the diverse conditions of different social

9. Note for instance how gullible or unsuspecting readers can believe wholly in purposely fake accounts, such as the papers reprinted in R. Baker (Ed.), *Psychology in the Wry* (Princeton, N.J.: Van Nostrand, 1963).

10. See, for example, J. Q. Wilson's structures on D. C. Thompson's "The Negro Leadership Class," *American Sociological Review*, 28 (December, 1963), pp. 1051-52.

11. Cf. B. Berger's review of J. Coleman's quantitative study, "The Adolescent Society" (*Social Problems*, 10 [1963], pp. 394-400); also J. Q. Wilson, *op. cit.* And whether analysis is quantitative or qualitative, later generations of scholars will discount it by placing it within a larger context of public rhetoric; cf. "Appendix: A Note on Imagery in Urban Sociology," in A. Strauss, *Images of the American City* (New York: Free Press of Glencoe, 1961), pp. 255-58.

12. For instance, when we read that someone has done field work with workers in a factory, we suspect that his interpretive account (even as it pertains to the workers) needs some correction because the admin-

structures, *invalidated* for other structures through the reader's experience or knowledge, and deemed *inapplicable* to yet other kinds of structures. It is important to note that when a theory is deemed inapplicable to a social world or social structure, then it cannot be invalid for that situation. It is not correct to say that because a theory "does not fit" a structure, then it is invalid. The invalidation or adjustment of a theory is only legitimate for those social worlds or structures to which it is applicable.

This ongoing discounting process by the reader allows the researcher to write his theory in general form, because the researcher knows that the reader will make the necessary corrections, adjustments, invalidations and inapplications when thinking about or using the theory. These are qualifications that the researcher could not begin to cover for even a small percentage of one type of reader; and, more important, they are qualifications that he must learn to gloss over or to ignore in order to write a substantive theory of some generality.[13] (It is also necessary to leave out qualifications in order to write a theory that is readable, because the rhetoric of qualification can be as onerous to read as to write.)

The researcher and his readers thus share a *joint responsibility*. The researcher ought to provide sufficiently clear statements of theory and description so that readers can carefully assess the credibility of the theoretical framework he offers. A cardinal rule for the researcher is that whenever he himself feels most dubious about an important interpretation—or foresees that readers may well be dubious—then he should specify quite

---

istrators have not been similarly studied. What correction is needed may not, of course, be so evident: for instance, some sociologists have studied state mental hospitals from a perspective borrowed from psychiatry and thus interpreted their structure and functioning from a quasi-psychiatric viewpoint. The needed correction was read in by at least one set of readers, who themselves later studied a mental hospital and came to a rather different conclusion about such institutions; see R. Bucher and L. Schatzman, "The Logic of the State Mental Hospital," *Social Problems*, 9 (1962), pp. 337-49. This latter instance suggests that readers are not always merely readers, but can also be or become researchers upon topics about which they have read.

13. Consider the discussion of social laws by Ernest Nagel, *The Structure of Science* (New York: Harcourt, Brace and World, 1961), pp. 459-66.

explicitly upon what kinds of data his interpretation rests. The parallel rule for readers is that they should demand explicitness about important interpretations, but if the researcher has not supplied the information then they should assess his interpretations from whatever indirect evidence may be available. These same rules apply to the reading of qualitative materials from libraries and organizational archives, as well as to the writing of those materials.

The Issue of Further Rigor

The presentation of grounded theory, developed through analysis of qualitative data, is often sufficiently plausible to satisfy most readers. The theory can be applied and adjusted to many situations with sufficient exactitude to guide their thinking, understanding and research. Given certain structural conditions under which sociologists work (such as designing specific action programs, or working in rather well-developed substantive areas), more rigorous testing may be required to raise the level of plausibility of some hypotheses.

Under these conditions, it should be a matter of empirical determination as to how the further testing can best be accomplished—whether through more rigorous or extensive field work, or through experiments or survey methods. The two essential points in this decision on method are, first, that the testing be more rigorous than previously (though not necessarily by the most rigorous method); and, second, that the more rigorous approach be compatible with the research situation in order to yield the most reliable findings. What should not enter into the determination of further testing are the researcher's ideological commitments (with associated career contingencies) to only one method; for instance, that a survey is a more rigorous mode of achieving a high degree of plausibility than field observation, and therefore the best and only mode to use in all cases. In the actual research situation, a survey may not be feasible nor worth the time or money, nor yield the type of information needed; it may even distort the information yielded. An approach to a necessarily higher level of plausibility should be based, therefore, on using the method or methods best suited to the socially structured necessities of the research situation.

This cardinal rule for determining which method to use for increasing the plausibility of theory is broken in another way by researchers who are ideologically committed to quantitative methods. They assume, out of context, that all research requires a rigorously achieved high level of plausibility; and that quantitative research, more rigorous than most qualitative methods, is therefore the *best* method to use in *all* research situations.[14] Thus, whatever qualitative research has been done is seen merely as a preliminary providing of categories to use in the ensuing quantitative research. As noted at the beginning of our book, this position neglects both the importance of discovering substantive theory based on qualitative research, and the fact that this substantive theory is more often than not the end product of research within the substantive area beyond which few, if any, research sociologists are motivated to move. Also, this view of the research as merely "preliminary," an attitude essentially focused on verification, inhibits the generation of theory.[15]

There are several reasons why substantive theory discovered through qualitative analysis is often the end product of research. First, those researchers who do try to move beyond substantive theory by testing it with quantitative data are often told by colleagues and editorial boards that they are simply proving what everyone knows sufficiently well already. They may be told that their quantitative work will be trivial and a waste of resources.[16] To "save" their work, they are

14. See Peter Blau's doctrinaire statement on this in Philip Hammond (Ed.), *Sociologists at Work* (New York: Basic Books, 1964), pp. 20-21. See also a fuller discussion of this position in our Epilogue.

15. Cf. Edward Shils, "On the Comparative Study of New States," in Clifford Geertz (Ed.), *Old Societies and New States* (New York: Free Press of Glencoe, 1963), p. 11.

16. For a few (or many) diverse comments of concern about the trivial results of "precise" quantitative research, see: on their laboring of the obvious, R. K. Merton, "Problem Finding in Sociology," in R. K. Merton, L. Broom and L. S. Cottrell, Jr. (Eds.), *Sociology Today* (New York: Basic Books, 1959), IV-I; on their uselessness for theory construction, H. L. Zetterberg, *On Theory and Verification in Sociology* (Totowa, N.J.: Bedminster Press, 1963), Preface, pp. 36, 52, and 67; and on their worth in verifying what is already known, A. Etzioni, "Book Review," *American Journal of Sociology*, LXVII (January, 1962), p. 466.

forced to turn their quantitative work of testing the "already known" hypothesis into an effort to discover new substantive fact and theory in their data. In sum, quantitative data are often used not for rigorous demonstration of theory but as another way to discover more theory; [17] and qualitative data often result in a *de facto* conclusive analysis rather than a preliminary one.

Second, it is an old story in social science that once an interest in certain phenomena is saturated with substantive theory, attention switches to something else. This switch usually occurs long before satisfactory quantitative research on the phenomena has taken place. Meanwhile, informed laymen and social scientists manage to profit quite well from the merely plausible work of discovery published by sociologists who carefully analyze their qualitative data, and so the need for future highly rigorous research is forestalled.[18] Since the theory works well enough, it is typically only modified, if even that, and not even by further demonstrative research on a specific hypothesis but only by additional related theory. The researcher's primary effort in working with this related theory is to discover new theory, not to correct or test older theory. Once new theory is discovered and developed, any modification of older theory that then occurs will receive post hoc recognition.

Third, and most important, a great deal of sociological work, unlike research in physical science, never gets to the stage of rigorous demonstration because the social structures being studied are undergoing continuous change. Older structures frequently take on new dimensions before highly rigorous research can be accomplished. The changing of social structures means that a prime sociological task is the exploration—and sometimes the discovery—of emerging structures. Undue emphasis on being "scientific" is simply not reasonable in light of our need for discovery and exploration amid very considerable structural changes.

---

17. See Lipset's discussion of how he started to test but then turned to generate more theory, in Hammond, *op. cit.*, pp. 107-20.

18. "While we cannot count on very many research workers being stimulated to conduct crucial tests of middle-range theories, they are likely to be especially stimulated by the concepts that enter into such theories." H. Hyman, "Reflections on the Relations Between Theory and Research," *The Centennial Review*, 7 (Fall, 1963), p. 449.

X

Applying Grounded Theory

In this chapter we shall discuss how grounded theory has been developed in order to facilitate its application in daily situations by sociologists and laymen. The practical application of grounded sociological theory, whether substantive or formal, requires developing a theory with (at least) four highly inter-related properties. The first requisite property is that the theory must closely *fit* the substantive area in which it will be used. Second, it must be readily *understandable* by laymen con-cerned with this area. Third, it must be sufficiently *general* to be applicable to a multitude of diverse daily situations within the substantive area, not to just a specific type of situation. Fourth, it must allow the user partial *control* over the structure and process of daily situations as they change through time. We shall discuss each of these closely related properties and briefly illustrate them from our book *Awareness of Dying*, to show how grounded theory incorporates them, and therefore why and how the theory can be used in practice.[1]

1. This chapter is reprinted with only minor changes from Chapter 14 of that book: Barney G. Glaser and Anselm Strauss, *Awareness of Dying* (Chicago: Aldine Publishing Co., 1965).
Applied theory can be powerful for exactly the reasons set forth by John Dewey, some years ago: "What is sometimes termed 'applied' science . . . is directly concerned with . . . instrumentalities at work in effecting modifications of existence in behalf of conclusions that are reflectively preferred. . . . 'Application' is a hard word for many to accept. It suggests some extraneous tool ready-made and complete which is then put to uses that are external to its nature. But . . . application of 'science' means appli-cation *in*, not application *to*. Application *in* something signifies a more extensive interaction of natural events with one another, an elimination of

Fitness

That the theory must fit the substantive area to which it will be applied is the underlying basis of a grounded theory's four requisite properties. It may seem an obvious requirement that a grounded theory, particularly a substantive theory, must correspond closely to the data if it is to be applied in daily situations. But actually, as we have discussed throughout this book, there are many pitfalls in the current ways of developing sociological theory that may preclude a good fit.[2] A sociologist often develops a theory that embodies, without his realizing it, his own ideals and the values of his occupation and social class, as well as popular views and myths, along with his deliberate efforts at making logical deductions from some formal theory to which he became committed as a graduate student (for example, a formal theory of organizations, stratification, communication, authority, learning, or deviant behavior). These witting and unwitting strategies typically result in theories so divorced from the everyday realities of substantive areas that one does not quite know how to apply them, at what part of the social structure to begin applying them, where they fit the data of the substantive area, or what the propositions mean in relation to the diverse problems of the area.

Deducing practical applications from formal theory rests on the assumption that the theory supplies concepts and hy-

---

distance and obstacles; provision of opportunities for interactions that reveal potentialities previously hidden and that bring into existence new histories with new initiations and endings. Engineering, medicine, social arts realize relationships that were unrealized in actual existence. Surely in their new context the latter are understood or known as they are not in isolation." *Experience and Nature* (Chicago: Open Court Publishing Company, 1925), pp. 161-162.

2. For many years, Herbert Blumer has remarked in his classes that sociologists perennially import theories from other disciplines that do not fit the data of sociology and inappropriately apply sociological theories developed from the study of data different from that under consideration. Cf. "The Problem of the Concept in Social Psychology," *American Journal of Sociology* (March, 1940), pp. 707-719. For an analysis of how current sociological methods by their very nature often result in data and theory that do not fit the realities of the situation, see Aaron V. Cicourel, *Method and Measurement in Sociology* (New York: Free Press of Glencoe, 1964).

potheses that fit. When the theory does not fit well, the consequences are a typical forcing and distorting of data to fit the categories of the deduced applications, and the neglecting of relevant data that seemingly do not fit or cannot be forced into the pre-existing sociological categories.[3] In light of the paucity of sociological theories that deal explicitly with change,[4] deduction of possible applications usually is carried out upon static, often logico-deductive, theories. This deduction tends to ensure neglect, distortion, and forcing when the theory is applied to an ever-changing, everyday reality.

Clearly, a grounded theory that is faithful to the everyday realities of a substantive area is one that has been carefully *induced* from diverse data, as we have described the process. Only in this way will the theory be closely related to the daily realities (what is actually going on) of substantive areas, and so be highly applicable to dealing with them.[5]

Understanding

A grounded substantive theory that corresponds closely to the realities of an area will make sense and be understandable to the people working in the substantive area. This understanding can be crucial since it is these people who will wish either to apply the theory themselves or to employ a sociologist to

3. Our position may be contrasted with that of Hans L. Zetterberg who, after some exploratory research to determine problems, bypasses development of substantive theory and goes directly to formal theories for help. He says, "We must know the day-by-day issues facing the practitioner and then search the storehouse of academic knowledge to see whether it might aid him." *Social Theory and Social Practice* (Totowa, N.J.: Bedminster Press, 1962), p. 41.

4. This is noted by Wilbert Moore in "Predicting Discontinuities in Social Change," *American Sociological Review* (June, 1964), p. 332; and in *Social Change* (Englewood Cliffs, N.J.: Prentice-Hall, 1963), Preface and Chapter I.

5. Thus, in contrast to Zetterberg whose applied social theory means rendering his data directly with a formal theory, we first develop a substantive theory from the data; it then becomes a bridge to the use of whatever formal theories may be helpful. By bridging the relation of data to formal theory with a carefully thought-out substantive theory, the forcing, distorting and neglecting of data by a formal, usually "thought-up" theory is prevented in large measure. See Zetterberg, *op. cit.*, Chapter 4, particularly pp. 166-78.

apply it.[6] Their understanding the theory tends to engender a readiness to use it, for it sharpens their sensitivity to the problems that they face and gives them an image of how they can potentially make matters better, through either their own efforts or those of a sociologist.[7] If they wish to apply the theory themselves, they must perceive how it can be readily mastered and used. It is more difficult for laymen in a particular area to understand a formal theory, because of its abstractness and presumed general applicability. It will have to be explained for them to understand its usefulness, and chances are they will not be able to apply it themselves.

In developing our grounded, substantive theory on awareness of dying, we carefully developed concepts and hypotheses to facilitate the understanding of the theory by medical and nursing personnel. This, in turn, ensured the close correspondence of our theory to the realities of terminal care. Our emergent concepts are both analytic and sensitizing, and these two features have enabled medical and nursing personnel to grasp the theory in terms of their own experiences. For example, our categories of "death expectations," "nothing more to

6. In contrast, both Zetterberg and Gouldner imply by their direct use of formal theory that the practical use of sociological theory is the *monopoly* of the sociologist as consultant, since, of course, these formal theories are difficult enough to understand by sociologists. See Zetterberg, *op. cit.*, and Alvin W. Gouldner, "Theoretical Requirements of the Applied Social Sciences," *American Sociological Review*, 22 (February, 1959). Applying substantive theory, which is easier to understand, means also that more sociologists can be applied social theorists than those few who have clearly mastered difficult formal theories to be "competent practitioners of them." (Zetterberg, *op. cit.*, p. 18.)

Another substantive theory dealing with juvenile delinquency, in David Matza, *Delinquency and Drift* (New York: John Wiley and Sons, 1964), provides a good example of our point. This is a theory that deals with "what is going on" in the situations of delinquency. It is *not* another rendition of the standard, formally derived, substantive theories on delinquency that deal intensively with classic ideas on relations between culture and subsubculture, conformity, opportunity structures, and social stratification problems, such as are provided in the formal theories of Merton and Parsons and in writings by Albert Cohen, Richard Cloward, and Lloyd Ohlin. After reading Matza's book, two probation officers of Alameda County, California, told us that at last they had read a sociological theory that deals with "what is going on" and "makes sense" and that they can apply in their work.

7. See Rensis Likert and Ronald Lippit, "The Utilization of Social Science," in Leon Festinger and Daniel Katz (Eds.), *Research Methods in the Behavioral Sciences* (New York: Dryden Press, 1953), p. 583.

do," "lingering," and "social loss" designate general properties of dying patients that unquestionably are vividly sensitizing or meaningful to hospital personnel; at the same time, they are abstract enough to designate properties of concrete entities, not entities themselves.[8] Further, these concepts provide a necessary bridge between the theoretical thinking of sociologists and the practical thinking of people concerned with the substantive area, so that both may understand and apply the theory. The sociologist finds that he has "a feeling for" the everyday realities of the situation, while the person in the situation finds he can master and manage the theory.

In particular, these concepts allow this person to pose and test his own favored hypotheses in his initial applications of the theory.[9] Whether the hypotheses are proved somewhat right or wrong, the answers are related to the substantive theory, which helps both in the interpretation of hypotheses and in the development of new applications of the theory. For example, as physicians (and social scientists) test out whether or not disclosure of terminality is advisable under specified conditions, the answers will be interpretable in terms of our theory of awareness contexts and of the general response that follows disclosure.[10] This, in turn, will direct these people to further useful questions, as well as leading to suggestions for changing many situations of terminal care.

In utilizing these types of concepts in our book *Awareness of Dying,* we anticipated that readers would almost be able to see and hear the people involved in terminal situations—but to see and hear them in relation to our theoretical framework. From this kind of understanding it is only a short step to applying our theory to the practical problems that both staff and patients encounter in a situation where a patient is dying. For instance, a general understanding of what is entailed in the "mutual pretense" context, including consequences that may be

8. On sensitizing concepts, see Herbert Blumer, "What is Wrong with Social Theory," *American Sociological Review,* 19 (February, 1954), pp. 3-10. Zetterberg has made this effort in choosing concepts with much success, *op. cit.,* p. 49 and *passim.*

9. Gouldner (*op. cit.,* pp. 94-95) considers in detail the importance of testing the favored hypotheses of men who are in the situation. However, we suggest that the person can test his own hypotheses too, whereas Gouldner wishes to have a sociologist do the testing.

10. Glaser and Strauss, *op. cit.,* Chapters 3, 6 and 8.

judged negative to nursing and medical care, might lead a staff to abandon their otherwise unwitting imposition of mutual pretense upon a patient. Similarly, the understanding yielded by a close reading of our chapters on family reactions ·in "closed" and "open" awareness contexts could greatly aid a staff member's future management of—and his compassion for —those family reactions. A good grasp of our theory also can help hospital personnel to understand the characteristic problems faced on particular kinds of hospital services, including their own, as well as the typical kinds of solutions attempted by the personnel.

Generality

In deciding upon the conceptual level of his categories, the sociologist generating theory should be guided by the criteria that the categories should not be so abstract as to lose their sensitizing aspect, but yet must be abstract enough to make his theory a general guide to multi-conditional, ever-changing daily situations. Through the level of generality of his concepts he tries to make the theory flexible enough to make a wide variety of changing situations understandable, and also flexible enough to be readily reformulated, virtually on the spot, when it does not work in application. The person who applies the theory will, we believe, be able to bend, adjust or quickly reformulate a grounded theory when applying it, as he tries to keep up with and manage the situational realities that he wishes to improve. For example, nurses will be better able to cope with family and patients during sudden transitions from a closed context to one of pretense or open awareness if they try to apply elements of our awareness theory, continually adjusting the theory in application.[11] The person who applies theory becomes, in effect, a generator of theory, and in this instance the theory is clearly seen as *process:* an ever-developing entity.

The sociologist should also be concerned with the theory's being general enough to be applicable to the whole picture. Because of the changing conditions of everyday situations,

11. Glaser and Strauss, *op. cit.*, Chapters 3, 8 and 9.

it is not necessary to use rigorous research to discover precise, quantitatively validated, factual knowledge upon which to base the theory. "Facts" change quickly, and precise quantitative approaches (even large-scale surveys) typically yield too few general concepts, and relations between concepts, to be of broad practical use in coping with the complex interplay of forces characteristic of a substantive area. A person who employs quantitatively derived theory "knows his few variables better than anyone, but these variables are only part of the picture." [12] Theory of this natue will also tend to give the user the idea that since the facts are "correct," so is the theory; thus hindering the continual adjustment and reformulation of theory that are necessitated by the realities of practice.

Because he is severely liimted in meeting the varied conditions and situations typical of the total picture, the person who applies a quantitatively derived theory frequently finds himself either guideless or trying to apply the inapplicable—with potentially unfortunate human and organizational consequences. This kind of theory typically does not account for enough variation in situations to allow appreciable institution and control of change in them. Also, such theory usually does not offer sufficient means for predicting the diverse consequences of any purposeful action on other aspects of the substantive area, which one does not wish to change but which will surely be affected by the action. Whoever applies this kind of theory is often just "another voice to be listened to before the decision is reached or announced" by those who do comprehend the total picture.[13]

Accordingly, to achieve a theory general enough to be applicable to the total picture, it is more important to accumulate a vast number of *diverse* qualitative "facts" on many different situations in the area. This diversity facilitates the development of a theory with both a sufficient number of general concepts relevant to most situations and plausible relations among these categories to account for much everyday behavior in the situations. These relations among categories are continually subject to qualification and to being changed in direction and magnitude by new conditions. The by-product of

12. Zetterberg, *op. cit.*, p. 157.
13. *Ibid.*

such changes, occasioned by the application of grounded theory, is a correction of inaccuracies in observation, and reintegration of the correction into the theory. The application is thus, in one sense, the theory's further test and validation. Indeed, field workers use application as a prime strategy for testing emerging hypotheses, though they are not acting as practitioners in a substantive area. In the next section, by illustrating how a grounded substantive theory guides one through the multi-faceted problem of disclosure of terminal illness, we shall indicate how one can apply a sufficiently general theory to the total picture.

Our method of discovering a sufficiently general substantive theory based on a multitude of diverse facts—and then seeing this theory as being in a continual process of reformulation and development as it is applied—tends to resolve the two problems confronting the social scientist consultant, who, according to Zetterberg, is both (1) "dependent on what is found in the tradition of a science," and (2) apt to "proceed on guess work" when tradition fails, so as not to "lose respect and future assignments." [14] Our method resolves these problems in large measure because its generality of scope and conceptual level are not limited by the dictum that Zetterberg's consultant must follow: "Only those details were assembled by the consultant and his co-workers that could be fitted into the categories of sociology, i.e., phrased in sociological terminology." [15] We do not believe that "only" the "categories of sociology" can be directly applied to a substantive area initially without great neglect, forcing, and distortion of everyday realities. A substantive theory for the area must first be *induced* with its own general concepts, or else a grounded substantive or formal theory that fits the area for application must be found. Then the concepts of these theories become a bridge to more formal sociological categories (if they deal adequately with change).

14. *Ibid.*, pp. 188-89.
15. *Ibid.*, p. 139. This dictum is based on the idea: "The crucial act here is to deduce a solution to a problem from a set of theoretical principles." Theoretical principles refer to laws of formal theories.

Control

The substantive theory must enable the person who uses it to have enough control in everyday situations to make its application worth trying. The control we have in mind has various aspects. The person who applies the theory must be enabled to understand and analyze ongoing situational realities, to produce and predict change in them, and to predict and control consequences both for the object of change and for other parts of the total situation that will be affected. As changes occur, his theory must allow him to be flexible in revising his tactics of application and in revising the theory itself if necessary. To give this kind of control, the theory must provide a sufficient number of general concepts and their plausible interrelations; and these concepts must provide the practitioner with understanding, with situational controls, and with access to the situation in order to exert the controls. The crux of controllability is the production and control of change through "controllable" variables and "access" variables. We shall not consider here the ethical problems involved in controlling situations. However, we must emphasize that this discussion concerns only the partial, beneficial, shifting, often benign controls that people already engage in without theoretical guides—*e.g.,* the nurse controlling her patient's care. We are not referring to a proposed, absolute, diabolic control over man.

Controllable variables. A theory with controllable concepts of sufficient generality, that fits and is understandable, gives anyone who wishes to apply these concepts to bring about change a *controllable theoretical foothold* in diverse situations. The controllability of a conceptual variable is enhanced by its being part of a theory that guides its use under most conditions that the user is likely to encounter. The theoretical use of a controllable concept may be contrasted with the unguided, ad hoc use of an isolated concept, and also with the use of abstract formal categories that are too tenuously related to the actual situation.[16]

16. At a lower level of generality, in much consulting done by sociologists for industrial firms, hospitals, social agencies, and the like, what is usually offered is "understanding," based upon an amalgam of facts given

For example, the prime controllable variable of our study of dying in hospitals was "awareness context"—the total situation of who knows what about the patient's dying. Doctors and nurses have much control over the creation, maintenance and changes of various types of awareness contexts. Thus they also have much control over the resultant characteristic forms of inter- action, and the consequences for all people involved in the dying situation. Also, we specified the interactional modes that are highly controllable variables; doctors and nurses deliberately engage in many interactional tactics and strategies.

If a doctor contemplates disclosure of terminal illness to a patient, by using our theory he may anticipate a very wide range of plausibly expected changes and consequences for him- self, the patient, family members and nurses. By using the theory developed on disclosure of terminal illness, he may judge how far and in what direction the patient's responses are likely to go, and how he can control them. By using the theory on closed awareness contexts, he may judge what consequences for himself, nurses and patients will occur when the context is kept closed; and by referring to the theory on open awareness contexts, he may weigh these against the consequences that occur when the context is opened. Also, he may judge how advisable it is to allow the characteristic modes of interaction that result from each type of awareness context to continue or be changed.

From these parts of our theory on awareness of dying he also may develop a wider variety of interactional tactics than ordinarily would be in his personal repertoire. If maintaining a closed awareness context will result in the nurse's managing the patient's assessments of his condition too greatly (an interac- tional mode), thereby possibly decreasing the patient's trust in

---

intuitively by references to formal theory and some loosely integrated substantive theory developed through contact with a given substantive area over the years. (Sometimes this is abetted, as in consumer research, by relatively primitive but useful analyses of data gathered for specific pur- poses of consultation.) Providing that the amalgam "makes sense" to the client and that he can see how to use it, then the consultation is worth- while. Conversely, no matter how useful the sociologist may think his offering is, if the client cannot see it, he will not find the consultation very useful. See also Zetterberg, *op. cit.*, Chapter 2.

the whole staff when he discovers his illness is terminal, it may be better to change the context to allow the nurse to respond more honestly. The doctor may also review our chapters on the family's awareness for judging to what degree opening the context by disclosure will lead to problems in controlling family members, and how the disclosure may affect their preparations for death. The entire book deals with the effect of disclosure on the doctor's relationship with nurses.

Resting the decision about disclosure upon our theory allows the doctor much flexibility and scope of action, precisely because we have provided many general concepts and their probable interrelations closely linked to the reality of disclosure, in order to guide him in considering the many additional situations, besides just dealing with the patient, that will be affected. Simply to disclose the imminence of death in the hope that the patient will be able to prepare himself for it is just as unguided and ad hoc as to not to disclose because he may commit suicide. Or to disclose because the patient must learn (according to formal theory) "to take the role of a terminal patient" is too abstract a notion for coping with the realities of the impact of disclosure on everyone concerned.

This example brings out several other properties of controllable variables, and thus further indicates why grounded theory is suited to practical applications. First, the theory must provide controllable variables with *much explanatory power:* they must "make a big difference" in what is going on in the situation that is to be changed. We discovered one such variable for dying situations—awareness contexts. As we have reiterated in *Awareness of Dying,* much of what happens in the dying situation is strongly determined by the type of awareness context that prevails.

Second, doctors and nurses, family and patients are already purposefully controlling many variables delineated in our substantive theory. While the doctor exerts the most control over the awareness context, all these people have tactics that they use to change or maintain a particular awareness context. The patient, for example, is often responsible for initiating the pretense context. Still, all these people, in our observation, control variables for very limited, ad hoc purposes. Grounded substantive theory, therefore, can give participants in a situation a broader guide to what they already tend to do, and perhaps help them to be more effective in doing it.

Controllable variables sometimes entail controlling only one's own behavior and sometimes primarily the behavior of others— the more difficult of the two. But control usually involves the efforts of two parties; that is, *control of the interaction* between two people by one or both of them. When a patient is dying, it is not uncommon to see patient, family, doctor and nurse all trying to control each other for their own purposes. Those who avail themselves of our theory might have a better chance in the tug-of-war about who shall best control the situation.

Objects and physical spaces are of strategic importance as variables that help to control situations and people's behavior.[17] We noted how in the hospital doctors and nurses use spatial arrangements of rooms, doors, glass walls and screens to achieve control over awareness contexts. By making such controllable variables part of our theory we have given a broader guide to the staff's purposeful use of them. For instance, to let a family through a door or behind a screen may be more advisable than yielding to the momentary urge of shutting them out to prevent a scene. Letting family members come in may aid their preparations for death, which in turn may result in a more composed family over the long run of the dying situation.

Access variables. A grounded theory to be used in practice must also include access variables. These are social structural variables that allow, guide, and give persons access either to the controllable variables or to the people who control them. To use a controllable variable one must have a means of access to it. For example, professional rules give the doctor principal control over awareness; therefore the nurse ordinarily has a great deal of control in dying situations because of her considerable access to the doctor, through or from whom she may try to exert contol over the awareness context. Professional rules, though, forbid her to change the context on her own initiative; they require her to maintain the current one.

Thus the organizational structure of the hospital, the medical

17. Elements of "material culture" should not be neglected in development of substantive theory. Gouldner suggests that they are the "forgotten man of social research" (*op. cit.*, p. 97).

profession, and the ward provide both doctors and nurses with different degrees of access to control of awareness contexts. Our theory of awareness contexts delineates this matter. Family members have more access to a private physician than to a hospital physician; thus they may have more control over the former. They can demand, for instance, that their private physician keep a closed awareness context because of the control they exert over him through the lay referral system (upon which he may depend for much of his practice).[18] In a closed context the patient has little access to a doctor in order to control changes of context. However, like the nurse, he has much access to everyday cues concerning his condition—they exist all around him and he learns to read them better and better. Thus, his access to strategic cues gives him an opportunity to control his situation—and we have discussed at length in our book how he can manage cues to gain control.

Access variables also indicate how best to enter a situation in order to manage a controllable variable while not otherwise unduly disrupting the situation. As an example, we delineated the various alternatives that a nurse can use to gain control over the "nothing more to do" situation in order to let a patient die.

Conclusion

In generating a grounded theory, particularly a substantive one, the researcher can increase its potential for practical applications by including controllable and access variables if they do not emerge by themselves. Grounded theory, generated in the way we have suggested, will fit, be general enough, and be understandable. One property of an applied grounded theory must be clearly understood: The theory can be developed only by professionally trained sociologists, but can be applied by either laymen or sociologists. Further, as John Dewey has clarified for us, grounded theory is applicable *in* situations as well as *to* them. Thus people in situations for which a grounded theory has been generated can apply it in the natural course of daily events.

18. On the lay referral system, see Eliot Freidson, *Patients' Views of Medical Practice* (New York: Russell Sage Foundation, 1961), Part Two.

We feel, as many sociologists do and as Elbridge Sibley has written, that "The popular notion that any educated man is capable of being his own sociologist will not be exorcised by proclamation; it can only be gradually dispelled by the visible accomplishments of professionally competent sociologists." [19] By attempting to develop theory that can also be applied, we hope to contribute to the accomplishments of both sociological theory and practice. Social theory, as John Dewey remarked thirty years ago, is thereby enriched and linked closely with the pursuit and studied control of practical matters.[20]

19. *The Education of Sociologists in the United States* (New York: Russell Sage Foundation, 1963), p. 19.

20. See "Social Science and Social Control" in Joseph Ratner (Ed.), *Intelligence in the Modern World, John Dewey's Philosophy* (New York: Modern Library, 1939), pp. 949-954.

XI

Insight and Theory Development

In this concluding chapter, we shall address ourselves briefly to a crucial issue: what is the relation of insight to theorizing from data? The discussion will center on the researcher as a highly sensitized and systematic agent. Those adjectives can be translated as follows: the researcher has insights, and he can make the most of them (as we have argued) through systematic comparative analyses.

Insight as a Source of Theory

The root sources of all significant theorizing is the sensitive insights of the observer himself. As everyone knows, these can come in the morning or at night, suddenly or with slow dawning, while at work or at play (even when asleep); furthermore, they can be derived directly from theory (one's own or someone else's) or occur without theory; and they can strike the observer while he is watching himself react as well as when he is observing others in action. Also, his insights may appear just as fruitfully near the end of a long inquiry as near the outset.[1] This

1. For excellent discussions of insight in relation to creative work, see Eliot D. Hutchinson, "The Period of Frustration in Creative Endeavor," *Psychiatry*, 3 (1940), pp. 351-59; "The Nature of Insight," *Psychiatry*, 4 (1941), pp. 31-43; and "The Period of Elaboration in Creative Endeavor," *Psychiatry*, 5 (1942), pp. 165-76. For an extensive bibliography and summaries of literature relevant to "insight," see Morris Stein and Shirley Heinze, *Creativity and the Individual* (Glencoe, Ill.: Free Press, 1960).

summation of the obvious has some methodological corollaries that are worth exploring.

The first corollary is that the researcher can get—and culti-vate—crucial insights not only during his research (and from his research) but from his own personal experiences prior to or outside it. To illustrate this point, we shall tell a story:

Recently a group of sociologists was discussing a colleague's article, "The Cabdriver and His Fare: Facets of a Fleeting Relationship." [2] This paper was based on the actual experience of the author, who had driven a cab while in graduate school. One sociologist asked whether field notes had been taken during his work as a cabbie; if not, he implied, then the article was really not based on field work—which is, after all, an intention-ally systematic enterprise. The author explained that he had taken virtually no field notes, and indeed had gotten his prin-cipal guiding ideas for the paper long after giving up the job. He admitted that the paper was not based on field work as such, but asserted that his experiences nevertheless seemed akin to field work data.

Our point is that his principal insights were based on his personal experience as a cabbie. Some insights that formed the basis of his later systematic theorizing undoubtedly occurred while he was still a cabdriver, and others—perhaps the major ones—occurred later when he reviewed his earlier experiences. The moral of the story is that one should deliberately cultivate such reflections on personal experiences. Generally we suppress them, or give them the status of mere opinions (for example, opinions about what is true of fraternities, having belonged to one before becoming a sociologist), rather than looking at them as springboards to systematic theorizing.

A related corollary is that such insights need not come from one's own experience but can be taken from others.[3] In this case the burden is on the sociologist to convert these borrowed experiences into his own insights. The validity of this point is easy to grasp if one thinks of an interviewer beginning to theo-

2. Fred Davis, *American Journal of Sociology*, 65 (1959), pp. 158-65.
3. Many years ago, Florian Znaniecki cogently advocated using personal experience and others' experiences as sociological data, but his focus was .principally on the validity of data; that is, on the verification function of experiences. See his *The Method of Sociology* (New York: Farrar and Rinehart, 1934), pp. 157-67 and 186-98.

rize on the basis of an insight gotten from an interviewee's words. The anthropologist also does this when he listens to informants. If we can do this with an interviewee or an informant, why not with the author of an autobiography or a novel? What is more, the insider (interviewee, informant, novelist) may not give us the insight unwittingly; he may offer it intentionally, fully aware that he is doing so. If the researcher accepts that offer at face value, there is no sound methodological reason why he cannot begin to build, or further build, theory upon it.

A third corollary pertains to how fruitful insights can be gotten from existing theory. As we have frequently remarked, researchers often stifle potential insights by virtue of too strict adherence to existing theory, particularly "grand" theory. Nevertheless, no sociologist can possibly erase from his mind all the theory he knows before he begins his research. Indeed the trick is to line up what one takes as theoretically possible or probable with what one is finding in the field. Such existing sources of insights are to be cultivated, though not at the expense of insights generated by the qualitative research, which are still closer to the data. A combination of both is definitely desirable (see Chapter III).

Some men seem to handle the precarious balance between the two sources by avoiding the reading of much that relates to the relevant area until after they return from the field; they do this so as not to interfere with personal insights. On the other hand, some read extensively beforehand. Others periodically return to one or the other source for stimulation. There is no ready formula, of course: one can only experiment to find which style of work gives the best results. Not to experiment toward this end, but carefully to cover "all" the literature before commencing research, increases the probability of brutally destroying one's potentialities as a theorist.

Because new insights can appear late in the inquiry, a final, corollary is that important new insights should be cultivated until the inquiry's conclusion. But they should be cultivated *within* the framework of the developing theory by joint theoretical sampling and analysis. Late insights should be fostered deliberately, for they can enrich the theory by forcing elaboration and qualification. (Wholesale qualification is impossible now, providing the theory is soundly grounded.) One example, referred to earlier, will do: late in the study of the terminal care of patients, deliberate visits to foreign hospitals were made, not to check the theory but to force further qualification and elaboration of it.

Development of Theory from Insights

An insight, whether borrowed or original, is of no use to the theorist unless he converts it from being simply an anecdote to being an element of theory. This, of course, is part of his sociological enterprise; his job (as discussed in Chapters III and V on theoretical sampling and analysis) is to transform insights into relevant categories, properties, and hypotheses. He does so by employing all the usual strategies for developing theory. Yet a few implications of that obvious point should be noted.

The first implication, or corollary, is especially important because many sociologists do not recognize its existence: that is, insights cannot be fruitfully developed, and are even unlikely to occur, unless the theorist goes beyond public discussion about any given area. In addition to the principal corrective of comparative analysis, there are at least two other strategies by which he can do this. The most intuitive is to sense that a given statement about the area under study—whether made by participants or by scholars—is simply part of an ongoing public discussion. For instance, a sociologist may sense, or even charge, that another's views of poverty, delinquency or social mobility represent current ideology rather than actuality—or at least are vitiated by his limited social perspective.[4]

A more systematic method (one to be recommended heartily) is that the researcher regard all statements about events pertaining to the area under study as being data. This means that the statements and writings of colleagues are data as much as those of laymen. Sociologists also must be considered as part of the social structure; and a developing theory must therefore take them and their statements into account as a slice of data.

4. See, for example, Marshall Clinard (Ed.), *Anomie and Deviant Behavior* (New York: Free Press of Glencoe, 1964).

Unless such steps are taken, one's insights will only be elaborated into variations on the public discussion, as in past and present writings in so many areas (urban sociology, delinquency, mental health, social mobility).[5]

A related corollary pertains specifically to existing theory. Not only must this theory be subjected to the procedures suggested above, but the theorist should also develop comparatively the implications of his personal insights regarding it. That comparison may mean initially pitting one's insight against a well-respected theory. For instance, in *Boys in White,* Howard Becker and his coauthors pitted their initial insights about students in general, and medical students in particular, against Robert Merton's well established theory of medical students' socialization.[6]

Any contest between insights and existing theory becomes a comparative analysis that delimits the boundaries of the existing theory while generating a more general one. Thus a few days spent in observing a mental hospital was sufficient to counteract Goffman's "total institutions" view of mental hospitals and the careers of mental patients; and to set up initial theorizing that took his theory into account rather than merely negating it or ignoring it.[7] A too-frequent practice in sociology, however, is to accept the existing theory and simply elaborate on it, thus suppressing or ignoring much rich data as well as potentially rich insights that could *transcend* the theory. An instructive example is *Women's Prison;* the authors have simplistically assumed that since the theory about prisons is based on men's institutions, a study of a women's prison will both qualify the theory—by pointing up differences between men's and women's prisons—and support the theory by underlining similarities between the prisons.[8] They do not, however, under-

5. Cf. A Strauss, *Images of the American City* (New York: Free Press of Glencoe, 1961), Appendix.

6. H. Becker *et al., Boys in White* (Chicago: University of Chicago Press, 1961); and Robert Merton, George Reader, and Patricia Kendall (Eds.), *The Student Physician* (Cambridge: Harvard University Press, 1957).

7. A. Strauss *et al., Psychiatric Ideologies and Institutions* (New York: Free Press of Glencoe, 1964).

8. David A. Ward and Gene G. Kassebaum, *Women's Prison* (Chicago: Aldine Publishing Co., 1965).

stand that such a comparison limits them to generating theory within the framework of existing theory, nor do they recognize that more effective comparative analyses would permit them to transcend it.

A third corollary is that the ambitious theorist should not only cultivate insights until his inquiry's close, he must actively exploit their implications. Two examples from the inquiry reported in *Psychiatric Ideologies and Institutions* will emphasize this point.

Almost from the first, the researchers focused on the lay personnel working either under professional command (as in private hospitals) or relatively autonomously (as in state hospitals). Differences of perspective between laymen and professionals were assumed and discovered early. But not until relatively late did an insight suggest that even when nursing aides were in contact with nurses and doctors for a long time, and under conditions of excellent "communication," they did not have the remotest idea of what "psychotherapy" meant to the professionals—but they believed they did. That insight and its implications were developed systematically, and checked out by further field work.

Again, during this research, after all essential theory had been developed, it was realized that its boundaries extended not only to the hospital staff but to the patients themselves, who had not been at the focus of the study. That insight was speedily but systematically developed, and briefly if perhaps inadequately checked out.[9]

To summarize: the theorist's task is to make the most of his insights by developing them into systematic theory. His sociological perspective is never finished, not even when he writes the last line of his monograph—not even after he publishes it, since thereafter he often finds himself elaborating and amending his theory, knowing more now than when the research was formally concluded.

The chief safeguard against stopping the development of one's theory too soon is, as suggested throughout this book, the systematic use of comparative analysis. This gives a broad, rich, integrated, dense and grounded theory. Since all those topics

9. *Op. cit.*

have been discussed earlier, we need only remind the reader-as-theorist that his developing perspective may continue to develop from substantive levels to more formal ones. Indeed, he may first publish a monograph about a substantive field and then go on to a second volume dealing with related formal theory.

Epilogue

Several months after completing the first draft of this manuscript, we happened across seven pages published in 1964 by Robert K. Merton, which present in capsule form the basic elements of the very position on the relation of theory to research that we have tried to overcome and modify in this book.[1] This task has resulted in the "frank polemic" interjected into our discussion of strategies of generating grounded theory from qualitative data. Merton's few pages afford the opportunity to succinctly summarize how we have disagreed with and modified the position he represents.

1. Merton's principal observation is that *"sociological theory tends to outrun the inevitably slower pace of systematic empirical research."* This situation exists because people who share Merton's position feel (1) that generating theory can be based on speculation ("hypothetical tabulations" and formulations), with qualitative evidence ("apt cases in point") used merely for illustrating speculative theory after its generation, not systematically as a basis for generating theory; and (2) that "systematic research" can only be quantitative. Since most researchers can easily generate theoretical ideas when not required to base them on data (a far more difficult task) and since efforts necessary to assemble quantitative data that will indicate even roughly the categories of our theories are "time-consuming, costly and arduous," it is no wonder that this gap be-

1. Marshall Clinard (Ed.), *Anomie and Deviant Behavior* (New York: Free Press of Glencoe, 1964), pp. 235-42. All quotes are from these pages unless otherwise noted.

tween theory and research exists. Our position closes the gap: grounded theory allows no speculation, while qualitative research is faster, less costly and a richer ground for generating theory than is quantitative research.

2. But Merton says clearly that qualitative research does not produce "systematic empirical" data. He implicitly disqualifies our position (that one can be just as systematic with qualitative data as with quantitative data) by associating "qualitative" with phrases that denote less than systematic inquiry; such as "replaced by clinical, qualitative description" and "rather than impressionistically and qualitatively," and "clinical, qualitative descriptions and analyses of social process are easier to come by than systematic, quantitative descriptions and analyses designed to test qualitative descriptions." In reference to dealing "systematically with a social process" (for which qualitative research is surely well suited), he says, "such a conception empirically should evidently require the use of a panel analysis."

In disqualifying our position he implies that theory based on speculation is better than theory based on qualitative data —we find it difficult to believe that generating speculations is better than generating theory based on data, however poor. And he is so wedded to the quantitative method that he fails to consider that one should use the most appropriate method, whether qualitative or quantitative, to obtain data necessary to the task. As we have pointed out, qualitative research is often the best way—and often the only way—to get data on a subject. Furthermore, it is hard to believe that one could catch with panel analysis any developing, ongoing social process with many stages. A panel analysis becomes cumbersome after four waves, even if the quantitative data can be obtained (most often it cannot).

In his final devaluation of qualitative research, Merton virtually tells a large proportion of his colleagues that they are not really sociologists at all. He tries to enforce his methodological position by denying them their professional identities, stating: "For, in the end the difference between plausible ideas and the systematic empirical investigation of those ideas represents a central difference between the literary observer of the 'human condition' and the sociologist." Such an outrageous and flat dismissal comforts people who share Merton's position, while it ignores the important problems concerning qualitative research that we have tried to attack in this book: How can we further systematize qualitative research, and how can we systematically relate qualitative and quantitative research to obtain the best of both methods for generating grounded theory? These problems, with which many sociologists have been wrestling for years, obviously have many alternative resolutions, depending on the conditions and purposes of one's research. But turning one's back on qualitative research as not being sociology is hardly a solution.

3. In implying that theory can usefully be generated through speculation or reformulation of others' speculations, Merton opposes our position that a theory should fit and work, that is, be relevant to the area it purports to explain. In Merton's view, speculative theory can be assumed to have fit and relevance until this is disproven—therefore, it should be tested with quantitative data. His reasoning necessarily leads to the position *that data should fit the theory*, in contrast to our position that *the theory should fit the data*.

Merton's position allows several kinds of license to preserve speculative theory in the face of contrary evidence, or lack of evidence to fit the theory:

(1) The data may be forced to fit the theory. Indices may be constructed, no matter what injustice is done to their meaning. Thus tests can abandon the reality of data.

(2) Since data often cannot be fitted to the theory, the theory is seldom threatened. If clearly qualifying data cannot be found, it is not the fault of the theory.

(3) When data are brought to bear on the theory they are considered by Merton, in this era of crude sociology, as merely "rough empirical approximations to the requirements of the theory . . . and these in the nature of the case, prove indecisive." Thus the only tests available can easily be discounted— so again the theory is not threatened.

(4) Since speculative theory usually has many variables, and is continually adding more, the restrictive nature of quantitative research can only test a fragment of it, even if the data fit. Thus from time to time the theorist can, with immunity, gra-

ciously admit a slight modification of his theory. (This, of course, further indicates the importance of that theory, since others are working on it.)

(5) Since testing is assumed to accomplish the important task of finding out "the extent to which these theories have captured significant variables and processes that are actually involved in the phenomena under examination," the relevancy and the explanatory power of the theoretical categories are again seldom questioned, for tests are so hard to come by.

Our position on the generation of grounded theory, of course, allows the theorist none of this license in generating and preserving theory. *The simple fact that one cannot find the data for testing a speculative theory should be enough to disqualify its further use,* for this surely indicates that it just does not fit the real world! Therefore, why should we continue to assume it should fit or have relevant and powerful explanatory variables? Why not take the data and develop from them a theory that fits and works, instead of wasting time and good men in attempts to fit a theory based on "reified" ideas of culture and social structure? [2] Generating grounded theory is what most of us end up doing, even if we start out to fit an existing theory to our data. This is well indicated by the sociologists who have commented on Merton's theory of anomie, in the same volume with his presentation.

Merton believes that a problem endemic in *all fields* of sociology "is the gap between the character of current theories and the character of much current research that explains the difficulty of decisively confirming, modifying, or rejecting one or another aspect of the contemporary theory of deviant behavior." We believe that when sociologists engage in generating grounded theory, the problem no longer is so great or prevalent, when it exists at all.

2. *Ibid.,* p. 97.

INDEX

Index